What Your Colleagues Are Saying . . .

"Melanie Meehan's new book, *Every Child Can Write,* is a professional invitation filled with wisdom that is sure to launch striving writers on a success journey. Fueled by Meehan's deep belief that *all children can learn to write,* teachers will feel empowered by her thoughtful ideas, tips, and reflections within a visual celebration of student-centered photographs of entry points, bridges, and pathways in action. This book is sure to bring to life a shared belief that 'all children can learn to write!'"

—Mary Howard
Author, *RTI From All Sides* and *Moving Forward With RTI*

"All of us can likely think of a student who isn't yet excited, energized, or in love with writing. These are the students we think about constantly, whom we most want to reach. With compassion, understanding, and wisdom that comes from years of experience, Melanie Meehan offers us practical strategies to help all kids find their way into writing. Her writing style is accessible and her examples are clear so that all teachers have a way in as well."

—Jennifer Serravallo
Author, *The Reading Strategies Book* and *The Writing Strategies Book*

"With a searing practicality and an impressively broad vision, Melanie Meehan moves through each moment and aspect of writing workshops and all but comprehensively answers the question, 'Why is this not working for some of my students?' If you have a bunch of kids who keep you up at night worrying about their writing progress, if you have felt the pangs of frustration over a beautiful lesson that does not land, if you have found yourself in a writing teacher rut, this book will help. Meehan's strong mind and years of experience mark every page, and by the end of this resource you will have notebooks full of ideas to make your writing classroom great for every child."

—Kate Roberts
Literacy Consultant and Author, *A Novel Approach*

"With authenticity and compassion, Melanie Meehan speaks directly to every question you have ever had or will have about a striving writer. Her suggestions, tips, and examples will guide you in supporting all of your writers, including the students who keep you up at night. This book will show you how to develop entry points, bridges, and pathways to ensure every writer finds voice and purpose. It is practical, it is accessible, and it will be your go-to resource when the going gets tough with the writers in your classroom."

—Clare Landrigan and Tammy Mulligan
Coauthors, *It's All About the Books* and *Assessment in Perspective*

"No matter how long you've been teaching writing, there will always be students who lack confidence, have discomfort whenever they're asked to write, or whose learning differences mystify you. Melanie Meehan's book provides you with an array of entry points so every student can self-identify as a confident writer. When students feel successful, they develop a greater sense of pride and independence, which is what all of us want for every child who is part of a writing workshop."

—Stacey Shubitz

Literacy Consultant and Coauthor, *Welcome to Writing Workshop*

"Melanie Meehan has created a book that blooms with hope and humanity within the realities of the writing classroom. Writing is downright scary for many students, and this book shows practical and respectful ways of reaching out a hand to invite writers into the challenging, beautiful, and fulfilling world of writing. I wish I had this in my hands long ago, but thankfully, it is here now. Teachers and writers—you will forever see opportunity in every difficulty because of Meehan and this book!"

—Patty McGee

Author, *Feedback That Moves Writers Forward*

"My goal as a literacy coach is to ensure every child has an entry point into writing and a comfortable place at the table. Melanie Meehan's book provides that perfect invitation with practical and purposeful strategies that you will eagerly revisit again and again. Do yourself a favor and add this gem to your professional library."

—Paula Bourque

Author, *Close Writing* and *Spark!*

Every Child Can Write

Entry Points, Bridges, and Pathways for Striving Writers

Grades 2-5

Melanie Meehan

Foreword by M. Colleen Cruz

CORWIN

CORWIN
A SAGE Publishing Company

FOR INFORMATION:

Corwin
A SAGE Company
2455 Teller Road
Thousand Oaks, California 91320
(800) 233-9936
www.corwin.com

SAGE Publications Ltd.
1 Oliver's Yard
55 City Road
London EC1Y 1SP
United Kingdom

SAGE Publications India Pvt. Ltd.
B 1/I 1 Mohan Cooperative Industrial Area
Mathura Road, New Delhi 110 044
India

SAGE Publications Asia-Pacific Pte. Ltd.
18 Cross Street #10-10/11/12
China Square Central
Singapore 048423

Senior Acquisitions Editor: Tori Bachman
Editorial Development Manager: Julie Nemer
Senior Editorial Assistant: Sharon Wu
Production Editor: Amy Schroller
Copy Editor: Karin Rathert
Typesetter: Hurix Digital
Proofreader: Dennis W. Webb
Indexer: Molly Hall
Cover and Graphic Designer: Scott Van Atta
Marketing Manager: Deena Meyer

Library of Congress Cataloging-in-Publication Data

Names: Meehan, Melanie, author.

Title: Every child can write, grades 2-5 : entry points, bridges, and pathways for striving writers / Melanie Meehan ; foreword by M. Colleen Cruz.

Description: Thousand Oaks, CA : Corwin, 2020. | Includes bibliographical references.

Identifiers: LCCN 2019019720 | ISBN 9781544355078 (paperback)

Subjects: LCSH: Language arts (Elementary) | English language—Composition and exercises—Study and teaching (Elementary)

Classification: LCC LB1576 .M434 2020 | DDC 372.6—dc23

LC record available at https://lccn.loc.gov/2019019720

19 20 21 22 23 10 9 8 7 6 5 4 3 2 1

Contents

online resources

Visit the companion website at
resources.corwin.com/everychildcanwrite
for downloadable resources.

Note From the Publisher: The author has provided video and web content throughout the book that is available to you through QR (quick response) codes. To read a QR code, you must have a smartphone or tablet with a camera. We recommend that you download a QR code reader app that is made specifically for your phone or tablet brand.

Videos may also be accessed at **resources.corwin.com/everychildcanwrite**.

Foreword

I am certainly not the first person to compare being a teacher to being a chef, and this is for very good reason. Educators, like chefs, need to combine technical know-how with artistry, all the while never losing sight of the audience.

However, there is yet another way I think of teachers as being akin to chefs. When we eat many a master chef's food, it can feel easy to be intimidated: the elegant presentation, the complex flavors, the sophisticated techniques, the pairing of various elements. When we experience that sort of master chef's food, we can marvel at it, treasure the memory of it, but rarely does it affect the way we cook when we return to our own kitchens. It is just too perfect to feel like something we could ever approximate.

Luckily for us home cooks, there are other master chefs who strive for something different. Their food is just as elegant, sophisticated, and complex. However, the way these chefs communicate, break things down, and create an inviting atmosphere, all change the experience for the diner. As we taste the cuisine of a master chef who is willing and able to invite us in and reveal their secrets, we not only marvel, we also are inspired. They describe the green market they visit to find the freshest ingredients, the workable temperatures for the yeast, the right amount of jalapeño for the salsa. When they describe their food, they often describe their process. As we listen, we start to imagine all the ways we can take that inspiration back home to our own kitchens. They make their mastery feel doable.

Melanie Meehan is absolutely a master chef of a teacher. Rather than model herself on the first type, however, she aims for the latter. She's not the type of master teacher to simply serve up a beautiful classroom, with every student engaged and creating page after page of fabulous writing and expect us to ooh and aah and then go home. Instead, Melanie invites us to join her. She begins by naming the obstacles many of our writers face. She then, ingredient by ingredient, technique by technique, lays everything out for us. Melanie knows how to create a beautiful writing classroom that inspires and allows every writer to reach their potential, to be sure, but she is not content to simply show it to us. She wants to help us to create this place for our own students, too. And much like the great Julia Child, Melanie speaks the truth, with joy and a depth of understanding that is grounded in reality.

Melanie is passionate about her belief that every child can and should learn how to write. She believes that often the students teachers find the most challenging to teach can bring the most insight and passion to our writing classrooms. She knows that everything from classroom environment to writing supplies to the strategies we teach can make or break a child's belief in themselves as a writer. However, she doesn't hoard this knowledge. In this book, Melanie breaks it all down for us. No detail is too small.

This book is explicitly aimed toward helping us best teach the students in our class who face instructional obstacles in writing, and its timing could not be better. One only need spend some time scrolling through social media or surfing the Internet to know that as a country we are facing a crisis of writing skills. Considering the most recent NAEP scores, which tell us that approximately only one quarter of American students are proficient in writing, one might argue a majority of our students face instructional obstacles in writing. However, even if your class is teeming with strong and passionate writers, because this book is grounded in the tenets of Universal Design for Learning, much of what Melanie suggests as being helpful for students who have the most writing needs will also be applicable to and make writing more accessible for *all* of your students. The ideas Melanie shares with us in this book are not little tricks and tips that you would only use for particular kids. Instead, her ideas are grounded in strong universal pedagogy, making it possible for you to trust that what you learn in these pages will make writing instruction even more transformational for you and all of your students.

Much like when we discover a new restaurant with an incredible chef who makes us want to change our weeknight cooking habits and which we can't wait to tell all our friends about, I am excited to introduce you, your colleagues, and teachers everywhere to this feast of writing instructional know-how that Melanie has laid before us. In these pages, Melanie stands firm in her belief that every child can write—and even more, she shows how every teacher can teach them.

—M. Colleen Cruz

Director of Innovation, Teachers College Reading & Writing Project, Author, Writers Read Better: Narrative; Writers Read Better: Nonfiction*; and* The Unstoppable Writing Teacher: Real Strategies for the Real Classroom

Acknowledgments

Every day, I feel grateful that I have a job that I *get* to do and not one that I *have* to do. I get to work in a district that values writing. I get to work with teachers who want to learn. And I get to work with students who are brave and motivated to put their words out into the world. I am so grateful to the Simsbury School District for providing me my own entry points, bridges, and pathways to become the best teacher of writing I can be. When we teach children to write, we empower them to change the world. I feel honored to do this work. Betsy Gunsalus and Maggie Seidel, thank you for always nudging me to think a little harder, reach a little further, know a little more, and do a little better.

So many Simsbury teachers welcomed me into their classrooms, shared their spaces, and allowed me to try out teaching experiments, offering collaboration and reflection with an unwavering commitment to grow student writers. Lisa Jacobs, Michele Holcomb, Lisa Smith, Lesley Turner, Missie Champagne, Jane Perkins, Nicole Weaver, Pam Lindley, Peg Bruno, Nancy Forsberg, and Christine Neskie—thank you for sharing your resources, classrooms, and students. Heather O'Connor, you've been not only a co-learner in this journey but also an awesome and honest critic—thank you for your positive energy, your complete open-door policy, your generosity, and your friendship.

Much appreciation to my coauthors of *Two Writing Teachers*—Stacey Shubitz, Beth Moore, Kathleen Sokoloski, Betsy Hubbard, Deb Frazier, Lanny Ball, and Kelsey Corter—you all inspire me every day with your brilliance and dedication to teaching young people to write. Clare Landrigan, you have encouraged, validated, advised, and reminded me that this is a process with a great outcome. And Brenda Power—I would not have had the courage to start this project without your belief and encouragement. Deep gratitude to all of you.

My family has gone above and beyond supporting me in this book-writing process, from delivering coffee (or wine) to me, listening to me develop ideas even when they sounded more like a foreign language, reading early drafts, validating the challenge of labeling every last picture, and even offering to help sort through permissions and appendix material. Huge shout-outs and gratitude to my husband, Garth; my four daughters, Larkin, Julia, Clare, and Cecily; my mom, Lynn Cavo; and my super-fan and sister-in-law, Amy Meehan. I couldn't have made it through this process without you!

Finally, I feel incredibly fortunate to work with the Corwin Literacy Team. Tori Bachman, thank you for asking and answering questions, always at just the right time! You percolated this idea with me, imagined the possibilities, and shaped it into reality, balancing patience, perspective, and suggestions that constantly inspired me to rethink, revise, and improve. You have guided this project from chaos to cohesion, and I can't thank you enough for believing in it from start to finish. Sharon Wu, you guided me through the details with clarity and kindness—thank you for making me much more organized than I really am. And I'm grateful to the production and marketing teams at Corwin—Amy Schroller, Deena Meyer, Scott Van Atta, and Julie Nemer—for your tireless attention to detail and for helping me put this book into the hands of teachers.

Publisher's Acknowledgments

Corwin gratefully acknowledges the contributions of the following reviewers:

Paula Bourque
Author and Literacy Coach
Augusta, ME

Mark Weakland
Author, Literacy Consultant, Literacy Coach
Hollsopple, PA

About the Author

Melanie Meehan has been Elementary Writing and Social Studies Coordinator in Simsbury, Connecticut, since 2012. Within that position, she gets to develop curriculum and assessments, coach teachers, and work with students to send them off into the world as confident writers who love to express their ideas. Melanie is a coauthor of *Two Writing Teachers*, a blog dedicated to the teaching of writing, as well as a regular contributor to *Choice and Lead Literacy*. In addition to learning with both students and teachers, Melanie loves to spend time with her family, doing almost anything that has her close to the ocean.

Introduction

I lived to ride horses from about the time I was five. I wanted to be a professional rider when I grew up. I would do just about anything in order to have time in the saddle. Three horses lived in a field a mile up the street from our house. Dr. Davenport owned the three thoroughbreds—a somewhat trained eight-year old named Nordic and two barely broken younger horses. He needed someone to ride them, and at age twelve, I jumped on that challenge, literally and figuratively. I rode those horses in a field with holes. I used his saddle that was too big for me, his stirrups that were too long for me, and a bridle with the wrong type of bit. We built jumps out of whatever we could find, and Dr. Davenport had no idea how to teach a rider or train a horse.

Between the environment, the equipment, and the instruction, there was more of a chance that I'd get killed than become a better rider. Luckily for me, the turning point happened when I broke my finger from gripping the reins too hard, and my parents decided that lessons and leasing a horse through a reputable stable would be a better idea than risking other broken bones under Dr. Davenport's supervision.

My equine adventures remind me of the experiences some of our writers have in classrooms. I'm not talking about all writers. For the most part, I'm envisioning the writers who may be facing instructional obstacles in their processes. While some people think of these students as strugglers or high-need students, for the rest of this book, I will refer to them as our striving writers. While I grapple with *any* term, striving implies effort, and I want to believe that everyone is wired and willing to *try*; people don't *choose* to struggle.

Striving writers might have obstacles in their learning pathways that get in the way of their cognitive engagement. In addition to learning disabilities or processing disorders, they could also have inconsistent or incomplete skill sets from previous years. Our strivers may have missed out on instruction for various reasons, such as receiving some sort of intervention during writing time. Maybe they moved from a district without a strong writing program. Maybe they didn't master an earlier concept that was foundational to the development of other skills. For instance, many of the skills within writing are developmental, and a striving writer might have been not quite ready to learn how to form letters when this was taught, and without that skill, they missed out on how to create words and sentences. Whatever the case, a gap starts to form within the writing life of these students, and without intervention and targeted instruction, that gap has the potential to widen. We cannot allow this to happen. If you've seen that gap start to form or widen in your own students, you've come to the right place.

Before we go a step further, though, we must agree to believe two things:

1. All children can learn to write.

2. It is a fundamental imperative that we do everything in our power to teach the students in our care how to express themselves through words and through writing.

Frank Smith, a contemporary psycho-linguist, wrote *Writing and the Writer* in 1994, and I return to his beautifully written statement to fortify my own conviction that all children can write: "It is unproductive to regard writing as a special kind of activity that requires unusual talents or lengthy training and can only be used for a few specialized ends, which perhaps do not concern many people. It is wrong to regard writing ability as a particularly esoteric skill that only a few can achieve, and then usually with a great deal of effort. The power of writing could be open to anyone who can use speech" (Smith, 1994, p. 17). In other words, I hope that this book will help you find ways for all of your students—especially the ones who struggle—to find access and success with writing.

Nordic was unsafe for me as a young rider. The hurdles were too many and too high. The more figurative hurdles in our writing classrooms might not break fingers, but they break spirits—and they crush any interest in the power of written words. For our striving writers to overcome their hurdles, we must change their course, recognizing that learning can happen at a different rate and from a different place.

Why Our Work Matters

While I was writing this book, I attended a breakfast for a local foundation whose mission is to serve as a catalyst for change in the lives of women and girls. The keynote speaker shared her experiences of teaching high school women how to develop an entrepreneurial mindset, how to manage personal finances, and what to think about insofar as managing money. As I sipped my cold coffee, everything she did sounded important—and so quantifiable. I haven't been able to quantify my writing instruction in terms of dollars. What is the value of composing a coherent email? Weaving stories into a cover letter? Writing instructions for a process?

Later that afternoon, I had a conversation with myself—I do that—reminding myself of the importance of my work. I even wrote about it in my notebook that night. Just as managing finances falls into the realm of critical life skills, so does writing. Written expression is a gateway into opportunities and personal impact.

So many students pass through our schools without learning how to assemble their ideas in writing, how to express themselves to the world in a literate and permanent way. We excuse ourselves from teaching some of these students to write, falling back on their labels, their behaviors, or their unavailability. Just because a child has an IEP doesn't mean that they should have a scribe

PAUSE FOR PD

When I first envisioned this book, I proposed the title *Who Keeps You Up at Night?* While this title didn't last, these are the students I'm talking about—the ones who you think about at night, wondering how you can meet their needs, what you can do to make learning seem more possible.

- Make a five-column chart. Down the left side, write the names of the students who you would call your striving writers, beginning with the second row.
- Across the top, beginning with the second column, write the following headers:
  - What do you know about them as people?
  - What do they do well as writers?
  - What could be holding them back?
  - What could you do to make writing more accessible to them?
- Fill out the chart as best you can

Over the course of reading this book, my hope is that your chart will develop and that you will revisit, reflect, and develop your knowledge and understanding of your students as people and as writers and your repertoire of tools and strategies for developing them as writers.

and be excused from creating their own written work. Likewise, fine motor skills shouldn't excuse a child from writing their own ideas. Behavioral issues that happen during writing are often caused by feelings of incompetency and vulnerability. Maybe those children would benefit from different entry points and invitations into the process.

Throughout this book, I will ask you to "Pause for PD" with a recurring text feature that presents a short exercise of professional development. Here's your first one, as I ask you to think about the striving writers who exist within your classroom, within your reach, within your impact.

Regardless of genre, regardless of platform, students need to develop their voices as writers and then use these voices to entertain, inform, and change the world. We have a responsibility as educators to teach students to write. Furthermore, we have a moral imperative to ensure that we provide pathways for *all* students to learn to write. We must teach our students to express their ideas so that they can share them with others. We must equip our students with courage, skills, and tools to do this. Communication is imperative, not only for careers and work but also for participation in a modern democratic society.

Entry Points, Bridges, and Pathways

It's common to get caught up in standards and what we are supposed to cover within our curriculum. In this mindset, when we sit down with a young writer, we see more that's wrong with their work that what's right. Our reaction sends a message to the writer. If we are going to correct everything on that page, our inadvertent messaging tells them to only put what's perfect on that page. That's paralyzing. If we are going to grow writers, we have to encourage imperfection. We have to invite our young writers to take risks and discover what works and doesn't work for them. This concept can be elusive and difficult to grasp, especially since so much of the writing we read is published and has the benefit of many drafts and revisions. We see the final perfect product, as opposed to the messy process that preceded it. This introduction was overhauled, revised, and wordsmithed several times before you were able to read it. If I thought that everything I wrote had to be perfect, I would freeze. This introduction, let alone this book, would not exist.

In order to let go of perfect, our striving writers need safe environments and accessible entry points. Sometimes these entry points are at different levels, and they may be different than other students' writing gateways. Our striving writers need bridges as well—various structures that can scaffold them and provide access from their entry points to other points further along their writing pathways. When we provide these entry points and bridges, we open up new pathways for our striving writers—pathways that lead to courage and risk-taking, growth, and achievement.

OUR SHARED BELIEFS ABOUT WRITING INSTRUCTION

For the first seven years of teaching, I worked in a residential school for emotionally disturbed students. Rather than embroil ourselves in constant power struggles and behavioral challenges, we teachers were always on the lookout for ways to engage and inspire our learners. It was 1992, a few years after *The Art of Teaching Writing* by Lucy Calkins had been published. The work of Donald Graves in and around children and writing workshops was well under way, and my colleague, Ann, and I signed up for a week-long course about writing instruction from Katie Wood—before she was Katie Wood Ray.

Many of the ideas behind that course boiled down to choice and process. Within all components of our writing instruction, we empowered our students to make decisions for themselves, to work their way toward a possible product by celebrating the growth and learning that happened through the process. Choice and process led to higher levels of engagement than Ann and I had ever experienced with our students—and they grew as writers.

When I returned to teaching after staying home with children for several years, I worked as a special education teacher within a district dedicated to workshop practices. I went on to become the elementary writing coordinator, and my current work entails training new teachers and planning professional development around workshop philosophy, strategies, and practices. Our district works closely with staff developers from the Teachers College Reading and Writing Project (TCRWP), and I pay close attention to their research and latest thinking around literacy practices. Therefore, many of the concepts within this book have been developed within the structure of a workshop with a minilesson, independent writing time, and a share time. A sense of authentic purpose and choice guide the work I do within writing classrooms.

With that said, I have tried to provide on-roads for a variety of instruction and classrooms. You don't have to be a workshop teacher to access the concepts within this book; there are many different ways to teach students to write. The important thing is that we all share these guiding principles:

- A commitment to standards-based instruction: My practices are based on the Common Core State Standards, but no matter where you teach, you also have a set of standards guiding your work.
- A quest for differentiated instruction that provides access points for learners who have a variety of strengths and needs: We want to meet kids where they are.
- A belief that all students want to learn and can succeed when given the right learning conditions.
- A willingness to relinquish the need for perfection in favor of process and choice.

The opening line of *Visible Learning for Literacy, Grades K–12* by Douglas Fisher, Nancy Frey, and John Hattie is "Every student deserves a great teacher, not by chance, but by design" (2016, p. 2). My hope is that you will find inspiration within the following chapters to reach for greatness when it comes to providing writing instruction for all students—that you will envision and then design a classroom in which every student can write and feel successful, that it's not left to chance.

How This Book Is Organized and What I Hope You'll Gain From Reading It

Madison, a third-grade student who admittedly did not like writing, did everything but listen to the instruction. She took a while to gather her materials. Then, she went to the back of the classroom to get a drink before heading to the front of the classroom where the instruction was taking place. Once she was there—midway through the lesson—she drew in her notebook and whispered with other students. Her teacher addressed her behavior, but her disruptions continued.

After observing this a few times, I invited Madison to have a conversation.

"You weren't listening to much of that instruction," I said. "Why not? What was in your way?"

Madison stared at me for a minute, maybe evaluating in her head if I was serious about my question (I was), maybe figuring out how to respond. I waited.

And then she answered.

"I need lessons that are at my level," she said.

I need lessons that are at my level.

Madison's statement has stayed with me. Many striving writers are not ready for lessons that their peers understand and integrate; how do we manage our classrooms and instruction to accommodate and differentiate for those children? If they're not paying attention, then they're not learning. It is my hope that the chapters in this book can help you reflect, identify changes that could be made, and implement some different processes so your students can become more confident, competent, and courageous writers.

Engagement is greater in classrooms where tasks are hands-on, challenging, and authentic (Marks, 2000), but as with so many things in life, we have to balance challenges with opportunities for success. Sometimes the balance is tenuous, and sometimes those entry points are elusive; my hope is that you'll gain confidence in discovering and differentiating entry points for striving writers through my mistakes, reflections, and repeated attempts.

Another hope is that the framework of these chapters affirm and validate predictable problems. The concepts underlying Universal Design for Learning (UDL) support guiding principles about the instruction of writing and the ideas and strategies I share that serve as bridges and alternative pathways for striving writers. UDL is a relatively recent framework in the history of learning and education. Anne Meyer and David Rose, researchers and educators, have led the work of the Center for Applied Special Technology (CAST) and laid out the principles of UDL in the 1990s. The main commitment of UDL is to make learning accessible and effective for all. The three principles of UDL are that learners should have multiple means of engagement, representation, and expression.

Let's think about what these three things—engagement, representation, and expression—might look like for our striving writers. They may need alternative ways to understand the reasons for learning and to stimulate interest and motivation for learning. They may need information presented in different ways, and they will likely benefit from having multiple ways to express what they know and are able to do.

If students can't do a task without us, then they can't do it. Our job requires that we expand our teaching repertoire, providing students with multiple means for engagement, representation, and expression so that they can do more and more at higher and higher levels—without us. The early chapters of this book focus on the conditions we need to establish within our classroom environment and management, so that all students can access our instruction and develop a mindset for learning.

Teachers who provide clear expectations and instructions, strong guidance during lessons, and constructive feedback have students who are more behaviorally and cognitively engaged (Jang, Reeve, & Deci, 2010). Engagement matters to learning, but how do we create that elusive concept for our students, especially our striving writers? How we set the stage matters, and the beginning of this book explores how we can create optimal environments for instruction and learning. Loris Malaguzzi, the founder of preschools in Reggio Emilia, Italy, believed that the environment plays such an important role in the learning lives of children that it serves as a third teacher, along with teachers and parents. We can adapt Malaguzzi's thinking to elementary classrooms at both lower and upper levels. Students must feel safe in their classrooms, but they also should recognize the tools and resources they can access in order to be independent, self-directed learners.

With a safe, supportive, and inspiring environment in place, we can think about management. How do we set up systems, routines, and expectations so that we maximize the minutes we spend with our students? And once we do that, how do we respond to the learning needs of our students, welcoming them into the learning process with expectations and entry points that align with their present levels of functioning? Chapter 2 provides actionable strategies for maximizing instruction as well as independent writing time for all writers, especially our strivers.

If the difference between what a student writes independently and what that same student writes during class time is significant, then it could be that you are doing too much of the coaching, which means the expected product is too far away from the student's current independent processing level. If we have to teach so hard that the work is more ours than theirs, then we're not creating an optimal learning situation. On the other hand, when we aim instruction at that place just beyond what students can do independently and we cheer on approximation, we have a much better shot at high learning rates. This place coincides with what Lev Vygotsky (Vygotsky & Cole, 1978) identified as the zone of proximal development (ZPD). Chapter 3 addresses many of the ideas around how ZPD has the potential to increase the impact of our instruction by helping us find entry points for our striving writers.

Once we relocate entry points for learners like Madison, we can begin to think about bridges, which is what we'll start to do in Chapters 4 and 5. In other words, how do we provide platforms and scaffolds that support our learners, albeit temporarily, so that they can develop skills and confidence? The middle of this book evolves into these sorts of structures. Chances are that at some point, the striving writers who show up in our classrooms weren't ready or weren't present for instruction during previous years, and we have to bridge those gaps, filling in holes and rebuilding foundations of skills and knowledge so that they can access the next levels of expectations.

Ultimately, we want students who can forge their own pathways in their learning process. I have designed Chapters 6 and 7 to take you along my thought process as I work to help striving writers discover their own pathways to independence. We don't want to minimize the importance of their eventual written products, but we do want to maximize the value of their process. Each individualized process should forge pathways of growth and achievement, as well as an understanding of and appreciation for the importance of writing in their lives as productive and contributing citizens. This is how writing skills transfer—how students start to own their learning and think of themselves as writers.

Because all writing leans on spelling and conventions—elements that Smith refers to as transcriptive components (Smith, 1994)—Chapter 8 delves into how we can incorporate spelling and punctuation lessons into the lives of our striving writers. How can we automatize some of those skills and processes so that the cognitive demand can balance between developing and communicating ideas and doing so in a way that readers can experience without translation? I admit that in my focus on process over perfection, I tend not to dwell on these elements of writing, but I know they are important.

The final chapter of this book presents a case study from a third-grade classroom in which I worked with a teacher to overcome some of the obstacles her striving writers were facing. In a relatively short amount of time, we were able to improve the writing scores of many of the students and provide them with momentum to keep growing their skills and feeling success. While I could not incorporate every concept, idea, and strategy from the preceding eight chapters, you will read about how many of the components come together in order to create a learning experience where students begin to see themselves as writers—begin to believe Frank Smith's conviction that the power of writing is available to everyone.

Throughout all of the chapters, you will come across some recurring text features, like the "Pause for PD" above. You will also encounter "Tips," where I offer pointers from my own experience. Closely related are the "Thinking Out Loud" boxes, where I share some insights and related thinking to what I've written about. There are a few "Lesson Plans," where I have created a lesson to demonstrate a skill or concept you can teach to students. While my instruction centers on workshop practices, these lessons could be given through various instructional practices.

My hope is that you will use my tools and ideas, but also tinker with them. Revise them, modify them, change them up entirely in order to engage, inspire, and empower the striving writers who sit near you. Every child can write—sometimes they just need different entry points, bridges, and pathways to find success.

Part 1

Creating a Productive Environment

CHAPTER ONE

COME IN AND LOOK AROUND!

How does the classroom environment support our writers who face instructional obstacles?

> The classroom environment holds so much potential for increasing student learning and achievement. At any point, students should be able to look around and find tools to support their learning, empowering them to be independent, self-directed members of their community. Chapter 1 contains specific strategies to increase the importance and power of the environment.

When I first started teaching, I loved going to a teacher's store, and I had to hold myself back from buying all the cute materials I could hang on the walls. Alphabet charts, punctuation posters, grammar explanations, parts-of-speech with elaborate graphics filled my shopping cart, but what I've come to realize is classrooms have white noise, and many of those purchased products are disruptive and distracting rather than productive or inspiring. Recent research recommends that at least 20 percent of available wall space should be clear (Fisher, Godwin, & Seltman, 2014). Too much on the walls is distracting and overstimulating, especially for striving writers.

Photo 1.1 Too much on the walls can be distracting to students, as it can become sensory overload, as in this photo.

I'm not saying that classroom walls should be bare. For the nine or ten months that students spend in a given classroom, they spend more waking hours within that space than anywhere else. Just for that reason alone, first and foremost, the walls should feel welcoming! Students also should know and understand how to work within those walls—and they should enjoy their work, as well. The more they feel a sense of ownership and belonging, the more they grow as learners in that space (Barrett, Barrett, & Zhang, 2015). Perhaps before we do anything else for our striving writers, we should think about the environments we are providing for their learning that set all students up for success in writing. Environments matter. Instruction and learning happen within environments, and it's our job to set them up to be as conducive to achievement for everyone as we possibly can.

The second principle of Universal Design for Learning (UDL) is that we should provide multiple means of representation, and our classroom walls should do just that. Our classroom environments offer opportunities for us to present information and for learners to access it, especially with visual alternatives. My good friend and colleague, Missie Champagne, is a fourth-grade teacher, and I once heard her say to her class, "Everything in this room is made for you or by you." The students looked around, and maybe with a bit of surprise, they realized the truth in Missie's words. When you walk into your classroom next, look around. How does your environment offer learning and reinforcement of the concepts you are teaching?

Photo 1.2 All of the charts in Missie's room have been created in front of the students as part of the lessons so that students understand the meaning and rationale for what is on them.

The Reggio Emilia approach to education is frequently associated with young children. However, the concept that the environment can function as a third teacher (after the classroom teacher and a parent/guardian) should apply to classrooms regardless of age and level. In the following pages, I address challenges we face in designing and maintaining classroom environments that support all learners—keeping our striving writers top of mind.

THE BIG IDEAS

1. **Our striving writers benefit from an organized environment, and they need routines in order to maintain that organization.** Students can spend a lot of time looking for things before getting to their writing. When they understand where to find their materials and develop systems for keeping themselves organized, their productivity and growth increase.
2. **Our classroom's spaces should contain only materials that foster student learning and independence.** When students look around their classrooms, they should be able to explain how *anything* in there helps them learn. Just as we tend to collect clutter in our homes, we also tend to collect it in our classrooms. One of the most common comments I hear from teachers is "I don't have enough space for all the stuff." Yet, when we really think about it, much of the "stuff" we have in our classrooms does not help students learn and become independent. We want to be mindful of clutter, space, and tools that can scaffold learning.
3. **The more we create, provide, and encourage the use of tools for independence and repertoire, the more learning will happen in our classrooms.** Once students recognize that the environment has tools and resources that can help them, you can suggest that they access those materials instead of waiting for adult availability. And co-creating tools with students gives even more agency. Not only will their productivity increase because they are not waiting around for you to solve their problem, but also their sense of self-efficacy will increase.

Our striving writers benefit from an organized environment, and they need routines in order to maintain that organization.

I don't know about you, but sometimes when I take on a project, I spend a lot of time finding the materials I need. Even when I am baking, sometimes I have to spend time looking for the bottle of vanilla or the box of baking soda—we can't seem to establish once and for all where they should be stored in our house.

One of the differences between me as a baker and many of our striving writers is that I *want* to make those brownies, while many of our striving writers might prefer to avoid writing altogether. They want to look busy, and if they don't want to write (or don't know how), they can look *really* busy by looking for things. All writers benefit from having time to write (Graham et al., 2012), so the better we can establish routines to organize striving writers, the more time they have to practice, and the more they can grow as learners. We all have our preferences when it comes to working environments, but the truth is almost everyone functions better with a sense of organization and an understanding of where to find materials and tools. In the most productive spaces, we don't spend time *looking* for things; we spend time *doing* things. Therefore, it's important to create and revise classroom environments that support the community members with what they need *when* they need it. While this custom-made environment benefits all learners, our striving learners—the ones with attentional challenges, processing differences, or gaps in their mastery—especially benefit when there are accessible tools and resources.

SETTING UP STUDENTS' PERSONAL SPACES

While the classroom has many levels of organization, the first one to consider as we're thinking about striving writers—all writers, actually—is the individual writer's personal space. Leighton, a fourth grader, is the first student that comes to my mind when I think about the need for organization. His teacher and I called him the absent minded professor; he was full of great ideas that frequently evaporated somewhere between his brain and his fingertips. If we were lucky enough that those ideas made it to paper, then chances were that Leighton's paper would end up crumpled at the bottom of his desk. The first two times I worked with him, we spent at least ten minutes trying to locate his work from the previous writing session. By the third session, I anticipated the struggle, and we worked on a system for putting his writing away.

Spend time teaching into where writing is kept, and create simple organization systems that work for each child. Like Leighton, **striving writers will need practice with how to put their writing away**.

THINKING OUT LOUD

Many teachers ask me about how to decide on small group instruction. We can offer small group instruction for skills, and we can also offer it for behaviors and routines. Just as our striving writers may need additional lessons for skills, they may also need additional lessons for routines. It's more than okay to pull a small group and reteach those!

Many of our striving writers have inadvertently (or intentionally) become experts at making their writing disappear or at least take a while to reappear. Here are some ideas to grow good routines:

- Provide each student with a two-pocket folder, with one side for completed work and the other side for work in progress, labeled clearly.
- Plan and directly teach in small group time around the routine of students putting their work away.
- Build in an extra minute or two at the end of your writing time for students to put away their work neatly.
- If your students are using an electronic device, help them set up an organizational system within that device. For instance, they can create a folder for works in progress and a folder for completed work, just as you would with papers. (This is another small group instruction opportunity!) You can even meet with a student one-on-one to determine what system works best—knowing modifications may be needed as the year progresses.

By all means, take the time! If students learn to organize their work early on, they will have more time throughout the year to work on their writing. More time means more practice means more growth.

TIP!

When a unit is over, take the time to clear out the folders! So often pieces of writing straggle from unit to unit, taking up space in folders and making it difficult to find current pieces of work. Make it a practice to collect and keep representative pieces of student writing in a portfolio that is located away from students' desks.

SETTING UP SUPPLIES

While it's great to think that students will always have a pencil sharpened and ready to go or a pen that's easily findable, gathering materials is another chance for students to avoid writing. Here are some ideas to overcome this right from day one:

- Have two containers for pencils, one for sharpened pencils and one for pencils that need attention. This two-container system will create more writing time for your strivers who know how to make sharpening a pencil take a long, long time.
- Decide on and teach into a system for having a pencil ready to use. It could be that one person is responsible for sharpening pencils during a specific time period of the day. It could be that pencil sharpening happens at the beginning of independent writing time, and after that, if pencils break, students get fresh ones from the "sharpened pencil" can.
- Give serious thought to using pens for writing. Their tips don't break, and students can't spend time writing, erasing, and writing again.
- If your students are using an electronic device, then set up time in the beginning to establish routines for their efficient use. I probably don't have to tell you how long a student like Leighton can take to sign onto a device. Until they absolutely know their login credentials, keep these taped to their work stations. And then, once they know them well, make it clear that logging in should take less than a minute. If they can't handle this, they use paper. (Every student I know gets faster when there are consequences in place.)

THINKING OUT LOUD

Just as you take the time to set up the use of folders, take the time to teach students how to access and put away computers. Striving writers might need individualized instruction on how to put away their paper writing, and they may also need extra coaching on how to follow a system for computer use. Make sure this system is in place, that it's understood, that it's possible, and that there are natural consequences in place if it's not followed. Digital writing is an accommodation and a privilege. Students can be productive with computers, but only if they learn to use them efficiently, independently, and responsibly.

SETTING UP A WRITING CENTER

Many high-functioning writing classrooms have communal writing centers for materials and supplies. Give some thought as to how to provision these centers and how to teach for the use of them. Writing centers should reflect the various needs and habits of the writers who live in the room, and the more that we create a feeling of communal ownership, the more we create a culture of responsible writers.

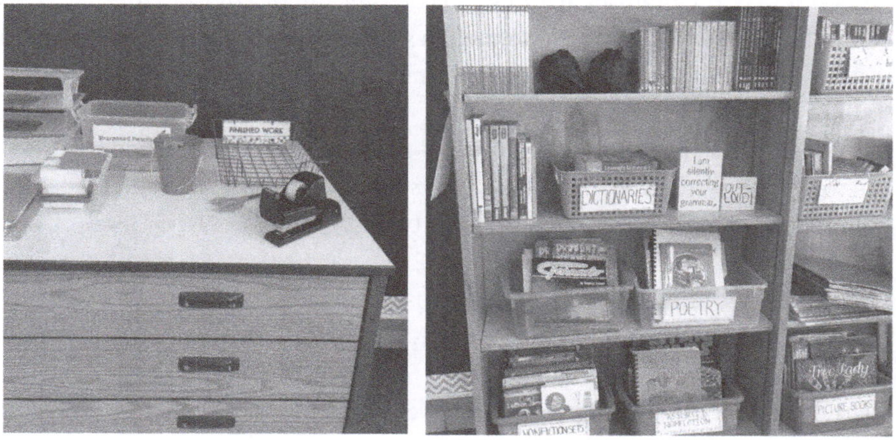

Photos 1.3 and 1.4 Missie's classroom has a well-stocked writing center of materials students use during writing workshop (Photo 1.3). Additionally, her shelves offer students dictionaries, thesauruses, and mentor texts to use when they feel the need (Photo 1.4).

At the least, writing centers should include these tools for writing:

- Paper—Aside from a writing utensil, paper is the most important tool. Give some serious thought as to how to set up the choices for paper, giving students power and responsibility with the choices they make. (Chapter 5 delves into the power of paper choice for striving writers.)
- Paper strips—As you teach about revision, paper strips become more and more important in your writing centers. Paper strips can be various sizes and colors, contain lines or no lines, and they are designed to be taped or stapled onto drafts of writing. For many striving writers, paper strips are an important tool because they offer a small space that feels less intimidating for trying out a new skill. Paper strips offer flexibility and differentiation options because they can be so many different sizes.
- Staplers—Just know that you may have to have lessons or at least small group instruction as to how to use them.
- Tape—See the note about the staplers!

Writing centers or classroom environments should also include models for writing, such as mentor texts and exemplar texts. At the Connecticut Writing Project 2018 Celebration, young adult author Matt de le Pena told students that "you can't be a good writer until you're a great reader," and he called books the very best teachers of writing. Mentor texts are pieces of literature we can return to again and again to help our young writers learn how to do what they may not yet be able to do on their own—showing, and not just telling, students how to write well (Dorfman & Cappelli, 2007, pp. 6–7). Mentor texts are powerful tools for teaching writing craft, and the more we can get students to recognize craft moves, the more that we can get students to use these craft moves in their own writing. When we model for students how to study craft moves and writing impact, mentor texts become important tools for students to build independence. Appendix A includes a list of my favorite mentor texts, as well as sample charts that map out the craft moves in several of them.

Exemplar texts are another resource and strategy to use with striving writers—as well as all writers. While mentor texts are usually far above the grade-level standards, we design exemplar texts to be representative of the level of work expected for the current unit of study. Exemplar texts are created by teachers or pulled from a collection of student-written pieces to offer models of what we are expecting students to produce as a result of our curriculum and instruction. Exemplar texts may contain examples of the grade-level standards at play without necessarily having the craft moves we might find in mentor texts.

Photo 1.5 Mentor texts occupy their own shelf and contain charts of pages and craft moves that students can try out in their own writing.

TIP!

What's important for students, especially students who struggle, is to realize that mentor texts don't have to be difficult-to-read, complex texts. The best mentor texts are ones students can read independently.

PORTFOLIOS TO HOUSE FINISHED WORK

Photo 1.6 A plastic bin works as a portfolio for student work. Folders hang on the insider of the bin.

Accessible portfolios are an important part of a classroom environment. Students benefit from self-assessing, reflecting, and making decisions about representative pieces of writing that they create throughout the year. These decisions foster the mindsets that we are all working through the process of continuous improvement, a mindset that striving writers frequently don't have!

A hanging folder box works well for portfolios, as students can have folders for their work, in alphabetical order. Color-coding the folders works well if you are collecting pieces from other subjects as well as writing.

Our classroom's spaces should contain only materials that foster student learning and independence.

What in the room is really for learning? What is just extra? We have all been in rooms that are bright and colorful and full—of just about everything. There are letter charts on the walls, motivational posters, laminated pictures of grammar rules and science processes and book offers and moon phases. Sometimes there's even student work. If there are teacher-created charts, there's tons of writing on all of them, and they overlap each other or poke out from underneath a layer of something else.

These rooms, while well intentioned, are the visual equivalent of very loud places with lots of different noises—music, chatter, maybe even a siren or two. Our striving writers benefit from environments that are quieter, both auditorily and visually. In a recent study, researchers found that children performed better when asked to complete tasks involving visuospatial attention and memory tasks in a low-load visual environment (Rodrigues & Pandeirada, 2018). Visuospatial skills help us imagine and then create, which is an important skill for writing—as is memory—so we definitely want to pay attention to how we can provide environments that contain the right amount of visual stimulation for our learners. So what can we do?

REDUCE CLUTTER

Spend time looking at your classroom the way a student might experience it. Sometimes the most productive classrooms have the least amount of extraneous materials. Just as we don't see the clutter in our own homes, sometimes as teachers, we don't see it in our own classrooms. A study conducted by the Princeton University Neuroscience Institute examined how people are able to focus when presented with multiple stimuli. The more that was presented to them, the more difficult it became to focus on the task presented. By using magnetic resonance imaging (MRI) to track emotional responses, scientists found that participants were more distracted, less able to process information, and less productive when facing disorganized stimuli. This study is relevant to classroom environments because we don't always think about how much students have to filter *out* information and stimuli in order to focus, concentrate, and learn.

Getting down and sitting at the level of a student may help you spot clutter you wouldn't otherwise notice, or better yet, invite a trusted colleague or friend to tour your room with a "where's the clutter?" lens. Look for the clutter that impacts *you* as well as the clutter that could impact students. Most of us know the feeling of not being able to find something, and we can think of the time we've taken to find it. Striving writers experience this syndrome often, so take some time to get rid of as much of the classroom clutter as you can. You might challenge yourself to do the following:

- **Clear out storage spaces.** Just as I clear my closet of clothes I haven't worn in three years, you can clear your cabinets and drawers periodically of materials you haven't used recently. How many yellowed posters have we kept and forgotten about? Once we have more physical space, it's easier to organize.
- **Rethink where materials are stored.** Maybe there's a set of books that takes a lot of space but isn't used often. With room in your cleared-out storage places, consider those books would be better elsewhere. What is used most often should be in the most prominent spaces.
- **Take a look at your walls.** Research suggests that classroom walls should be 20 percent clear (Fisher et al., 2014). Are yours? What on your walls truly supports student learning and fosters independence? If students aren't using it, then it probably doesn't need to be there. If you don't want to throw it away, you now have more space in your cabinets and drawers!

THINKING OUT LOUD

Think of your classroom as real estate. When we think about land and homes, the best land should have the best homes. The best classroom real estate is where students look and access the most often. Make sure that what they are looking at and accessing is what you *want* them to be using! What's the highest leverage use of your room and its environmental features, such as wall space, whiteboards, bulletin boards, shelves, and so on?

PARTNERING WITH CAREGIVERS

Consider sharing the ideas about organized work spaces and brain research with caregivers. Help parents understand the importance of a clutter-free environment both in school and at home for optimizing productivity and diminishing frustration.

ENSURE THAT WRITERS HAVE PHYSICAL SPACE TO DO THEIR WORK

Once there is less clutter, there is more room for useful materials and physical space for writers.

Photos 1.7 and 1.8 These pictures show the difference between a cluttered and clear workspace, which can make a huge difference for striving writers.

The striving writers I know need more physical space than most. As you observe your students at work, take inventory of how much space they are using and how much space they might need. For example, you may have striving writers who cram themselves into tiny spaces, yet you know real productivity requires some elbow room. Work with those students to find solutions they can be comfortable with: Perhaps instead of sitting in a reading nook to write, they sit at a desk with a cardboard divider that provides coziness but offers more room for paper and materials. Pay attention to your own writing life and recognize the amount of physical space you need in order to do your best work. It would be hard for most of us to write well if our papers were on top of other papers or our elbows were bumping other elbows. You might even pay attention to environmental cues that shift your brain into writing mode. For example, I do most of my writing in a chair in my bedroom, and there is almost always a cup of coffee by my side when I'm at my most productive writing self. Another writer I know leaves her desk and sits down on her sofa with her laptop to enter her world of writing. Students may benefit from hearing about these habits of writers and then developing some of their own patterns and rituals.

THINKING OUT LOUD

Choice is an important element to consider in all aspects of writing. We can offer choices of where students work, and it's important that they develop an awareness of where and how they are their most productive selves. We can explicitly offer students instruction on how to create optimal work spaces for themselves.

Whether your classroom is set up with desks or tables, some quick fixes for creating beneficial work spaces include the following:

- Make sure students put away materials from other subjects when it's writing time. Students are distractible, and writing requires concentration. Clear spaces and surfaces are much less distracting than ones with any sorts of *stuff*. If there's not room in desks for textbooks or pencil cases, designate a place in the room where those sorts of materials stay. When students are writing, they should have only what they need for writing in their immediate vicinity.
- Consider what communal supplies are accessible at which times. Communal bins are great, but a lot of the materials in them are not needed while drafting. Some shared supplies can be stored on a back counter when students aren't using them.
- Designate certain spaces in classrooms as "writing spaces." Some striving students may benefit from a physical shift that aligns with a cognitive shift. In my own home, my writing place is that bedroom armchair, and my brain seems to know and cooperate when I'm there. Striving writers also benefit from this sort of set-up if it is available within your classroom setting.

TOUR YOUR ROOM WITH DIFFERENT LENSES

Look around the room and ask yourself how what's there supports what you're teaching. Some considerations and questions to ask yourself include the following:

- Is what I see proportional to what my learning priorities are?
- Am I using what I'm seeing most on a regular basis?
- If someone walks into the room, can they figure out the recent learning emphasis?
- Are the learning priorities representative of the space on the walls and on the bulletin boards?

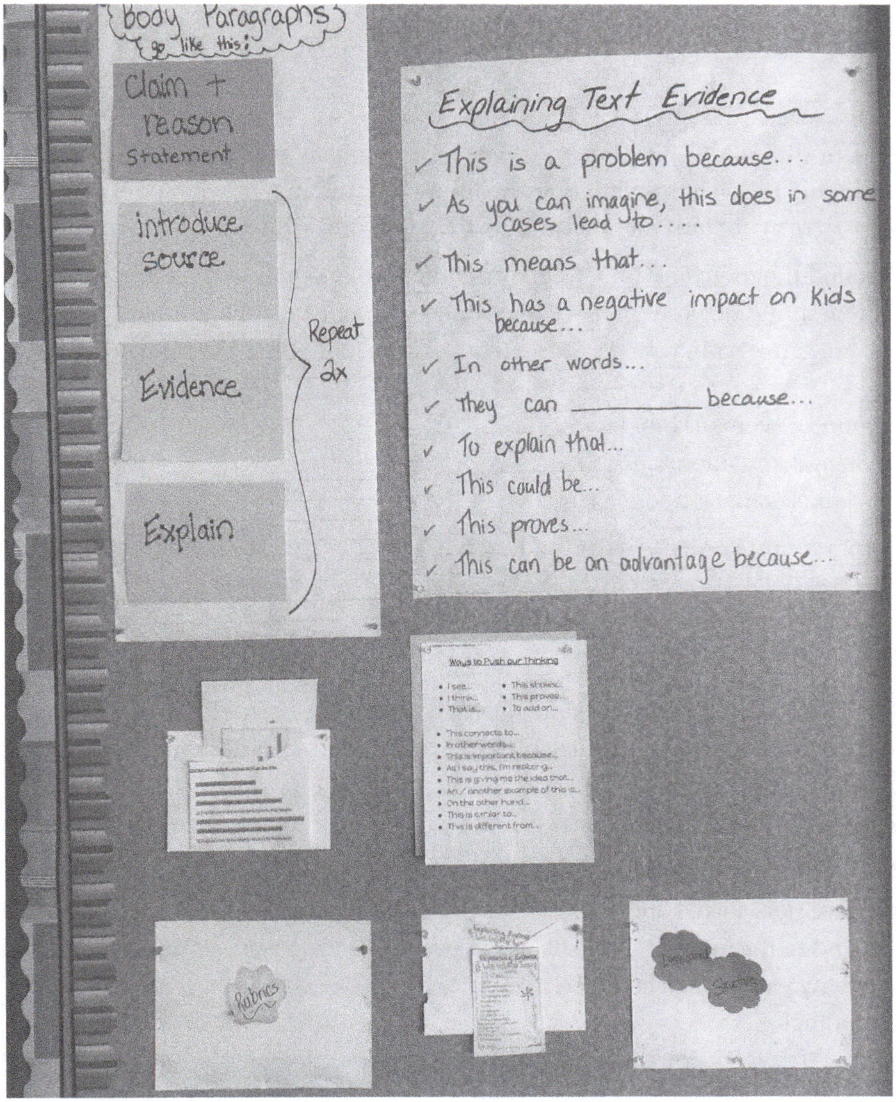

Photo 1.9 The materials on this bulletin board clearly support the learners as they develop their skills as essay writers.

In addition to *you* touring the room with a student-focused lens, it's also helpful to ask *students* what works for them. The lesson that follows can help you do this work with your students. This lesson can not only help clarify where clutter lives in your environment, but it can also help you recognize the tools and resources in your classroom that help students become independent, resourceful learners, the focus of the following section.

LESSON PLAN: *What Helps You Learn?*

MATERIALS NEEDED: Chart of directions, sentence stems, paper, writing utensil

INQUIRY QUESTION: What tools and resources do we have in the classroom that help you learn?

DEMONSTRATION: In our classroom, we have tools and resources that help us learn. Today, you're going to teach me what ones are important and maybe what ones we can take away. Here's your task: [Write the following steps on a whiteboard or chart.]

1. Look around the room and find 3 things that help you in your writing process.
2. Write these things down in order of importance (1 is the most important).
3. Get up and walk over to your #1. (Hint: It's OK if your #1 is different from other people's #1.)
4. Look around at your classmates.
5. Repeat Steps 3 and 4 for your other ideas.
6. Talk to your classmates about their choices.

During Step 6, present students with the following list of sentence stems, either individually or as a classroom chart:

SENTENCE STEMS TO USE TO EXPLAIN OUR CHOICES

- This set of supplies in the writing center helps me because ____________________.
- One of the places in the room that I look at most often in order to get ideas is ____________________.
- If the teacher is not available, then I can use ____ in order to help me work and be independent.

CLOSURE: You have now shared and heard about the tools and resources that we have here and now and in the future. I'll be looking for you to use them. Also in the future, if there's something you feel that could help you learn, let me know, and we'll try to get that up and running!

PAUSE FOR PD

Let's think about your classroom:

1. Draw a floor plan of your room, including the built-in features or immovable objects—the bulletin boards, windows, Smartboard, sink, closets, wall space, and so forth—like the one in the photo below. If drawing isn't your thing, take some pictures of your room and its spaces.
2. Working collaboratively with colleagues or thinking on your own, identify the high-leverage spaces. Where are students most apt to look? What spaces are the most accessible to them?
3. With those insights, plan what should go there. The most accessible places should have the highest leverage tools and resources. Use sticky notes on your original drawing to plan and revise how to set up classroom spaces.

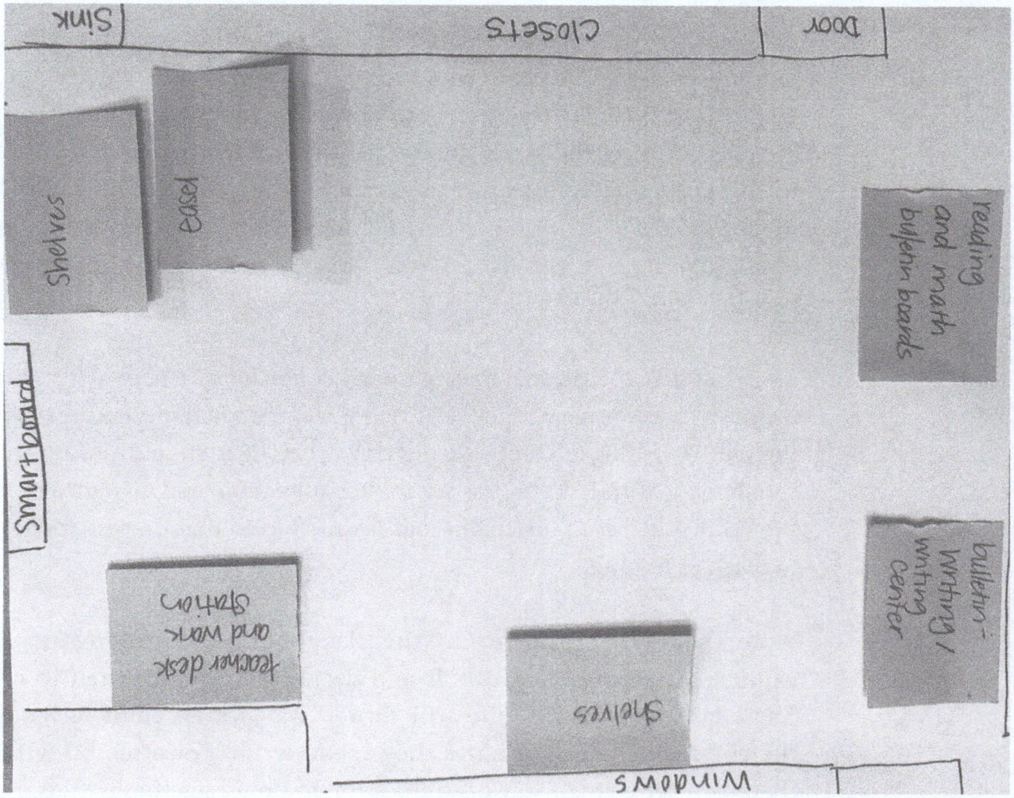

You can garner a lot of information by seeing where students go during this lesson. Students can also learn a lot through this process if you stop and reflect with them, asking why they chose what they did, having them share with one another what's helpful and why. Additionally, any time we can encourage students to learn from one another is a great opportunity to build collaboration skills—this is a quick and high-leverage activity for students to share their processes with each other.

It's important to realize that *if students aren't using it, then it's not needed.* Everything that's in your classroom should be geared toward helping students learn, which leads right into the idea of creating, providing, and encouraging the use of tools for independence and repertoire.

The more we create, provide, and encourage the use of tools for independence and repertoire, the more learning will happen in our classrooms.

Creating, providing, and encouraging the use of tools for independence and repertoire makes it easier for both students and teachers to do their work. One of our goals as teachers is to create independent human beings who are able to bring the skills they've learned within the walls of a classroom to the tasks they're asked to do in the outside world. The gradual release model speaks to scaffolding new learners with unfamiliar tasks, gradually removing those scaffolds so that the new learning is internalized and becomes independent.

Knowing that the gradual release model correlates to effective instruction and learning rates (Fisher & Frey, 2013), we want students to become captains of their own writing projects, identifying what they should do and how they should do it with less and less scaffolding, direction, and guidance from adults. We want students to internalize our instruction so that they no longer need us to teach or remind.

More than other students in the classrooms, our striving writers need explicit instruction about tools and deciding how and when to use them. These are the students who will sit and wait for an adult to be available, thereby reducing the minutes they spend writing or attempting to resolve their own problems. They need the strongest message that writers, regardless of their level, figure out ways to captain their own work and find tools that lead to independence. Creating bulletin boards that offer individually sized charts, such as the one shown in Photo 1.11 can help all students, especially striving writers, access support and strategies to help them find independent pathways.

The tools within a classroom are scaffolds; they don't exist in the real world, and we don't want children to use them forever. And yet, using classroom tools is a step toward independence and away from raising a hand or getting up to tap the teacher's shoulder. When a student realizes they need a tool and takes a step to get that tool, that student is on a pathway toward internalization and independence. Within the classroom environment, we have several options for providing access to tools for students.

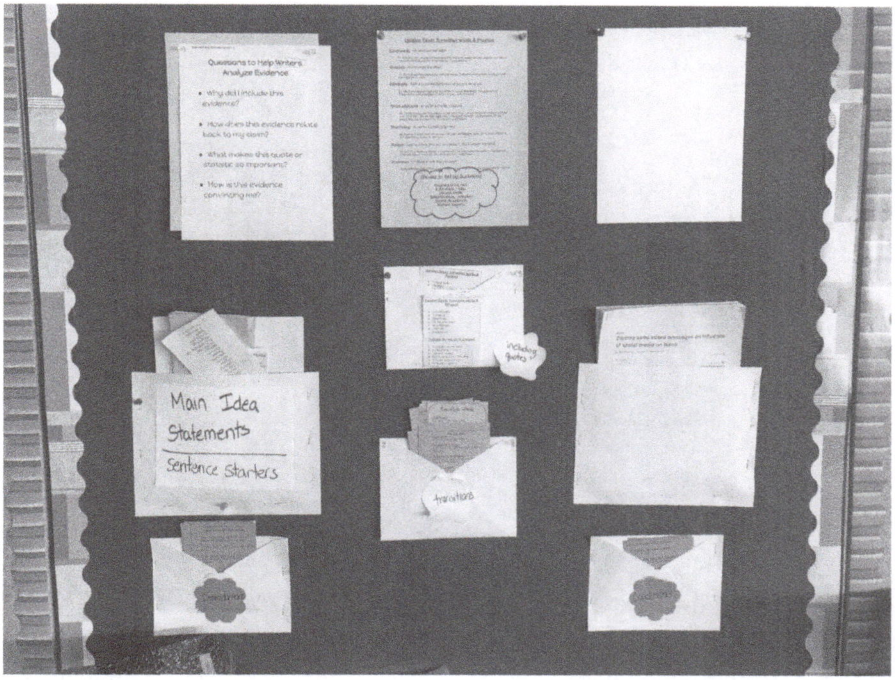

Photo 1.11 This interactive bulletin board is an important part of the environment, offering tools for students to take and borrow as they decide. You'll read more about charts in Chapter 6.

THINKING OUT LOUD

Self-advocacy is an important skill for many striving writers. As they move through the grades, they may find many situations—and not just in the realm of writing—where they'll have to speak up for themselves. You can help them build from dependence to independence by coaching them and reminding them to ask for what they need to do their best writing.

CREATE CHARTS THAT SUPPORT INDEPENDENCE

Within any environment of writing instruction, charts help student to be independent and develop repertoire. Returning to the second principle of UDL that emphasizes the importance of providing representation, when we create charts with students during explicit instruction, we have visual representation for when students are practicing the skill within their own writing. They can access the scaffolding as they need, provided by the charts in their environment. Our goal is for students to get to the point where they own the skills and strategies, and they don't need the visual reminders in order to demonstrate their knowledge.

Bulletin boards are the best place for charts, especially when there's a designated board that is explicitly for writing.

Photo 1.12 Bulletin boards offer students a central place to look for ideas and strategies for their writing. A variety of charts and even pop-out words can help students find what they're looking for quickly.

Many classrooms don't have access to bulletin boards, but there are other ways to display charts. In one classroom, wall space was minimal, so the teacher asked the custodian to hang a wire from one side of the room to the other. Then, she could use clothespins to hang charts—and easily remove them when no longer needed.

Chapter 6 delves into charts in terms of the various types, the ways we can use them, and how we can encourage students to use them. For now, think about where charts can hang in your classroom and how they can be organized so you maximize their impact on student learning.

Photo 1.13 Sometimes classroom environments do not provide bulletin board space. Hanging charts from a line is a possible solution for limited wall space.

THINKING OUT LOUD

Too many charts become overwhelming and fall into the dreaded category of clutter. This is often a tightrope walk! When students no longer need or use a chart, consider retiring it. When you switch to a different unit or genre of writing, charts from the previous unit should disappear, to be replaced by new ones to scaffold learning. All students, especially striving writers, will struggle to find the chart that helps them if there are too many hanging in the room.

CLEAR OUT SPACES AT THE END OF A UNIT OR LEARNING CYCLE

Bulletin boards should develop as lessons occur and students work on their writing. Likewise, bulletin boards should be cleared off to make space when units end or the type of writing that is happening within the classroom changes.

Any of the charts and tools on a bulletin board can be photographed or reduced if students aren't ready to work without them; I will say more about strategies to individualize the use of these resources in Chapter 6. Many striving writers will need direct instruction on organization and utilization of the tools you provide, but they will benefit from having fewer rather than more tools in front of them at any given time.

Photo 1.14 This empty bulletin board is cleared and ready to support the next writing unit.

TIP!

No matter whether you have one or ten bulletin boards in your room, start the year with blank bulletin boards. Yes, at the beginning of the year, greet students with a blank board. They can be pretty colors—fabric stores sell material for $3 a yard. This is your first step toward making your bulletin board beautiful.

Now, on your beautiful (and clutter-free) spaces, you can add various resources to the bulletin board, and it becomes a place where students know to look. Some of the best bulletin boards I have seen in terms of how they support student learning include the following:

- Charts that teachers have made with or in front of students.
- Examples of student work that serve as mentor or exemplar texts, even in pockets that students can take to their work space if they need to have it closer.

- Checklists that support or enumerate the goals and expectations of the current writing genre. Striving writers benefit from simpler checklists. Sometimes too many words are overwhelming. This is a great time to remember the mantra that oftentimes less is more. As striving writers begin to approximate and master some of the expectations, they can select more complex checklists. But it's helpful to provide a range.
- In some of the most organized classrooms, teachers have specific subjects cordoned off in specific places. Most elementary classrooms include a variety of subjects, and our brain wants to keep those subjects in somewhat of an organized way. If space exists to create separate bulletin boards for separate subjects, do it!

As you teach and create tools together, students start to recognize and use the charts and tools displayed on your bulletin board because they've been part of the process.

When we think about classrooms and how to make them as productive as possible for all members of the community, it's important to remember that everything should have a purpose and reflect what students are doing and learning—much like the artifacts in my daughters' rooms reflect their personal lives. While the girls live in their rooms, I want their walls to relay their stories—and while students live and learn in classrooms, those walls should contain the history of our instruction and students' progress toward independence and mastery. Just as I want my daughters to tell stories about the artifacts on their walls, I love when students can describe and tell the stories or rationales behind everything on their classroom walls. Remember Missie Champagne's words from the start of this chapter: "Everything in this room is made for you or by you."

End-of-Chapter Questions

1. Walk through your classroom with these questions in mind:
   a. Why is this _____ in the room? Do students use it?
   b. How does this _____ help students learn? How could it be more powerful?
2. How much space do the students have to do their work? Is it enough? How can it be more?
3. Are there tools available to students, and do the students know how to access and use them?

Take Action!

1. Go through your classroom as you might go through your closet. Like you'd give away clothes you no longer wear, get rid of materials you no longer use. Reduce the clutter.
2. Tour your classroom using various lenses, especially the lens of a student who is striving to engage in a writing project. What needs to change, move, or appear?
3. Consider ways to store communal materials away from students as they are working. Balance accessibility with distraction.
4. Observe students as they work, and make note of how much space they use and how they could benefit from having more space.
5. Commit to creating at least one set of tools that builds independence and/or repertoire for students. This could be anchor charts for genre-specific writing, strategy charts for specific targets, or checklists that support the learning targets. Create a set and make sure it's available to students. If you want to make additional sets or tools, go for it!

CHAPTER TWO

LISTEN, LEARN, AND THEN GO WRITE!

How can we set up classroom management and routines to support learning and independent writing?

Within any classroom, it's important that students are available to pay attention to instruction and then have protected time for independent and intentional practice. How can we set up routines and structures so that we deliver lessons with efficiency and students make the most of their writing minutes? This chapter has specific ideas for streamlining instruction and transitions in order to maximize practice and independent writing time.

Michele is one of the most reflective teachers I've ever worked with. Whenever she feels like students aren't making the growth she'd like to see, she stops into my office. Midway through the year, she came in and sat down. Michele looked frustrated. I knew her class was especially large and some of her students had behavioral challenges.

"They still don't listen at all," she said. "I can hardly get through a lesson."

She described how some students took forever to get their writing materials ready for their lesson. Many students had to wait for her to start teaching since others weren't ready to listen. And then, throughout the lesson, she had to keep stopping because they still weren't listening. When I went in to observe, I saw all these things taking place.

"Your lessons are taking a long time because you're managing so much behavior," I said.

Michele nodded.

"Let's get you teaching and not managing," I said. "That way students will have more time to write."

"I know," she said. "But how?"

Great question—but how?

When I think about behavior management in a writing class, I don't think about marble jars or sticker charts; I think about instruction and time for practice. Students need both in a flourishing writing class. The best form of behavior management is great instruction. If students are interested, they will listen. And writing, like any skill, requires practice. If children are not writing—and many times our striving writers aren't—then they are not practicing. Ask yourself these questions if you're frustrated with behavior and work habits: Are students paying attention to lessons? Really paying attention in a way that they learn? And then, is there time for independent writing time? And what are students doing during that time?

As part of my coaching work, I work through entire units of study with teachers, often for a six-week time period. When I first begin with a teacher, I focus my attention on students and what they are doing within three main components of

THE BIG IDEAS

1. **Transitions work best when everyone, especially striving writers, get to where they belong during instruction and independent writing time.** Students, especially striving students, take a long time with transitions. In fact, they take so long that by the time they get there, many of the other students—striving or not—are restless and having behavioral issues. When we teach explicit strategies for transitioning smoothly and efficiently, we not only have more time for instruction, but we also avoid behavioral issues that distract all learners from the task on hand.
2. **In order for instruction to be effective, students must not only listen to it, they must also understand it.** It's almost impossible to pay attention when we don't understand what's going on, yet striving writers may not always understand what we're teaching. More than other students, striving writers tend to fidget, talk, or zone out, so they don't engage in or internalize the concepts of the lesson. These students benefit from clarity, streamlined instruction, and the accountability that comes with a specific task.
3. **Independent writing time should involve independently writing.** Although we envision independent writing time as a time students are writing and practicing what we've taught in minilessons, striving writers may be distracted, distracting, or disengaged in their own writing. Sometimes, these blocks become times for students to find anything to do except *write.* Striving writers produce more work when they have tasks that they can do independently. They also benefit from knowing and understanding how, when, and why they lose focus and engage in off-task behaviors.

a writing class: transitions, instruction, and independent writing time. Students need clear expectations during these times. If we can resolve the predictable challenges, then we improve learning and achievement, especially for our striving writers—who are frequently the main offenders when it comes to either interrupting those important blocks of time or compliantly looking busy while producing very little.

Transitions work best when everyone, especially striving writers, gets to where they belong during instruction and independent writing time.

At one time or another, every teacher has experienced this: First one student needs redirection, and then all of a sudden another student needs redirection . . . then another, and another, and another . . . and you spend your entire teaching time asking for quiet or stillness or heads turned your way or eyes on you. There's an arcade game, Whack-A-Mole, where plastic moles pop up randomly and you have to keep hitting them on the head with a mallet; that's what this feels like. My advice? Teach students to transition efficiently. Once you've taught that skillset, expect them to do it ***every time***. Before you even start talking, before you even launch into your instruction, have some routines in place so that you're not spending time managing behavior before you even start teaching.

Once you know when your transitional times happen—and writing classes have some predictable ones, such as arrival or the beginning of class, the start of instruction, and the beginning of independent writing time—here are **three quick tips** to create smooth transition routines so that when you're ready to teach a lesson, students are ready to *learn* a lesson:

TIP!

The three quick tips for improving transitions are as follows:

1. Set clear expectations for what students should look like and where they should be when you are teaching.
2. Instead of singing or counting as students transition, consider having a story that starts your lesson and begin telling it as students are transitioning to instruction mode.
3. Use the power of visualization.

1. **Set clear expectations for what students should look like and where they should be when you are teaching.**

It could be that they stay at their desks, but in this case, they should know what materials to have ready and the expectation that their feet are on the floor, their head is up, and they are looking like learners. If they come down to the rug, they might need semi-permanent spots, such as a masking tape X or circle, so there's not a ritualistic debate of where they will sit. No matter what the routine, spend time early in the year discussing expectations—and practicing behaviors.

LESSON PLAN: *What Does a Great Transition Look Like?*

Materials Needed: Chart paper, marker

Inquiry Question: What does a great transition look like?

Demonstration: There are times during our writing class when we move from one activity to the next one. Transitions can happen as we switch subjects, but they can also happen within the same subject.

- Reveal a piece of chart paper with an inquiry question already written on it: Transitions are when we move from one activity to the next one. What does a great transition look like?
- Either take suggestions from students, ask students to turn and talk with a partner, or have students work in small groups to come up with suggestions.
- Record the responses and write the names or initials of the students who made the suggestions. (Nothing holds students more accountable than having the idea be publicly *theirs!)*
- Keep the chart in a prominent place or provide individual copies for each student until transitions no longer require any reminders.

Closure: We will keep this chart to remind all of us about what great transitions look like. If there's anything else anyone thinks of that should be included, let me know and we'll add it. In the meantime, we can all use this resource.

2. **Instead of singing or counting as students transition, consider having a story that starts your lesson and begin telling it as students are transitioning to instruction mode.**

I observed many students in a kindergarten classroom taking a long time to transition to their spots on the rug. A really long time! The teacher, Caroline,

Photo 2.1 This procedural chart of transitions was created by a third-grade class during an inquiry lesson. The question we posed was, "What does a great transition look like?"

used several strategies, including singing, counting backward, and even starting the lessons, but there were some students who still dawdled. Predictably, those were the students who needed to be there the most. I pointed out to Caroline that when she counted backward and kept the students who *had* transitioned waiting, she was negatively reinforcing their expected behavior. We talked about this and brainstormed.

Caroline began an incredibly successful practice of telling a story to the students who were ready and on the rug. Caroline's story spanned almost three weeks and was about two friends who were playing catch on the playground at recess when a giant bird swooped down and scooped them up. At each transition, she told about a new place the bird took the children, and the story ended when they finally made it home. By that time, her kindergartners were experts at getting to their instructional places with intention and efficiency. Not only were the students who did what was expected naturally rewarded, but the students who took their time stepped up their game because they wanted to hear the story!

TIP!

This story strategy works especially well if you add a little drama to it. Try keeping your voice low and your story less than a minute. Kids get quiet when they want to hear something, and they even shush each other if the story's really good.

Even though Caroline teaches kindergarten, her strategy can be adapted to older classrooms. While you don't have to create oral masterpieces each day, if you do it enough, students will get in the habit of listening to whatever you say.

When you begin this way, you build community and relationships, as well as a readiness to learn. What's more, if someone doesn't hear the story, it's not going to impact their learning of the impending lesson.

TIP!

If the idea of thinking up a fictional story seems daunting, share a personal story—it could be something you did yesterday, an anecdote about your pet, a funny story about a family member. Students love to hear stories about their teachers. They will not only transition better in order to hear your story, but also, they will develop stronger relationships with you, and that helps with their overall learning process. Relationships matter!

Along similar lines, whenever I teach a demonstration lesson in a classroom, I begin the lesson with a short story or a share that somehow relates to my subsequent teaching point. I try to weave in personal aspects of my life that most children want to hear. In most classrooms I'm in, children come to the front of the room for writing instruction, and I don't wait until everyone is there; if my story's good, they get there.

3. **Use the power of visualization.**

Asking students to picture themselves doing what we're expecting leads to much more success-oriented behavior. When a transition took longer than it should have, I asked the third-grade students to sit back down at their seats before their teacher said another word of instruction. "Picture yourself," I began, being a little theatrical, "sitting crisscross, watching your teacher, close to your classmates, but not touching anyone. Picture yourself thinking about how her lesson is going to work with your writing. Are you ready?" I asked. I even gave them a moment to close their eyes and really visualize themselves. When we invited students back to the instructional circle, they all were much more attentive throughout the rest of the lesson. Visualization works for me as an adult, and I've learned not to underestimate its power, even in young children. If we plan it, often times, we do it.

This visualization strategy works for other transitions as well. Sometimes I use it when students are heading off to write independently. "When you can picture yourself at your desk, opening your writing folder, rereading your work from yesterday, and getting started on your writing today, then go to it," I say to students.

WAYS TO ADDRESS STUDENTS AND SPECIFIC TRANSITION CHALLENGES

It's possible that, even after implementing the three tips above, you still have transitional outliers—those students who just can't get themselves ready—and these are often your striving writers. Once you have systems and routines in place for transitions and you're not playing Whack-A-Mole, you can teach into specific challenges. This can even be a conference or a small group instructional focus.

One of the charts that I keep in my notebook is flexible and can be customized given the challenge I'm seeing. Some students started calling it the Green Greatness Form, and the name has stuck. The Green Greatness Form is simply a T-chart with the following headers:

- What is not so great?
- How can I make it great?

This small form is a perfect one to pull out for a small group or an individual student who continues to struggle with transitions. Once I talk with students to name their challenge, we work together to find solutions. Initially, many students interpret these conferences as them being in trouble, but I work hard to explain that they are not in trouble. Instead, they have the opportunity to think about how they learn, what gets in the way, and what they can do about it. Revealing their learning constructs helps them to see themselves as learners (Graves,

1994), which in turn helps them grow as writers. In time, students can name the solutions that work best for them, which will help them self-advocate in the future. Once I conferred with a student who was having trouble getting to work after instruction. His response and solution is shown on his form (see Photo 2.2).

Photo 2.2 This form was filled out by a student who felt that a headset would help him get to his writing more quickly. I loved—and I think he appreciated—that he was part of the solution for his challenges in focusing.

Other responses I have gotten when I've asked students to think about what gets in their way include the following:

- I couldn't find a pencil.
- I didn't have my glasses.
- There wasn't any room for me to sit down.
- I didn't want to.

I begin the conversation with "Your challenge is transitioning from ____ to _____, and this challenge is getting in the way of your learning and your productivity. What can we do to help with this?" Students take it from there.

When we invite students to be part of the solution, we stand a better chance that they will internalize and commit to that solution. Striving students will benefit from this sort of proactive and responsive instruction regarding transitions, too. They will find themselves more in the mindset for learning and with more time on their hands for practicing.

TIP!

When you use the Green Greatness Form, or your own version of it, the students should be the ones writing. Point out to them the importance of their words on paper in order to relay a message and help them learn. Whenever there's a chance to fold in the message that writing is an important life skill, take it!

In order for instruction to be effective, students must not only listen to it, they must also understand it.

During my lesson on ways to begin a story, Colin, a striving writer, sat toward the back of the group. Just after I asked him to keep his hands away from his wiggly tooth, he gave one more yank. "It's out!" he announced. I tried to complete my sentence about the importance of establishing the setting in narrative stories, but the blood in his hand was way more interesting than any detail about an imagined place. I hit the pause button on my lesson while Colin got himself to the sink and then to the nurse.

It's tough to compete with wiggly teeth but important to remember that whenever we talk in front of students, we run the risk of them not paying attention to what we're saying. Students have many potential distractions, and they can look really compliant without internalizing a single word. However, there are some ways we can make it easier for them to pay attention:

1. **Be clear about what you're teaching.**

Whether you are using instructional objectives that are guiding your teaching throughout the course of a unit or shared learning targets that frame the lesson from a student's point of view, it helps to think about what students should be able to do as a result of the lesson (Berger, Rugen, & Woodfin, 2014). Teacher clarity is one of Hattie's top ten influences on student learning (Hattie, 2009), emphasizing the importance of communicating the intentions and success criteria of the lesson. Just as teachers should know what they are teaching, students should also know. Fisher, Frey, Amador, and Assof (2018) add an additional element: Students should not only know what they are learning and how they know when they're successful, but also students should understand the importance and relevance of the lesson.

Sometimes we try to teach too much at a time. As a rule of thumb, if you're trying to teach more than one clear objective during a ten-minute instructional block, that's too much. In a third-grade classroom, I taught students that I have a responsibility to say, "Today I'm going to teach you . . . ," and when I say those words, every student in the room should look like my dog does when I touch the cookie jar. We practice this, and it's pretty funny to watch them all try to simulate dogs about to get cookies when I say "Today I am going to teach you." However, I emphasize the seriousness of listening and learning as well. I recommend cueing students with a phrase that gives them clarity as to what you will be teaching. Both you and your students will have clarity as to what the lesson is really, really about.

THINKING OUT LOUD

All students—all people—have a harder time paying attention to material that is too difficult or not relevant. Pay close attention to the cognitive work that students are having to do in order to understand your instruction and modify it if need be. Any skill we teach students should have an underlying learning progression. What skills need to be intact for students to build new skills? What skills could follow? When we think in terms of progressions, we can provide differentiated instruction that meets students' learning needs.

Another strategy for increasing the clarity of instruction is to write down and post the teaching point for the day. Students—all students—benefit when your instruction becomes part of the teaching environment. As you teach, consider posting either your instructional objectives or your shared learning targets so that they remain visible to students throughout the writing unit (we'll dig into charts and how to develop more in Chapter 6). Two of John Hattie's ten mindframes of effective teachers involve having a common academic language and providing opportunities for students to have deliberate practice (Hattie & Zierer, 2018). When we provide artifacts of previous instruction, students continue to benefit, and we are living within those mindframes. Photo 2.3 shows a picture of a chart that will be created over the course of a unit. Each teaching point/objective will remain visible to learners throughout the unit.

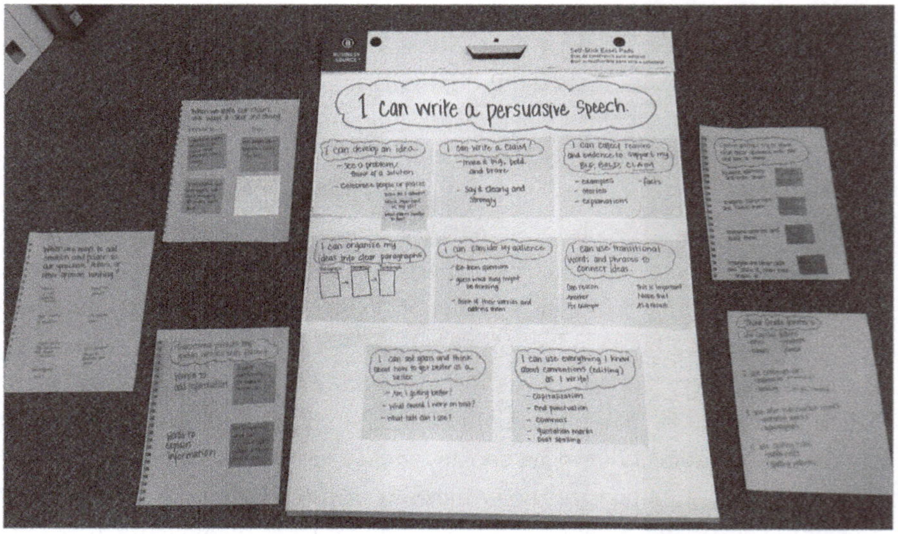

Photo 2.3 This photo shows a chart that we created before the unit but will be created as the unit is taught. Each large sticky note represents a teaching point of a lesson, and they will be added when the lesson happens.

THINKING OUT LOUD

Something that gets in the way of writing volume is students' tendency to do what was taught only *on that one day*: "Today, we learned how to write introductions, so once I've written an introduction, I'm finished for the day." Nope. Remind students instead, that "Today, we've added introductions to the repertoire of skills and strategies we are developing in this unit." This is a subtle but important shift in language that will result in a shift in thinking, and this mentality will dramatically increase the volume of writing that happens during independent writing time.

PAUSE FOR PD

As part of my work as our district's writing coordinator, I have created a series of videos of myself teaching minilessons. In order to keep my videos within four minutes each, I had to maintain clarity in both my teaching point and my instruction. The QR code leads to an example of one of my videos.

resources.corwin.com/everychildcanwrite

As you watch it, you might want to consider how I did the following:

- Engaged students
- Stated the teaching point for the lesson
- Instructed and demonstrated
- Offered students a chance to try it out
- Challenged students to incorporate this skill into their growing repertoires

You can learn a lot about your own clarity by videoing yourself at your desk or in another quiet place and delivering a short lesson to an imagined audience. Before you hit the record button, I recommend the following:

- Make sure you can state your objective clearly and concisely.
- Have all resources you need ready to hold up and share.
- Envision how you will model your own metacognitive work for your audience.

After you video yourself, watch and reflect on the following questions:

- Would students know and understand what they're expected to learn from this lesson?
- Have you demonstrated how to do what you're teaching?
- Do your visuals enhance the learning objective?

2. **During your instruction, think hard about questions that are being asked and their impact on learning.**

During a recent coaching cycle I said to the teacher, *"During the time you are teaching, there are no questions."* At first, this seemed counterintuitive to her, as it does to many teachers. "How will I know they're getting it?" she asked. She agreed to give it a try, and she realized that she would be able to assess students' understanding during a part of her lesson explicitly designed for them to try out the skill—and even more so from what they'd do during independent writing time.

No doubt you will come across students who want to ask questions at any (and every!) point during instruction. You have precious minutes to deliver instruction before attention spans are tapped. Don't let those minutes get taken up by questions that do not drive learning. Those minutes are *your* talking time. It's worth taking the time to teach students that during the "teaching part" of your lesson, there should be no hands raised unless it's an emergency that has nothing to do with the lesson of the moment.

TIP!

A few phrases work especially well for the chronic hand-raisers during instruction:

- "It's my turn to talk."
- "Wait and see if you still have your question at the end of the lesson."
- "I'll give you a chance to ask questions at the end of this lesson."

I used to ask students at the end of a lesson if there were any questions before I sent them off to independent writing. Predictably, hands would go up, and there'd be questions asked that did not benefit most of the learners. In fact, many questions seemed to hold the rest of the students hostage, keeping them away from their work. Therefore, now when I finish a lesson, I say to the group, "If anyone has a question, stay on the rug. Otherwise, the rest of you—off you go." All students, especially striving writers, benefit from having independent writing time—time to practice the skills we've taught. Providing daily writing time is a hallmark of effective writing instruction (Graham et al., 2012), but sometimes, questions from peers can eat away the time available from that precious independent practice time. On the other hand, striving writers may have different questions than their peers, and they should have the opportunity to ask those questions.

TIP!

If there is a question I think everyone would benefit from, I interrupt writing time quickly, honor the student who asked the question, repeat it, give the answer, and tell everyone to get right back to work.

3. **As part of your instruction, think about tasks students can do that require them to produce something.**

When students have to produce something, they are more accountable for learning, and you have an artifact that provides information to guide and inform your instruction. For example, when I taught a fifth-grade class about the different ways to elaborate in a narrative piece of writing, I asked students to create their own tools. During that lesson, I taught students that writers weave action, dialogue, description, and inner thinking into narrative text in order to elaborate and build tension during important parts. I asked them to think about which strategy or strategies they could work on, then asked students to create a tally sheet for themselves. The student whose work is shown in Photo 2.4 decided she would try to use all four techniques.

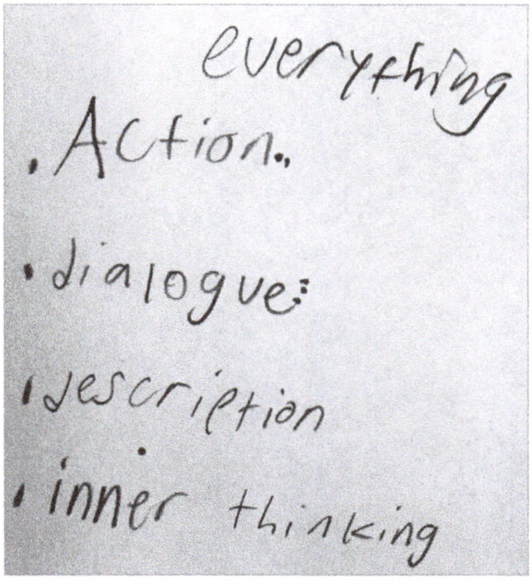

Photo 2.4 This photo shows a tool a student made for herself during instruction that she could use during her independent writing time.

Depending on the challenges of your students, you may want to have a few tally cards already made up and ready to hand out. Many striving writers struggle with fine motor skills, so the act of writing a tally sheet might distract too much from independent writing time. I have also said to the whole group, "You are in charge of your own learning. If you think you are ready to handle all four, then write down all four. If want to set your intention on two or maybe three, that's fine, too." This sort of statement empowers all learners, and striving writers especially benefit from having choice and ownership within their learning. The third principle of the Universal Design for Learning involves providing multiple means of action and expression, and challenging learners to create their own tools is a way to support planning and strategy development.

Another way to involve students in the lesson is to build in the practice of having them make their own tools. Keyrings work well for this, combined with a supply of cardstock with holes punched. During whole group, small group, or individual instruction, students can create learning tools for themselves, designed to help them hold on to key materials in a way that makes sense to them. Some examples of tools students have created are shown in Photos 2.5.

Tools don't need to be beautiful; they need to be effective. The more ownership and understanding of tools that students have, the more potential those tools have to support higher levels of learning and achievement.

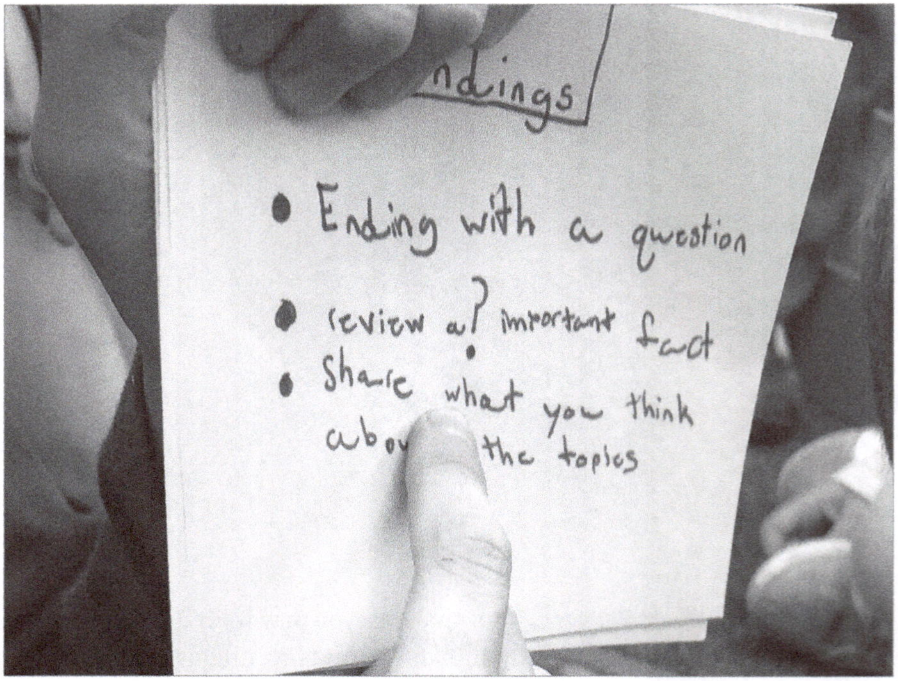

Photo 2.5 Card 1 focuses on the variety of ways to conclude an information piece, while Card 2 cues the student to remember the various ways to plan. Card 3 reminds the student to think about the order of his informational sections.

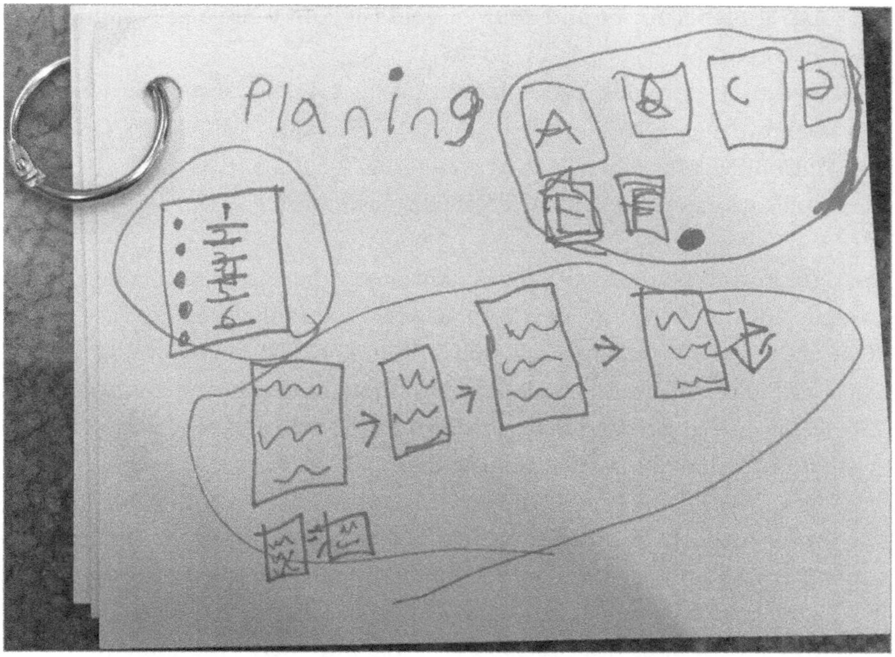
Planing
A

order is so important
1.
2.
3.
4.
5.
Add to the original

4. **Ask students *to set and share a goal* they may have as a result of the instruction.**

Goal-setting is engaging and empowering for students, especially when they are able to name what they are working on (Graham et al., 2012). One of our responsibilities as teachers is to provide tools for students to meet their goals. Let's look at what this could look like in a classroom.

Within an information writing unit, we should have a progression of lessons so that students learn how to write a grade-level informational piece of writing. One of the lessons could be about how writers include thinking when presenting facts and information. This skill develops throughout the elementary grades, so the lesson is relevant for various levels, with thought and differentiation given to the pieces students have in front of them.

As part of my instruction in a fourth-grade classroom, I provide students a list of suggested prompts (as in Photo 2.6) that can facilitate their own thinking.

The *goal* for many of the students is to include their own thinking in their writing. The chart shows them *how* to do it. I ask the students to create their

Photo 2.6 This chart can hang in a classroom or be made into individual-sized charts for students.

own tools, jotting down phrases they intend to use in their writing. During a recent lesson, one fourth-grade student listed some phrases he intended to use and then added checkboxes next to each one so that he could self-monitor his use of phrases (see Photo 2.7); his completion of his checklist was his evidence that he was on his way toward meeting his goal.

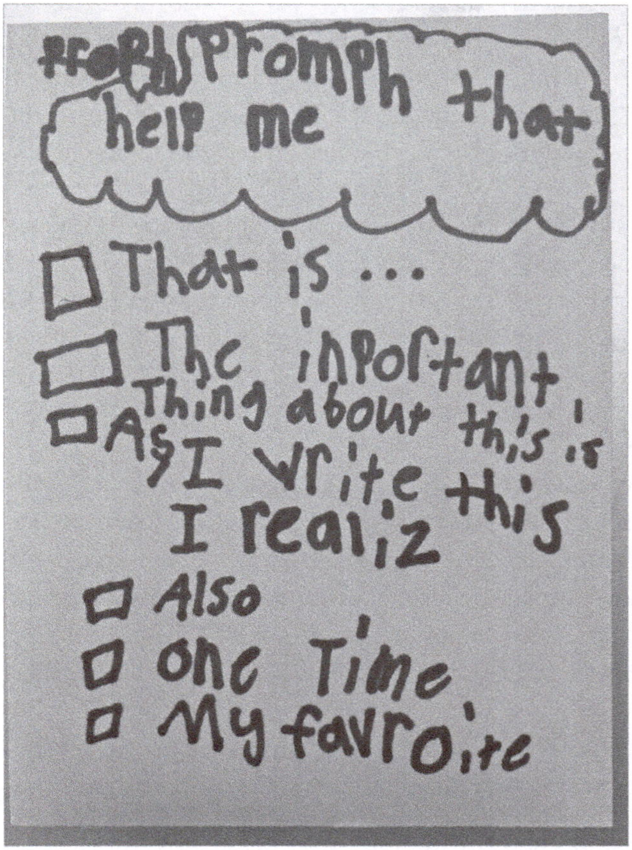

Photo 2.7 Madison made this tool for herself after a small group lesson on including her own thinking in her writing.

Having the boxes to the left of each strategy reinforced his intention to include those phrases and hence his own thinking into his writing. When I met with this student and asked him what he was working on, he could say, "I am working on including my own thinking into my writing. I've done it by using these phrases." When students set goals for themselves, they take responsibility for their own work, leading to increased engagement and higher levels of learning (Marzano, Pickering, & Pollock, 2001).

Independent writing time should involve independently writing.

Great writing lessons consist not only of a clear lesson but also of time for students to practice the new skill, as well as skills from previous lessons. We learn and improve through instruction, practice, and approximation—then a little more instruction, more practice, perhaps slightly better approximation. Whether we are five or fifty, in order to become better writers, we have to spend a fair amount of time . . . writing. All students need time to practice developing skills; our striving writers, especially, need time for independent practice, but many of them don't spend much time writing independently.

Often our strivers are the ones with adults beside them. Maybe the adult is a special education teacher, maybe a paraprofessional, maybe the classroom teacher—especially if the striver is someone who has behavioral challenges during independent writing time. Although all of those adults want to be helping students learn, a lot of the time, they're nurturing learned helplessness and a perpetual cycle of overreliance.

If striving writers aren't spending their independent writing time with an adult close by, then a lot of their time may be spent visiting the bathroom, sharpening their pencil, breaking their pencil, erasing their work, writing a word or two, erasing their work again. We need to figure out how to develop and use every strategy we can in order to facilitate words appearing on pages. What follows are three conceptual tips for increasing student engagement during independent writing time.

STRIVING WRITERS SHOULD BE WRITING MORE PIECES THAN HIGH-FLYING WRITERS

Striving fourth graders will attain more growth if they write several pieces that approximate lessons and standards than if they write one or two pieces with lots of coaching and scaffolds. Students who have frequent opportunities to write across genres show growth as writers (Graham, Harris, & Santangelo, 2015). However, when striving students work on longer pieces over extended periods of time, they often do not produce much writing on any given day. Furthermore, left to their own devices, heavily coached students will not be able to duplicate the process unless they've had a chance to try it out on their own through a model of gradual release, not through a model of step-by-step instructions.

THINKING OUT LOUD

Not every piece of writing needs to be perfect. Sometimes it helps teachers release the need for perfection by thinking about each piece being representative of a developing skill. If students write several pieces as opposed to one or two lengthy (or coached-to-perfection) ones, then they can work on planning for a piece, structure for another, transition words in another, and keep on going. That way, in later pieces, planning and structure become more ingrained, more part of that student's individual repertoire, which is exactly what we want to have happen.

PARTNERING WITH CAREGIVERS

Many caregivers have questions about how students can be "finished" with a piece, but there are still many mistakes. We can communicate how different pieces represent different goals and achievements. Not every skill of the unit will show up in every piece, especially in pieces that students write early on in the unit.

There are some relatively simple ways, I've found, to increase volume and productivity for striving writers that don't require a whole lot of extra prep or classroom time:

1. **Date the work.** Have a date stamp on hand or teach students to write the date wherever they begin their work. This process holds students accountable for production and makes what writing work they complete in a given period of time more visible to both themselves and to their teachers. Sometimes, just an awareness helps in terms of volume. We want students to know how much they typically write and begin to set goals for themselves in terms of actually getting words out on paper or onto a digital document.
2. **Get rid of erasers.** Really. Get rid of them. Teach students to make a single cross out when they make a mistake or want to make a change. Students who struggle to produce typically spend a LOT of time erasing. They've learned how to look busy without getting a lot of writing done.

(Continued)

(Continued)

3. **Consider using pens.** If your budget allows, provide students with a variety of colors and have students change colors each day. I know one teacher who bought big packs of pens in four different colors, and each day, everyone used a different color. Think about the accountability and the information you'd have if you could glance at a piece of work and see how much has been done on any given day. Similarly, you could teach students who compose on keyboards to switch their colors on a daily basis. It's a simple shift, and it provides lots of information.

VALUE THE PROCESS OVER THE PRODUCT

One of the most important reminders about life and especially about writing was years ago from a writing specialist in a neighboring town: "Don't let the perfect get in the way of the good," Hava Dunn often said. Whenever I can, I spread her wise words.

Most writing students produce will be nowhere close to perfect. I know that sounds obvious, but ask yourself, what do I really want this student to learn from writing today? Working in a fourth-grade classroom, I watched a striving writer struggle to read texts about Connecticut history that she was then expected to integrate with information from other texts before planning an informational writing piece of her own. Those are several complex tasks to complete before even beginning the actual process of writing. For Jaynessa, it made more sense to have her write about something in Connecticut that she already knew about—she was excited to write about a shopping mall. "But her piece isn't going to be like the others," her teacher worried. True, but Jaynessa could practice planning, creating structure, and drafting with a more familiar topic. By working through the process, she learned writing techniques that did make her final product better and, more importantly, allowed her to experience being a writer. Her product did not meet all of the fourth-grade standards when we considered the ones that dealt with research, but her process empowered her and enabled her to learn. She did not need to spend weeks on just one piece; she wrote her piece about the shopping mall quickly, and in subsequent pieces, she was able to transfer what she learned and was able to do to pieces that integrated increasing amounts of information. By focusing on Jaynessa's process—and celebrating the good without requiring perfection—she was able to get closer to expected grade-level products with independence and confidence.

THINKING OUT LOUD

Sometimes, when I first explain this concept to people, they misunderstand and think that I am giving up on these striving writers. Not at all. Instead, we are offering them repeated practice within their zone of proximal development, so that they can feel success, develop mastery, and then be ready for subsequent skills without feeling overwhelmed, frustrated, or in need of constant adult support. In Chapter 3, we will get into Vygotsky's zone of proximal development and how his important theory impacts how we can think about entry points for writers.

CLOSELY RELATED POINT: NOT EVERY PIECE HAS TO HAVE EVERY TEACHING POINT REPRESENTED WITHIN IT

We are teaching repertoire to students. The process approach to writing correlates to student growth and achievement in writing (Graham et al., 2015), and in a classroom that is really implementing process writing, students should be working from different points of the writing process. Not everyone will be ready to use that teaching point on that day. It might be that the relevance will come later, but because you've posted it and there's an understanding of how to use teaching points and build independence and repertoire, the teaching point of the day may show up on a different day. Furthermore, our goal should be to provide students with strategies they can use. Not every published story or piece of writing contains every strategy we teach students. Their pieces don't need to either.

SPEND TIME SIMPLY OBSERVING STUDENTS DURING INDEPENDENT WRITING

One of the most important things you can do is to observe your students every now and then as they work (or don't work) independently. You won't get to all the conferences and small groups you think you should, but you will gain important information about the work habits of your class that you can share with your students.

I have formalized my student-watching procedures by using engagement inventories. Jennifer Serravallo (Serravallo & Calkins, 2010) has inspired much of my thinking about engagement inventories, and I almost always create my own version of one when I am working in a classroom (see Photo 2.8). Along the left column of a table, I list students, and across the top, I list times. From there, I create a list of codes. In most classes, my codes include the following:

- On-task writing: OTW
- On-task conversation: OTC
- Staring into space: SS
- "Preparing" (which includes getting supplies, sharpening pencils, taking out folders, signing on to a computer): P
- General nonproductivity: GNP

Photo 2.8

Writing Engagement Inventory

Also available for download at resources.corwin.com/everychildcanwrite

WRITING ENGAGEMENT INVENTORY

NOTE TO TEACHER: Kid-watch and record student behaviors during 5–10 minute increments.

KEY: W = Writing, GR = Getting paper, sharpening pencil, opening folder, starting up computer, LT = Looking or waiting for teacher, T = Talking, LA = Looking Around, Z = Zoning Out, AB = anything but writing (bathroom, noseblowing, water-getting. . .)

Name	Time	Time	Time	Time	Notes

Not all engagement inventories will have the same list of codes. As you get to know your class, your list will develop! Other possibilities include W (writing), GP (getting paper/opening folder/starting computer), LT (looking for teacher), and so on. Use whatever codes make sense for the data you want to collect from your observations.

There are several ways we can use the information we collect by doing engagement inventories. When we commit to completing them on a regular basis, we notice patterns. Sometimes, I've sat down with students to analyze, talk about, and reflect on those patterns. I may start questions along the lines of the following:

- What do you notice about your row of data?
- Why do you think that is?
- What could you do to continue that pattern or change that pattern?

I may also use the data to inform small group instruction or individual conferences. For students who are not productive, I may take a more direct approach: "I notice that during independent writing time, you spend a fair amount of time reading, rereading, looking around, and getting ready. I'm going to teach you some strategies that could help you be a more productive writer in terms of what you actually get down on paper." From there, I would teach them about using different colored pens, setting goals in terms of page production, and using date stamps to reflect on what they can get done. I may also have a conversation with them about what they feel gets in the way of the physical act of writing, too, and from there, brainstorm some possible solutions with them. Remember the Green Greatness Form? This is a great time to bring one out, inviting students to be part of the solutions.

Here are two quick strategies that help students self-monitor their on-task behavior:

1. **Teach them to "Take Inventory."**

I love this phrase. Every so often, when I am working in a class, I say, "Writers, take inventory." I teach them that when they hear me say this, they are to freeze and think about *what they were doing* when I said it. Were they writing? Talking about their writing? Erasing? Sharpening a pencil? Moseying their way back from a drink of water?

I emphasize that they are not in trouble, that I am not looking to catch them. I am looking to help them understand their own work habits as writers. As your writing community develops, if you use this phrase regularly but at different times, I know you will find that most students will take pride in being able to say they were working—really working—when asked to take inventory.

2. **Give a finger-based self-assessment.**

Another effective way for students to self-assess their writing engagement is to ask them to "rate themselves with their fingers." Five fingers means they were spot-on and super on task, three fingers means they may have needed a reminder or two but were mostly okay. One finger indicates there's some work to be done.

Productivity, engagement, and growth are closely related concepts. Regardless of the activity, we need to practice in order to become better. Sometimes, routines help us get to work, and sometimes having more awareness of where the tasks get hard helps us increase our commitment to dig, put our head down, and plow through what might feel difficult at first. Striving writers benefit from these concepts. Because they don't have a lot of experience with the satisfaction that comes from achieving a goal or accomplishing a challenge, their fallback, consciously or subconsciously, is avoidance or even disruptive behaviors. When we teach explicit routines and expectations, we set the stage for success for all writers in our rooms.

End-of-Chapter Questions

1. Think about your classroom management from the standpoint of blocks of time, as well as through the lens of setting goals:
    a. Where are there issues? During transitions? Instruction? Independent writing time?
    b. What can you do to address the issues and thereby create more time for writing and instruction?
2. How much clarity do you have in your daily teaching points? What are some strategies you could use so that both you *and* students are able to say what the day's lesson is about, how to know if it's successful, and why it matters?
3. Are students engaged in their writing during independent writing time? If they are not, how do you know and what are you doing to help them use that time more productively?

Take Action!

1. Recognize and list the transitions that exist within writing instruction. Decide on and set up systems that work for students to transition within the classroom. Teach those systems and stay consistent with them across the day and content areas.
2. Commit to shortening your instruction if you haven't already. It's hard for all of us—and especially hard for striving writers—to pay attention for stretches of time that are longer than ten minutes.
3. Establish a way to monitor student engagement during independent work times. The more you know how much *all* of the students in your room are producing, the better you can manage the output and the learning that is happening.

Part 2

Finding Entry Points and Building Bridges

CHAPTER THREE

FIND THE PLACE WHERE WRITERS CAN JOIN THE WORK

How can we provide entry points so all writers get to experience success within the writing process?

When people face a task that feels too hard, they often feel anxious or defeated before they even begin. These feelings are common for our striving writers. Chapter 3 shows how to use the zone of proximal development within our writing instruction. How do we know where to begin for our striving writers? How can we anticipate obstacles, and how can we empower writers to self-assess and participate in their own learning process?

One Thanksgiving morning, we made plans as a family to go to my friend's yoga class. Even Julia, who would rather have a hard-core cardio workout, agreed to come. However, she suggested running to the studio.

"You can do it, Mom," she said. "It's less than three miles."

Even though I knew three miles was three too many for me, I agreed. The idea of making holiday memories was tough to resist. (It shouldn't have been.)

Julia kept me going for over two miles with funny stories and encouragement. My husband, who was wise enough to say no, offered me a ride about 500 yards from the studio, and I shamelessly took it. Yoga was tough. Cooking was tough. Walking the next day was tough. And the experience confirmed in my own head that running is not for me. I think I've tried to run once since then. The thing is, running three miles was way outside my training zone, yet I jumped right in. What might have been different if I'd worked up over time to running that distance?

Whenever we are learning a new skill, we need opportunities to feel successful, moments when we feel a glimmer of hope that we can do this. When students believe that they can successfully complete a task, they have self-efficacy, and self-efficacy is correlated to higher learning levels (Hattie & Zierer, 2018). Therefore, it is incumbent on us to know and understand our students' current level of functioning. That way, we can provide non-overwhelming entry points into the landscape of writing.

Lev Vygotsky defined the zone of proximal development (ZPD) as "the distance between the actual development level as determined by independent problem solving and the level of potential development as determined through problem solving under adult guidance or in collaboration with [a] more capable peer" (Vygotsky & Cole, 1978, p. 86). In other words, the ZPD is the place where students need a bit of scaffolding to be successful—a place where they don't feel frustrated. While the size of the ZPD may vary in individuals, the consistent finding is that we learn at our highest rates when we take on tasks that are just beyond what we can do independently. We might need some scaffolding or guidance, but the task should not feel impossible. When we work and learn within this range, our ZPD shifts, and we are able to take on progressively more difficult or complex tasks and learning.

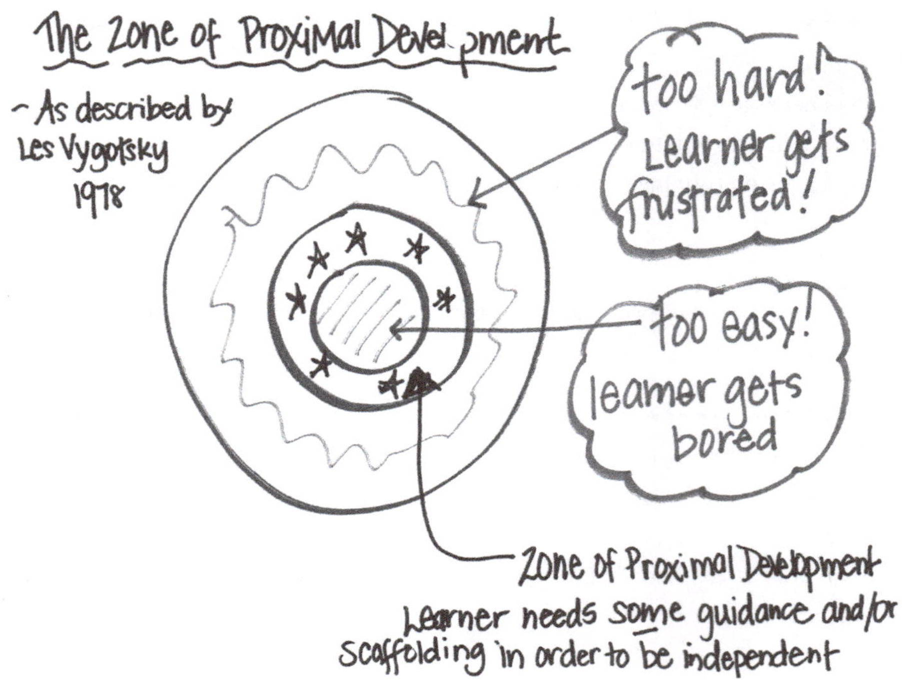

Photo 3.1 This diagram shows Vygotsky's zones with concentric circles representing where the task is too easy, just right, and too difficult.

Vygotsky's thinking guides my work around entry points within writing instruction. Lucy Calkins (1994) emphasizes the importance of considering the ZPD when conferring with young writers. In order to grow, writers need instruction and feedback that aligns to their functioning level and next steps as writers. Remember Madison from the introduction to this book? She was the third grader who avoided instruction. When I asked her why, she told me she needed lessons at her own level. If she were to use more academic language, she might have said that the instruction was beyond her ZPD. But locating ZPDs for individual students is challenging.

My running foray on Thanksgiving morning was an experience well beyond my ZPD. I felt exhausted, my muscles ached, and I was anything but inspired to try again. When I talk to teachers about this, I use the analogy of training for a road race. If, on Day 1, my coach said to me that I should run five miles, I would quit. (Or I'd do something really stupid, like try to keep up with Julia for three miles.)

I'm nowhere close to being ready for a five-mile run. On the other hand, if he asked me to run a half mile, I'd give it a shot. A half-mile run would be my entry point. And maybe the next day, I'd agree to a mile. I'd get to five over time, but I'd need to train and prep my legs and lungs. This analogy always helps me when I am working with striving writers.

THE BIG IDEAS

1. **We can use what we know about standards and progressions of writing to help students grow within their ZPD along the continuum of mastery.** The Common Core Writing Standards were written in a progression, with skills developing over time. The better we understand the progression, the more effectively we can know where to welcome students into the process.
2. **When we determine where and how students get stuck in their process, we can help them find the right entry point.** We have to be able to know where and how students get stuck in their process in order to provide meaningful instruction. Just as we know and recognize predictable problems in other skills, we have to know the steps and progressions of writing so that we can guide students from those areas.
3. **We empower students and engage them in their development as writers by teaching them to self-assess their process—and progress.** The more students are able to participate in the process and learn how to self-assess, the more we empower and engage them as writers. Self-assessment is a critical skill for all learners, especially our strivers, as it's a precursor for self-efficacy and self-advocacy.

We can use what we know about standards and progressions of writing to help students grow their ZPD along the continuum of mastery.

Because most elementary teachers teach all content areas, they have many standards and expectations to know and remember. While it's challenging enough to learn, know, and remember one set of grade-level standards, it's even more so to know and understand the standards that come before and after. Furthermore, "meeting grade-level standards" in writing is not always clear for teachers and students, especially when that expectation is out of reach—as is the case for our striving writers. Teaching to those standards is frustrating at best, ineffective at worst. Therefore, the more we can create tools, resources, and systems that clarify the progression of skills and standards, the better we can differentiate instruction in more attainable ways for striving writers. Striving writers take on many tasks that are far from their ZPD. Consequently, they feel defeated before they even get started, and it's no wonder they want to give up. Just as I need entry points into a long run, our striving writers need entry points into the writing process—entry points where they can experience and build on success.

1. **Think about learning progressions.**

Learning progressions, more than any other tool, have the potential to help identify where students are in the process. Learning progressions are, simply stated, skills students need to master in order to step to the next place along the path to mastery. James Popham (2007) defines a learning progression as "a carefully sequenced set of building blocks that students must master en route to mastering a more distant curricular aim. These building blocks consist of subskills and bodies of enabling knowledge" (p. 83).

Writing is a complex task that involves the integration of fine motor, memory, and integrative skills, but steps still exist within the process. The steps along the process toward mastery of those multiple skills make up the learning progressions for written expression, and the more that we can identify those steps, the better we can understand where to initiate our instruction—the entry points—for striving writers.

2. **Think about the writing standards.**

Staying within Popham's concept of building blocks, we can think about the CCSS for the first three writing standards. I have created documents for these standards where I've copied and pasted the standards for progressive grade levels into one document. Figure 3.1 shows an example of what this looks like. (See Appendix F for all three genres, K–6.)

THINKING OUT LOUD

While the CCSS does include expectations for figurative language and understanding craft in the writing process, there is not a specific standard for poetry. For this reason, the focus of this book stays with the three genres: narrative, information, and opinion/argument. Many of the ideas and concepts can work during poetry instruction, but I am not explicitly addressing those connections in this book.

Figure 3.1 The Progression of Opinion Writing Standards From CCSS

KINDERGARTEN

Use a combination of drawing, dictating, and writing to compose opinion pieces in which they tell a reader the topic or the name of the book they are writing about and state an opinion or preference about the topic or book (e.g., *My favorite book is . . .*).

GRADE 1

Write opinion pieces in which they introduce the topic or name the book they are writing about, state an opinion, supply a reason for the opinion, and provide some sense of closure.

GRADE 2

Write opinion pieces in which they introduce the topic or book they are writing about, state an opinion, supply reasons that support the opinion, use linking words (e.g., *because, and, also*) to connect opinion and reasons, and provide a concluding statement or section.

GRADE 3

Write opinion pieces on topics or texts, supporting a point of view with reasons.

- Introduce the topic or text they are writing about, state an opinion, and create an organizational structure that lists reasons.
- Provide reasons that support the opinion.
- Use linking words and phrases (e.g., *because, therefore, since, for example*) to connect opinion and reasons.
- Provide a concluding statement or section.

GRADE 4

Write opinion pieces on topics or texts, supporting a point of view with reasons and information.

- Introduce a topic or text clearly, state an opinion, and create an organizational structure in which related ideas are grouped to support the writer's purpose.
- Provide reasons that are supported by facts and details.
- Link opinion and reasons using words and phrases (e.g., *for instance, in order to, in addition*).
- Provide a concluding statement or section related to the opinion presented.

(*Continued*)

Figure 3.1 (Continued)

GRADE 5

Write opinion pieces on topics or texts, supporting a point of view with reasons and information.

- Introduce a topic or text clearly, state an opinion, and create an organizational structure in which ideas are logically grouped to support the writer's purpose.
- Provide logically ordered reasons that are supported by facts and details.
- Link opinion and reasons using words, phrases, and clauses (e.g., *consequently*, *specifically*).
- Provide a concluding statement or section related to the opinion presented.

GRADE 6

Write arguments to support claims with clear reasons and relevant evidence.

- Introduce claim(s) and organize the reasons and evidence clearly.
- Support claim(s) with clear reasons and relevant evidence, using credible sources of the topic or text.
- Use words, phrases, and clauses to clarify the relationships among claim(s) and reasons.
- Establish and maintain a formal style.
- Provide a concluding statement or section that follows from the argument presented.

TIP!

When I make a progression, I try to repeat the words and sentences from the previous level. That way, students aren't spending cognitive energy on decoding and understanding the words; their energy is on understanding the differences in the levels so that they are better able to reproduce them in their own work with their own ideas.

PARTNERING WITH CAREGIVERS

Caregivers gain deeper understanding of the expectations for writing when we share the standards with them, especially when we show them the standards in conjunction with examples of writing. The more caregivers understand the process and the expectations, the better they are able to support their children as they grow and develop as writers.

3. **Create exemplar texts that integrate the progression with the standards.** Once we have these standards in front of us, we can write our own exemplar texts that align to them, creating a progression of how the writing might develop throughout various grades and levels. We can do this for any genre, spanning a variety of grades. As an example, in Figure 3.2, I have taken the first part of the narrative writing standards from Grades 3 through 6, and I have written beginnings of a story that meet the description of the standard.

Whenever I use progressions with students, I want them to study the progression and make decisions about which level they're ready to aim for. I emphasize that *any* of the levels are okay—that the intent is the most important part. What are you trying to do and how are you doing it? These are the questions I want

Figure 3.2 Learning Progression of a Narrative Beginning

Grade Level	The Standard Says	Example That You Can Reach For
3	Establish a situation and introduce a narrator and/or characters	Cecily stood at the edge of the diving board. Today would be the day she jumped off. Her sisters and her best friend Kate were sitting at the side of the pool.
4 and 5	Orient the reader by establishing a situation and introducing a narrator and/or characters	Cecily stood at the edge of the diving board, her heart beating hard. Today would be the day she jumped off. Her sisters and her best friend Kate watched from the side of the pool, and they were ready to cheer for her.
6	Engage and orient the reader by establishing a context and introducing a narrator and/or characters	"I can do this," Cecily whispered to herself. She wasn't sure she believed herself, though. She stood at the edge of the diving board, her heart beating hard. Today would be the day she jumped off. She'd promised her sisters and her best friend Kate she'd do it, and they were watching from the side of the pool.

THINKING OUT LOUD

I normally include only three grade levels in a writing progression. In this example, the Common Core State Standards for what should be included in a narrative beginning is the same for Grades 4 and 5. Therefore, this progression spans Grades 3 through 6.

students to be able to answer. In this lesson, I emphasized that whatever choice they made was *okay!* The important thing was they understood what they were working on.

I can use this tool in a variety of ways. One of my favorite ways is to show it to students and challenge them to make decisions as to where they want to aim. Photo 3.2 shows a chart where I have written out a progression of information

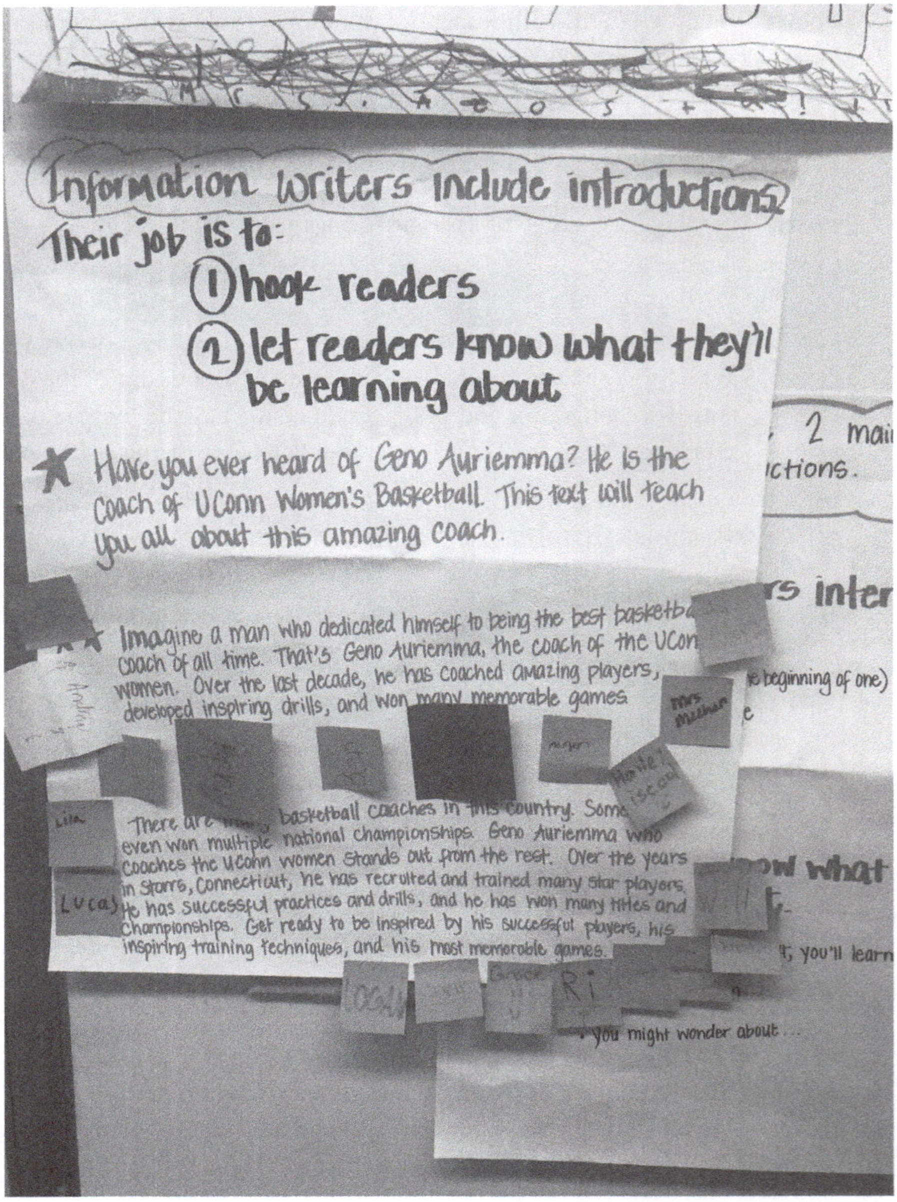

Photo 3.2 A chart that shows a progression of information introductions and students' goals for their own work.

introductions and then challenged fourth-grade students to make decisions as to what level they will try for in their own introductions. As you can see in the picture, students wrote their names on sticky notes and posted them to their goal levels.

I can also use progressions and exemplars to recognize where a writer is functioning and what my next instructional step could be. This way, keeping in mind the ZPD, we can identify teaching points that hover between writers' current abilities and just a little beyond. For example, I can show students a progression and ask them to decide how their work compares. Then, students can see a clear pathway for improvement of both my exemplar and their own writing. In Photo 3.3, students are analyzing their informational endings.

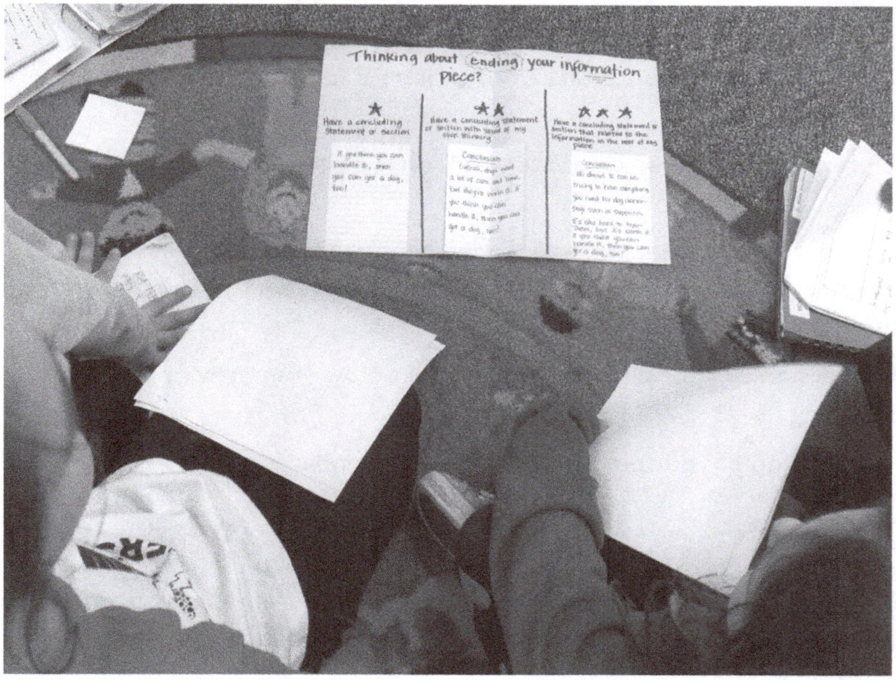

Photo 3.3 A small group of students studies the progression of an informational ending before deciding what they will try to accomplish in their own writing.

TIP!

The idea of creating exemplar texts for various levels may seem overwhelming. One idea for managing this task is to enlist students. Enlist student volunteers to study the standards and writing progressions, give them a topic, and challenge them to write a series of pieces at each level. Strong writers will enjoy this sort of a task, and you will have an immediate set of progressions and exemplars.

THINKING OUT LOUD

As confidence grows, so does the band of the ZPD. However, many striving writers have been receiving messages that they're not good writers for a while, and their band could be narrower than one would expect.

PAUSE FOR PD

Think of striving writers in your own instructional realm. What is the area in which they struggle? Maybe it's writing across pages. Maybe it's having a clear beginning, middle, and end. Whatever it is, break that skill down into a sequence. What are the precursor steps in the sequence, and what are your students' functional levels? Create a progression that could take your writers back to a place of independent functioning.

1. Decide which genre you will use to create your series and decide on a topic or story idea.
2. Look at the standard that is two or three grades *below* the one you teach. Capture the concepts from the standards in the most kid-friendly language you can. Consider including this on your chart.
3. Write the first version of your piece at least a level below your striving writer's current functioning level.
4. Write a second version of your piece that meets the standards of the subsequent level.
5. Write a third piece that meets the standards of the next level.
6. If you are doing this as a group, reflect on the differences together. If you are doing this individually, consider annotating your pieces with sticky notes that specify the differences.

Striving writers will find these exemplar progressions helpful because they can identify where they see themselves, and from there, they can work incrementally. Sometimes the work we show our striving writers is so much better than what they feel like they can do that it's easier to give up than get started. Most of our striving writers have foundational gaps in their skills and understandings; they will feel more confident and grounded if they experience success completing pieces that are more within their independent functioning level.

We can make progressions for any of the elements within genres. Sometimes I align my examples to stars as opposed to grade levels. If students are especially sensitive to being below grade level, then stars is a good alternative. That being said, I do think it's important for students to know their functioning level, just as I know that (if I were to run), I would run about a ten-minute mile.

In Appendix C, I have included examples of progressions that I have made for various skills. If you use my progressions, or better yet, ones that you design yourself, the important question to ask when working with students is "Where do you want to aim for your own writing?" And be prepared to help students set goals to meet that mark, based on the entry point that matches their current ZPD. Writing progressions work really well when we are working on goal setting with students. We can ask students to decide for themselves how many stars or what level they want to try for; to an extent, any one of the columns is an okay place for students to aim for, as long as they are making it and then pushing themselves to move across the progression in the next piece or in a revision.

When we determine where and how students get stuck in their process, we can help them find the right entry point.

We have to be able to know where and how students get stuck in their process if we are going to provide meaningful instruction. In John Hattie's 2018 updated list of factors related to student achievement, cognitive task analysis is noted with the fourth highest influence (Hattie, 2018). Cognitive task analysis is when we break down the implicit and explicit knowledge that is involved in completing a complex skill (Clark, Feldon, van Merriënboer, Yates, & Early, 2008). Complex skills involve the integration of both automatic and developing knowledge, which writing definitely does. When we apply this concept to writing, students benefit when they understand the steps in the process and have a clear idea of a progression of attainable goals within that process, regardless of level, regardless of genre.

Think about how we usually teach narrative writing. We teach students how to generate ideas, how to plan, and how to begin the drafting process. Once they are drafting, we can teach them more sophisticated ways to begin stories, to develop them by adding details and dialogue, and to end them. And somewhere along the line, we teach about conventions and maybe even some grammar. In many ways, those skills all stand on the shoulders of the previous skills, as well as the learning that has happened in previous years.

But what happens when there's a breakdown?

Sometimes I make the analogy of breakdowns in writing skills to Swiss cheese when I am talking to teachers. "You have to take action on the cheese if you want to fill in the holes," I say. "Think about heating up the cheese and then think about reteaching the students." Maybe an electrical circuit is an even better analogy for some of our striving writers. In a circuit, if we are missing a connection, the light bulb won't glow. Similarly, if students are missing a step in the writing process, they will stop producing and completing pieces. If they can't think of an idea, they can't plan. If they can't plan, they can't draft. If they can't draft, how will they add details or try out conventions or improve their grammatical/language skills?

So, let's think about the progression of skills across the narrative genre—not so much about the standards, but about the steps in the process—to complete a cognitive task analysis. If we break down the steps of writing a story, it looks somewhat like this:

1. Think of an idea.
2. Plan how your story will go—this could be through talk, pictures, or written words.
3. Decide on the important parts (at the very least, the beginning, middle, and end).
4. Draft, making sure to pay extra attention to the important parts.
5. Include elaboration such as
    a. Action
    b. Description
    c. Talking
    d. Thoughts
6. Use the best capitalization, punctuation, and spelling that you can.

TIP!

For younger students, I replace the third step with sketching across the pages. Their drawings provide the same scaffold as the beginning, middle, and end decisions. It's more important that they think sequentially and get words onto the page than it is for them to recognize the important parts of their stories. Sometimes drawings can serve as an entry point for our older striving writers. Drawing is an important precursor to writing that is frequently overlooked in upper elementary classrooms.

When students hit the expectation that some types of writing involve research—usually in fourth or fifth grade—then the number of skills that have to be intact for them to get to a final product increases. Not only do they have to think of an idea, plan, and draft, but they also have to read, take notes, categorize and integrate information, keep track of sources, and understand the differences between paraphrasing and quoting. Almost always, striving writers are striving readers, so many of these skills are challenging if not frustrating if not demoralizing.

Once students know the steps of the process, they can better identify the places where they get stuck, where they struggle, or where they need instruction. Let's walk through what this looked like with Madison below. I knew that Madison was able to think of narrative ideas. She did, however, struggle to initiate her written work. Talking and drawing are precursors to writing (Horn & Giacobbe, 2007), so I could lean on my task analysis to jump-start Madison's writing with talking and drawing as an entry point:

1. Telling the story
   Using a three-page booklet, I had Madison tell me her story across the pages—beginning, middle, and end. I did NOT write for her in this step, but I did have her tell me her story more than once.

   With repeated tellings, students clarify their stories in their own minds, and they add details, as well. Having students tell their story multiple

THINKING OUT LOUD

If I know that students have memory issues, and they won't be able to draw or write the whole story in one sitting, then I may challenge them to think of one or two words to write on sticky notes that will help them remember. I still do not write the words for them; I have the child write the words.

Photo 3.4 Madison drew pictures in her notebook of her story about Imani having her hair done.

THINKING OUT LOUD

Sometimes drawing can turn into an avoidance tactic. I try to pay close attention to how much time a child *who is able to write* spends on drawing. If I think they are using the artwork to avoid writing, I will suggest that they move their drawing along. Many times, I discourage them from using colors since the purpose of the pictures is to plan and remember the story.

times also helps them to remember their story, which is sometimes a stumbling block for striving writers.

2. Drawing the story
   I gave Madison a choice of how to draw her story. She chose to draw it in her notebook. Although her pictures are more detailed, colored, and elaborate than I would have liked, they worked to help her hold onto her ideas (see Photo 3.4.).

3. Writing the story
   Madison was able to begin writing her story. When she faltered, I could refer her to the pictures, and she was able to regain her writing momentum.

> Pictures are powerful scaffolds for students since they remind them of what they were thinking. Writing involves memory, and many striving writers are faster sketchers than they are word makers.

Distilling sequential steps in the writing process helps strivers because it offers them the language to express their challenges, too. And it seems more approachable, more chunkable. We teachers also gain instructional insight because we can focus our efforts on high-leverage entry points for students.

We empower students and engage them in their development as writers by teaching them to self-assess their process—and progress.

The more students are able to participate in the process and learn how to self-assess their own process, the more we empower them and engage them in their development as writers. The identification of the ZPD is largely the responsibility of the teacher, while the development of a task analysis could be a teacher's responsibility or the collaborative effort of teacher and student. Making tools that clarify the progression of standards is also a teacher responsibility. However, if we continue to think about Hattie's influential factors that relate to student achievement, self-reported grades is the second-highest factor in Hattie's 2018 list. While self-reported grades may seem to relate more to high school students, we can open the gates for self-assessment in elementary writing classrooms, as well, involving students in our assessment and evaluation work. Over and over, educators agree about the importance of students understanding what they are learning (Marzano, Pickering & Heflebower, 2010) and why they are learning it (Fisher, Frey, Amador, & Assof, 2018). Assessment is an area where we can absolutely invite students into the process, involving them and engaging them in their learning lives.

Self-assessment is a critical and lifelong skill for all learners. When we ask students to self-assess, we allow them space to think through the process themselves, to problem solve and to tell us what they need from us. Yet they need guidance in order to self-assess effectively. Following are ways I've been successful with guiding students toward self-assessment.

MAKE SURE THAT STUDENTS UNDERSTAND THE ACADEMIC LANGUAGE OF WHAT WE'RE ASKING THEM TO DO

Self-efficacy and engagement grow when students set goals for themselves and then seek out strategies and lessons that help them meet those goals. I'm frequently amazed at how many students are able to identify areas of growth. However, students need a common academic vocabulary in order to name their goals, and oftentimes our striving writers don't have that. Sometimes, we assume that they understand the steps within the process, but when asked about their goals as a writer, their typical answers are along these lines:

- To be a better writer
- To get a good grade

This is the equivalent of a soccer player saying that their goal is to win a game. Yes, that can be the ultimate goal, but there better be some more tangible and measurable ones in the process, such as dribble better, kick farther, pass more precisely. If our students can't name the skills that underlie the goals, then before we expect them to identify their own goals, we have to make sure they understand the progression of skills; this is where task analysis and learning progressions again are helpful.

Once students have the steps listed, they can begin to speak about goals with an academic vocabulary. We can coach them into thinking about the progression through the steps so they can find their own areas of challenge and growth opportunities. Henry Ford is credited with the statement "Whether you think you can or whether you think you can't, you're right." Self-efficacy is our belief in our own ability to succeed in situations or accomplish a task. Bandura (1997) identified several factors that increase self-efficacy, and the most powerful one involves experiencing success. Therefore, it is imperative that we provide opportunities for students—all students—to feel success and mastery within their work.

CREATE AND USE CHECKLISTS THAT TAP INTO THE POWER OF A GROWTH MINDSET

Checklists are powerful for many tasks. Atul Gawande, author of *The Checklist Manifesto,* wrote about how a five-step checklist used in intensive care units to prevent infections was credited for saving over 1,500 lives over the course of eighteen months (Gawande, 2007). Checklists work at the grocery store, for wrangling daughters into completing household chores, and yes—even in writing instruction. In order to create a writing checklist, we can mine the

CCSS writing standards, the expectations for a unit of study or even for an assignment and create a list of learning targets or expectations in terms of a checklist. Photos 3.5 show checklists that could be created ahead of time or, even better, made with students in conjunction with anchor charts and expectations of the unit. Additionally, *Writing Pathways* (Calkins, 2014) contains complete sets of writing checklists that cover all three genres, from kindergarten through eighth grade.

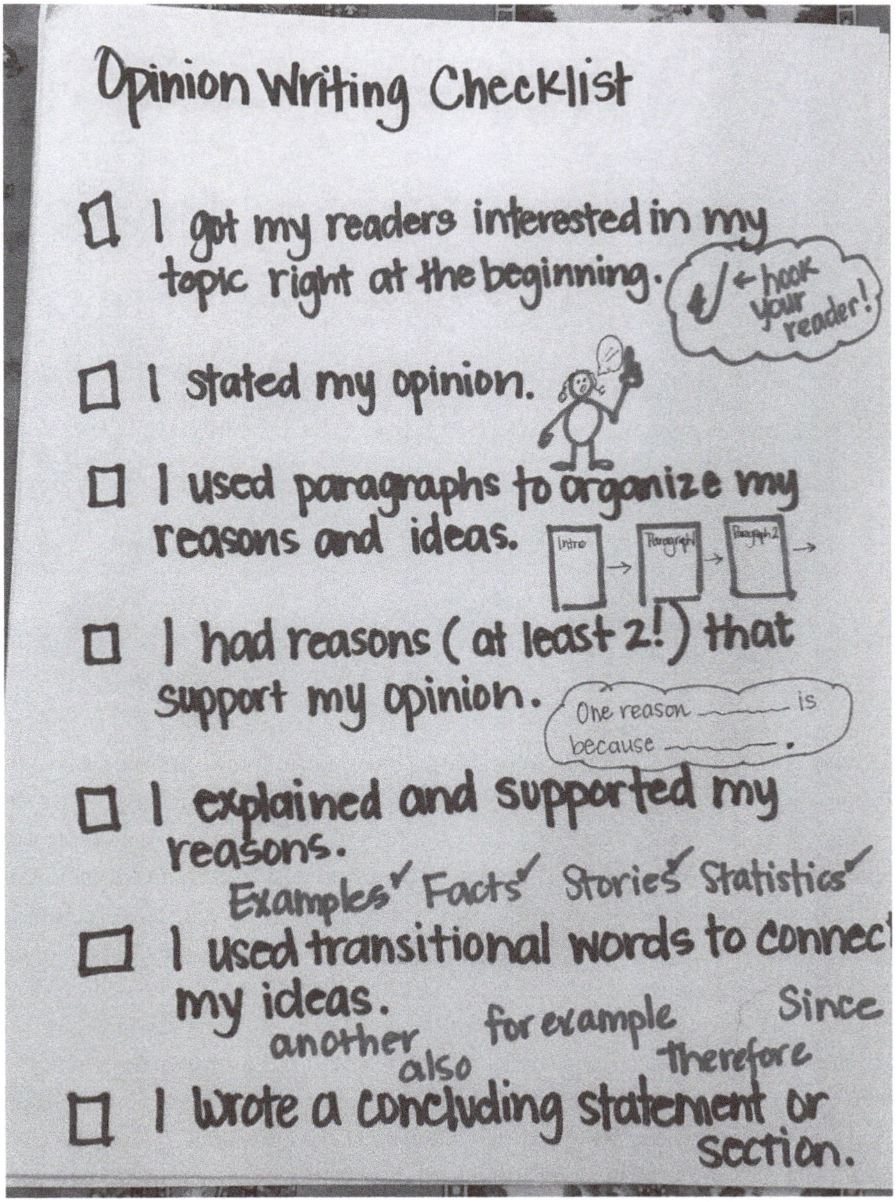

Photo 3.5(a&b)
A checklist like these for opinion and information writing can be created ahead of time or with students in support of their writing.

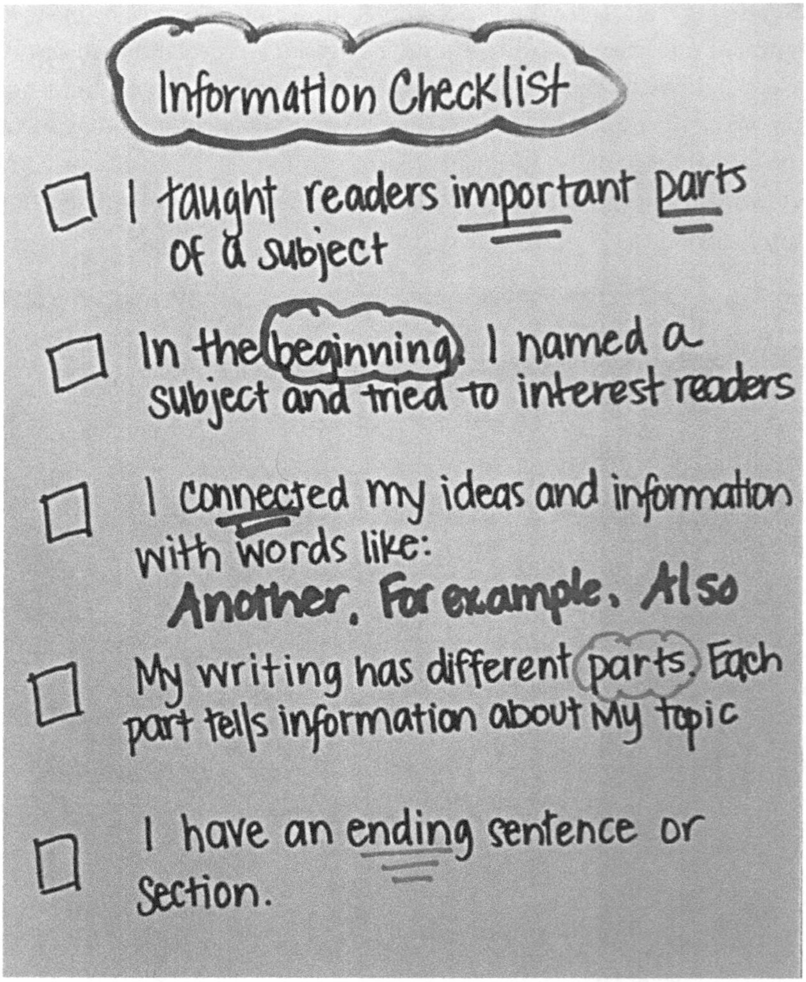

However you choose to obtain a checklist, keep in mind some important concepts about learning. First, learning isn't based so much on how smart you are but rather on how hard you persist through tough work; this is a major facet of growth mindset (Dweck, 2012). ***Yet*** is a powerful word, as it opens possibilities. When using checklists with students, it's beneficial to include three columns: yes, starting to, and not yet. This language keeps the doors of possibilities open, as well as makes a negative answer feel less defeating.

If you do create your own checklists, an activity that leads to a stronger understanding of the concepts behind them, consider designing them with students. Just as we need to understand the concepts, so do students. Additionally, using their own language is powerful because students are then intrinsically involved in the self-assessment process. In the book, *An Interpersonal*

Approach to Classroom Management, Davis, Summers, and Miller (2012) write that "the inclusion of cognitive engagement makes an important distinction between students' efforts to simply do the work and effort that is focused on understanding and mastery" (p. 23). Student involvement in creating checklists leads to understanding on their part, and when they understand, they are better able to move along the ladder of mastery.

The checklist that was used in intensive care units—the one that saved lives—only had five items on it. When presenting or creating checklists for written work, remember this! Sometimes less is more. Since striving writers are often striving readers, they may have to do some cognitive work just to read the indicators. You don't want them to use all their cognitive energy reading the checklists, so prioritize your indicators. Checklists are scaffolds, and scaffolds should be designed with a plan for removal. As students gain confidence, integrate skills, and demonstrate mastery, you can also have mini-celebrations with students where they cross off indicators and add different ones. That way, there's a cognitively manageable number at any given time.

THINKING OUT LOUD

As long as we don't overwhelm striving writers with too many indicators or items, checklists have the potential to help students self-assess and identify challenges in their own processes. Whatever checklist you use, keep in mind a few additional reminders:

1. The indicators should be at or just a little above students' present level of functioning. Sometimes it's even more effective to offer checklists to striving writers with lower indicators so that they can experience success. (Don't forget Bandura's wisdom and provide opportunities for success!)
2. You don't have to give everything all at once! Maybe offer students indicators that have only to do with structure at first. Gradually add development and conventions as students build confidence, vocabulary, and understanding.
3. Even consider giving these indicators individually. Some teachers I've worked with have created laminated keyrings of their checklist, and students only ever have one indicator in front of them at a time.

USE YOUR OWN WRITING AND BE THE LEAD SELF-ASSESSOR

If you are not yet a teacher who writes, please consider becoming one. One of the most important things teachers can do to be more effective teachers of writing is to write themselves, thus deepening their understanding of the metacognition involved in writing, as well as providing opportunities to reflect on their own practice (Newman, 1991). "Students need to see that writing can be a struggle; that there is nothing wrong with them if they do not find writing easy, or if their efforts are often less than perfect" (Smith, 1994, p. 220). That way, when we have conversations with students about what is hard, our validation is authentic. Additionally, we can pay attention to the metacognitive processes that writing requires. Trust me—you will be a better teacher of writing if you work your way through the process yourself.

While we become better teachers of writing when we experience the process firsthand, we can also use our own writing to model self-assessment. Revision is a scary step in the writing process; most writers struggle with reworking what's already on paper. We are vulnerable and sometimes even defensive when our words receive critiques. When we model that vulnerability, we send the message that we value risk-taking, another high-leverage quality of classrooms where learning happens at high levels (Marzano et al., 2010). Working in a third-grade classroom, the teacher wrote and demonstrated with her own piece of writing throughout the unit. During a lesson about transition words, I co-taught with her, nudging her to not only teach transition words but also to teach them in terms of function; there are transition words to introduce information, as well as words and phrases that explain or contrast information. With a revised chart, she realized in front of her students that her piece did not have much explanation, and she revised right then during the lesson. Students not only learned about transition words, but they also learned about the importance of revision through their teacher's willingness and commitment to make her writing better.

Returning my thoughts to Julia—the daughter who talked me into a run on Thanksgiving morning—she thrives on physical activity. She went to college thinking that she would be okay without being a member of a sports team, and she was wrong. She transferred her sophomore year to a school where she could play soccer. That was all well and good, except that she had a long way back to return to her playing condition. She recognized her level of functioning, and she designed a program for herself to return to peak condition. Her program followed a clear progression of the skills and fitness measures she'd need to master and accomplish. She recognized her entry point back into soccer, she set goals, and she established a pathway she could follow and self-assessed her progress in order to achieve them. Our writers, regardless of their functioning level, need and deserve the same. We can help them find their entry points and give examples of the progressions their writing can follow so that they can see their pathway for learning and growth.

End-of-Chapter Questions

1. How does our understanding of ZPD lead to greater empathy and better instruction for our striving writers?
2. How can a cognitive task analysis benefit our understanding of the writing process, as well as our students' understanding?
3. What tools and resources might you lean on in order to identify high-leverage teaching points?
4. What are some important considerations around involving students in their own self-assessment process?

Take Action!

1. Teach your students and any adults who work in your classroom about the zone of proximal development so that part of your conversation with learners involves where they feel like they are in terms of the visual representation of the ZPD.
2. Construct a cognitive task analysis of a writing task, thinking about not only the standards associated with it but also the series of skills that have to be intact in order to complete it.
3. Sit down with a striving writer and make a personalized checklist with them. Keep it minimalistic. Challenge your writer to think of three goals that will move them as a writer, and make sure that the checklist is used on a regular basis.

CHAPTER FOUR

CONSTRUCT BRIDGES FOR WRITERS TO JOIN THE JOURNEY

How can we change the steps and the process so that all writers can participate and produce?

Sometimes writers who face instructional obstacles benefit when they start their writing process at a different entry point. Maybe they spend so much time thinking of ideas that they never get drafting. Maybe they spend so much time reading and researching that they don't finish their essays. Maybe specific skills get in the way of their productivity. This chapter has ideas and strategies to provide bridges for writers to join into the writing journey from their particular entry points.

As a new driver, getting onto the highway scared my youngest daughter, Cecily, and it should have! We have a couple of different choices for entering the highway near our home. One involves a yield sign, and drivers have to wait until there's a space in the highway traffic before they can get on. Another entrance takes longer to get to, but it offers a long on-ramp before we have to blend in with other cars at a fast pace. Still now, after a few years of driving on her own, Cecily almost always chooses to take the long way to the more welcoming ramp. Only when there's no chance of traffic will she make a different choice. I wish that I could magically create bridges for her to have a safe route onto the highway, as once she gets on, she feels confident and able to navigate lane changes and faster speeds.

I'm sure many teachers would also love magical bridges for their striving writers. Writing can be like a highway. We stop and start, we try to figure out what we're going to write, map the route to get there, and if we're lucky, if the conditions are great, we enter the highway of writing. And even people who do a lot of writing or who have solid writing skills understand the jolts and jitters of finding our on-ramps.

Sometimes our striving writers need different and earlier entry points, as we thought about in Chapter 3, but sometimes these writers benefit from a bridge of some sort. In Chapter 3, I shared task analyses for various writing tasks, and while these steps in the process are important to know, we also have to understand that learning to write does not always follow a specific sequence of steps. As Smith (1994) puts it, "Writing develops as an individual develops, in many directions, continually, usually inconspicuously, but occasionally in dramatic and unforeseeable spurts. And, like individual human development, writing requires nourishment and encouragement rather than a restrictive regiment" (p. 220).

Bridges allow us to travel from one spot to another, avoiding difficult or impassable terrain. Striving writers may experience steps in the writing process that aren't yet passable, but once through those steps, they can rejoin the process. Oftentimes, we teach sequentially, but sometimes it's beneficial for learners when we pause and identify where and how they get stuck in the process. Just as Cecily struggles with the on-ramp but is okay on the highway, some of our writers can't quite see or figure out the on-ramp for themselves to begin working on a piece of writing, so they benefit from bridges to slightly different entry points. Experiencing success is important for learners and can result in an increased willingness to take risks and, consequently, be able to grow at higher rates (Bandura, 1997.)

Emmett, a striving writer who was masterful at every task-avoidant behavior I have described, produced almost no actual writing in his fourth-grade informational writing unit. As I began work with him, I made it clear to him that our goal together needed to be about volume.

"I just get stuck," he said.

"So let's get you unstuck," was my response.

I shared an information piece I'd written about Nathan Hale, but I explained that I'd left the introduction and conclusion for him. Within ten minutes, Emmett wrote an introduction and a conclusion, both meeting the expectations of fourth-grade writing.

In subsequent days, we planned his lessons in a backward fashion. We gave him bullets of information to write into a paragraph form—as well as introductions and conclusions. Next, we had him add to notes we'd already started before we had him initiate an organizational structure for his notes. While initially his teacher thought this would be a lot of additional work for her, when we talked it through, she realized that she could create teaching tools that would support her instruction in subsequent years and for many other students.

By the end of the unit, Emmett wrote several pieces—he was stunned and proud of how much writing he produced. Although he did not complete a piece from start to finish all on his own, he grew as a writer, and both his teacher and Emmett recognized his growth. Because he produced written work, we could provide feedback to him, and he could set goals about next steps. He also had metacognitive realizations about environments and tools that help him as a learner.

In order to produce writing and grow as a writer, Emmett needed a few bridges throughout the unit. While the work I did with Emmett was a mixture of shared writing, backward chaining, and strategic writing, I have isolated these strategies within the three main genres of writing: narrative, information, and opinion. The strategies I share in this chapter lean on the thinking and knowledge of colleagues in other grades and fields. My hope is that you develop your own toolkit and repertoire of strategies that you can reach for when you are working with your own Emmetts in your classroom.

THE BIG IDEAS

1. **Even though choice is a critical feature in many writing classes, sometimes we need to remove choice in order to provide the temporary scaffolds that get students writing.** Choice leads to agency, no doubt, but it can also lead to minimal production and low volume. We're not going to move writers if they're not producing and practicing. While shared writing is usually associated with early primary classrooms, it is a powerful strategy we can implement in upper-level classrooms in order to inspire striving writers to get writing.
2. **The bridges we provide for our striving writers may need to be placed in different parts of the process.** In terms of thinking of an idea, making a plan, and drafting, writing is a linear process. However, sometimes if we provide entry points later in the journey, building a bridge that even skips a step or two, our striving writers are more willing to try the earlier steps, which are more accessible. We can use principles of backward chaining, a model used by behavioral specialists, when building bridges with striving writers.
3. **Sometimes isolating skills is an effective way to improve overall performance.** Writing is a process and, as such, involves many different skills. Sometimes writers need more practice to strengthen specific skills instead of the entire process. Just as athletes or musicians isolate individual skills to practice in order to improve their overall performance, improving specific writing skills can help build confidence and achievement within the entire writing process, providing a bridge from one point to another in the process.

Even though choice is a critical feature in many writing classes, sometimes we need to remove choice in order to provide temporary scaffolds that get students writing.

Any writer—even those of us who *want* to write and consider ourselves fairly competent—will tell you that there have been times in their writing life when they just couldn't think of what to write. In many writing classes, we expect students to generate their own ideas. But if they are at all insecure or resistant, that first initial step frequently stalls the process. For many students, I lean on components of early education to jump start writers, specifically shared writing.

"So what are you going to write about?" I hear myself ask when I am in classrooms.

"Don't know," "trying to decide," or a shoulder shrug are common answers.

Maybe these responses are because the writers really can't think of a topic, and maybe these responses are because the writers have learned that no ideas leads to not having to initiate and engage in a task they don't like. Or maybe they have an idea but not the courage or the confidence to share it with the world outside of their head. In any case, not thinking of an idea leads to not writing. And we can't have that. Remember, writing is a practice, and striving writers especially need to write more volume in order to find areas of growth and challenge.

In an early elementary classroom, shared writing is an important component of balanced literacy. Shared writing is a supported writing experience in which the teacher and students collaborate to compose a text. Students generate ideas and talk through the plan and process, while the teacher does the actual writing, possibly using prompts, questions, and suggestions to strengthen the work. Teachers of strivers in upper-elementary grades can borrow ideas from primary educators and create shared-writing experiences for their students as well. Let's look at how it could look across the genres.

SHARED NARRATIVE WRITING

Students and teacher generate a character together, as well as a setting. The following chart works well:

Character	Setting	Trouble	Out of trouble

Photo 4.1 shows a chart I created with three fifth-grade striving narrative writers. Together, they agreed on a character, CJ, and they thought of some different places CJ hung out. We brainstormed various "troubles" CJ could have in his different settings, as well as how he'd get out of trouble. This process set the students up to think about the beginning, middle, and end of stories, as they each practiced telling the different sections of the stories.

The students worked to decide on the most effective beginnings, middles, and ends before they divvied up the work. These conversations involved higher-order thinking, as the students debated and evaluated the strengths and downfalls of each section.

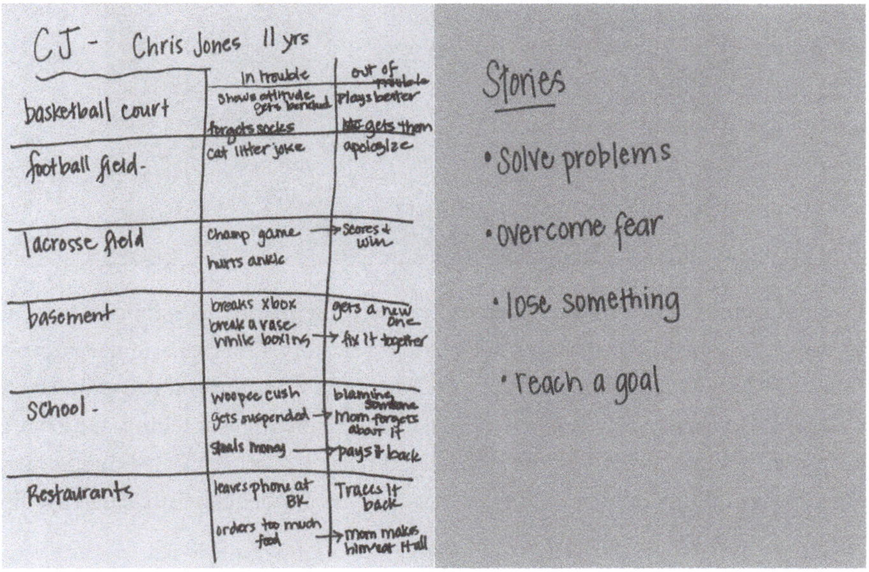

Photo 4.1 The students used these two charts as they developed their stories.

Once they felt confident about their collaborative story, each student took on a section, and within a day, they had a complete story that they all three felt responsible for. They annotated and revised the story, paying attention to how the plot unfolded, as well as how details emerged (shown in Photo 4.2).

Photo 4.2 Once students had written their parts of the shared story, they suggested revisions for each other.

While the entire process took less than three writing periods, the students were able to verbalize how it helped their understanding of story structure and development. Many striving writers spend many days on the same story without being able to give a clear plot summary. Striving writers benefit from thinking—or telling—and writing a structured story clearly and quickly; shared narrative writing helps them practice these skills and then transfer the skills into their own independently created stories.

THINKING OUT LOUD

In this example, I wrote the chart of story ideas for CJ. Whenever I make the decision to write *for* students, I make sure they know this is a task I expect them to take over.

We can use shared narrative writing in a variety of ways, depending on the ages and levels of students. In a primary classroom, students might develop the story through talk, and the teacher could write the story. In an upper elementary like the one in the example above, we might pull a few students into a small group. Depending on their level, we could go through this process with *one story*. Then, we would talk out *another* one of the story ideas, and each student would write *their own version* of it. Everyone is responsible for creating their own product, and even though the premise of the story is the same, the creations are different. Remembering the concepts of gradual release and volume, the group of writers now have a list of story ideas, and they can work through more stories. They get practice establishing clear beginnings, middles, and ends, and they can begin to work on developing the details that lead to better storytelling.

"Can I do this with my own character?" is a question I begin to hear from these students.

It's fun to respond sort of theatrically when I hear them ask this!

"Do you really think you're ready? You have a character and some trouble in mind?"

They nod, and then, just like that, they're working on their own story, and not our shared one.

SHARED INFORMATION WRITING

Recently, I joined a group of students as they ate lunch, and we all started talking about money. I happened to be sitting with a few students who had been having a tough time thinking of what to write about in their information unit, and I pointed out to them that they knew a lot about money.

"I think we should write an information book about money," I said.

They first looked at me like I was a little crazy, but then they got excited as they thought about the different topics they could create. By the time we got back to class, they were all on board. I met with four students who I knew had issues with thinking of topics and creating structure for themselves. They brainstormed topics, and I wrote the ideas on sticky notes. Bills, coins, how to make money, how to spend money, and the different forms of money were our final sections. During the course of one independent writing time—about thirty minutes total—Ryan wrote all about the different bills, August filled two pages describing the various coins, and Aidan had a lot to say about the various ways to make money. Max took a little longer to get going but was able to fill about a page with ways to spend money. Since Aidan finished first, he took on the task of writing an introduction for the entire piece, and August was able to complete a conclusion. They were thrilled to have a complete book.

Maybe more importantly, they made some insightful realizations about writing information pieces. Aidan had been planning a piece about sharks, a topic he didn't actually know that much about.

"I just realized that I could write a better piece about cell phones," he said. "I actually know a lot more about them than what I know about sharks."

August had been struggling to keep each chapter about one thing. Since he knew others were writing about specific topics, he knew he couldn't or he'd be writing "their information." Somehow, the process created a sense of ownership that helped him understand organization better and the idea that each chapter needed to be about one overall idea without overlapping other chapters or straying into material that didn't align. Photo 4.3 shows the shared writing piece our group wrote about our school.

LESSON PLAN: *Shared Writing With Students*

Materials Needed: Sticky notes, paper for informational writing

Teaching Point: Working through the complete process of writing is an important part of learning to write. Sometimes we can do this more efficiently by collaborating and completing a piece together.

Demonstration:

1. Find a topic that everyone knows about from personal experience—I've had success thinking about a local grocery store, the school's media center, money, and sleep. The most powerful way to find a topic is to *talk* with students and *listen* to them. Since we are taking choice away, it's that much more important for them to write about something that interests them.
2. As a group, brainstorm subtopics. I do this with sticky notes. This is the only part of the process when I am the scribe, and I write down as few words as

possible—just enough to capture the ideas. When we wrote about money, my sticky notes said *coins, bills, ways to make,* and *ways to spend.*

3. Have students choose their subtopics. I have never had issues with this, but if two students absolutely wanted to do the same section, I'd let them. My purpose is to bring students into the process of writing, get them thinking with structure, and use strategies of drafting; if we have two sections of the same thing *and the students know and recognize that,* the process is still serving my purpose. Remember to focus on the process and not the product.
4. Have students tell each other and collaborate on what they plan to write. Verbalizing and envisioning have the potential to help striving writers a lot.
5. Have students choose their paper. Bringing choice back into the mix, I show students three paper options with varying numbers of lines, asking them if they envision being able to write a little, a medium amount, or a lot. This is an important step for knowing your students' current functioning level. Offer a paper choice that is slightly below the lowest functioning level of productivity so all contributors feel empowered, within their ZPD, and that contributing is in their realm of possibility.
6. Send students off to write their section. Students may choose to work wherever they feel most productive—another option for choice when we've removed it from the topic. While they are drafting, you can offer them some key words to try to work into their piece—*also, another,* and *for example* are words I put in front of them, as well as *this is important because, therefore,* and *as you can see.* I may give these words to students on a sticky note or on a small piece of cardstock.
7. If someone finishes their section before the others, suggest that they write an introduction or conclusion. Sometimes I write the introduction while they are working, but usually it's a student who's finished. If more that one student finishes early, they might *both* write introductions and then compare how they did it.
8. Once everyone finishes their section, they can all write an introduction if no one else has—same for the conclusion. Then, make copies for everyone and celebrate the book they wrote together.

CLOSURE: We can all have copies of the piece we wrote together so we can see how we separate our sections, create and introduction, and provide an ending. We are working toward creating an entire informational text all on our own.

Photo 4.3(a-e) Shared Information Book About Our School

(a) I wrote the introduction once everyone committed to the section they would write.

Welcome to Latimer Lane! Latimer Lane is a school in Simsbury, CT. Character traits are an important part of this school – you'll love them. There's a great playground and wait until you ~~here~~ hear about the teachers!

(b) At a playground, you can have fun, make friends, and play different games. You can do tag, swing, soccer, basketball, hide and seek, and cops and robbers.

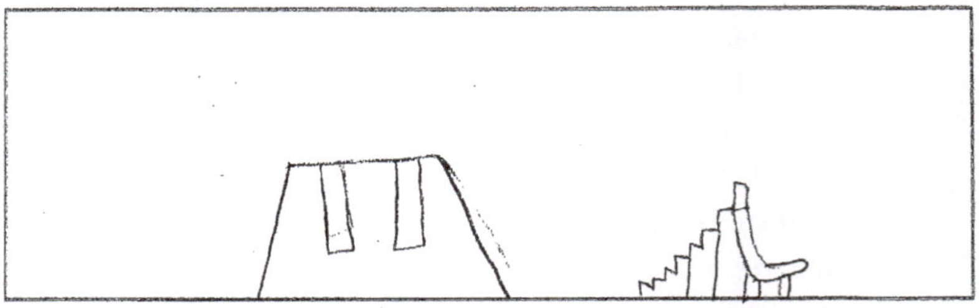

at a play grawnd you can Make frends and difrent play games. You can do tag swings and baskitball hide and Seak and COPS and robers.

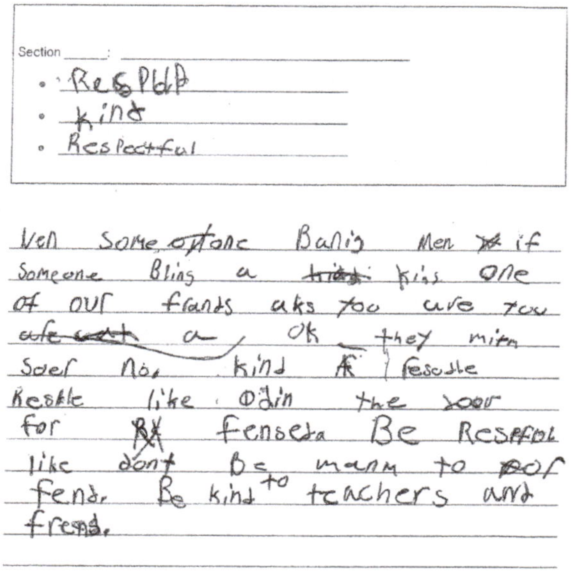

Section ____: ________________

- ~~RespDP~~
- kind
- Respectful

Ven some ~~ofton~~ Banis men ~~x~~ if someone Blins a ~~tran~~ kis one of our frands aks you are you ~~afe ant~~ a ok they mitn saer no. kind ~~K~~ Resosle Reskle like opin the door for ~~RX~~ fensets Be Resffol like don't Be manm to por fend. Be kind to teachers and frend.

(c) When someone is being mean if someone is being a kind. One of our friends asks you are you ok. They might say no. Responsibility like opin the door for friends. Be responsible like don't be mean to your friends. Be kind to teachers and friends.

One of the techers named Mis. Mcabe. is rally nice Becquse she reads rall funny Books. And she tackes ~~os~~ ~~ose~~ os on lots of feld trips. another is Mis. Snyder Becqs she was rally funny and nice.

I rally wanr you guse to hear obot the library there is a rally nice techer named mis bergenty. She loves to read books to little kids like fist graders and senkit graders and When you walk in ~~one~~ on one side there is cumputers and in fror you see a lot of Books.

(d) One of the teachers named Mrs. McCabe is really nice because she reads really funny books and she takes us on lots of field trips. Another is Mrs. Snyder because she was really funny and nice.

I really want you guys to hear about the library. There is a really nice teacher named Mrs. Brighenti. She loves to read books to little kids like first graders and second graders and when you walk in on one side there is computers and in front you see a lot of books.

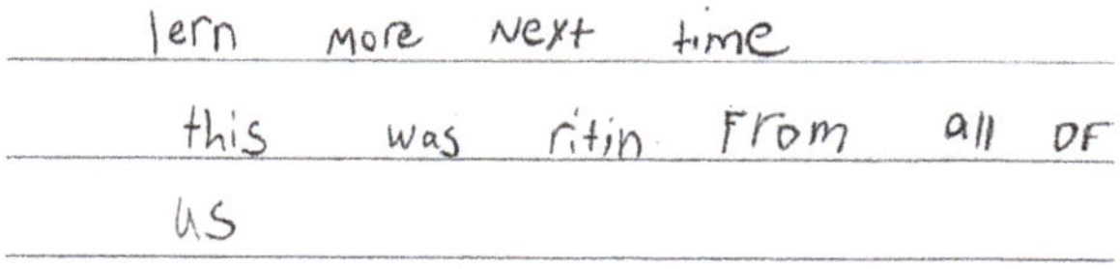

lern more Next time this was ritin From all OF us

(e) Learn more next time. This was written from all of us.

THINKING OUT LOUD

For these samples in Photo 4.3, I have provided translations in the caption for the pieces that are difficult to read. You'll see that with these students, I did not focus on spelling and punctuation. At this point in the lives of these writers, I want them to *write*. Sometimes we don't know what a striving student truly can or can't do because they've become *so* resistant and reluctant to write due to spelling and punctuation challenges. Once a student produces writing, however, we can decide on our next important instructional move. Should it be more about idea generation and composition? Or should we shift our focus to conventions and spelling? We can make those decisions when students have produced a body of work. Chapter 8 tackles spelling and punctuation challenges.

SHARED OPINION WRITING

The process for shared opinion writing is similar to that for information writing. Topics can vary, ranging from an issue students care about, a change they'd like to see, or even a letter of appreciation they'd like to write to someone in the community. Specific topics that have worked well include the following:

- Letters to custodians, lunch workers, or office staff. Children often come into contact with these people on a regular basis and can generate ideas and reasons to appreciate them.
- Letters to teachers or principals (or anyone with decision-making power) about what they wish would change. Ideally, these topics are ones that potentially *could* change because then students see the power of their writing. Some topics that have worked well include the following:
    - We should be allowed to chew gum.
    - We should be allowed to choose our own seats in the cafeteria.
    - We should be allowed to take out more than __ books at a time.

As with information writing, we can think about progressions and gradual release in terms of what we ask students to do once we have a topic. Students struggle with organization in opinion writing more than in the other forms, and by third grade, the CCSS have the expectation that students begin to approximate paragraphs. Therefore, it is even more beneficial to have an opinion piece be a shared project because the division of work parallels the separation of paragraphs. In other words, there is a *physical* separation that parallels a *conceptual* separation; *one* student writes about *one* reason, and so on and so forth. Photo 4.4 shows an example of a model piece that was created as part of a professional development session with adults.

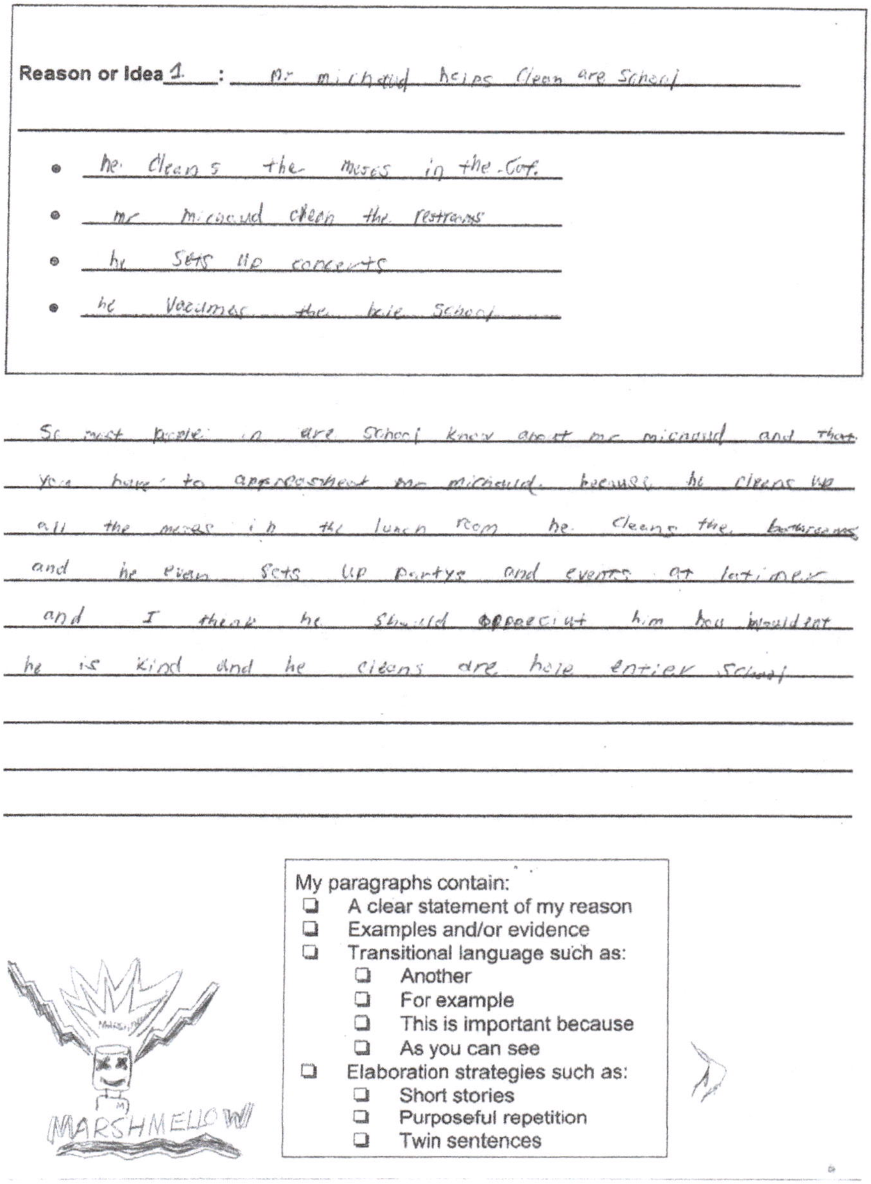

Reason or Idea 1 : mr michaud helps clean are school

- he cleans the meses in the caf.
- mr micaud clean the restrooms
- he sets up concerts
- he vaccumes the hole school

So most people in are school know about mr micaud and that you have to appreshent mr michaud because he cleans up all the meses in the lunch room he cleans the bathrooms and he even sets up partys and events at latimer and I think he should appreciat him hou wouldent he is kind and he cleans are hole entier school

My paragraphs contain:
- ❑ A clear statement of my reason
- ❑ Examples and/or evidence
- ❑ Transitional language such as:
  - ❑ Another
  - ❑ For example
  - ❑ This is important because
  - ❑ As you can see
- ❑ Elaboration strategies such as:
  - ❑ Short stories
  - ❑ Purposeful repetition
  - ❑ Twin sentences

Photo 4.4 In this example of shared writing, each student has written about a separate reason for their shared claim.

(Continued)

(Continued)

Reason or Idea 2: Mr. Michaud is always Kind.

- ✓ He help's clean.
- He helps the school.
- *✓ He moved our smart board.
- * He says hello to students.

Mr. Michaud is kind. For example he help's clean the class room and cafe and last the hallways. Another way he is kind is, he moves are smart board to the middle of the room. As you can see he is ~~verry~~ very kind. Another he says hello to students like every day. One last example he helps the school by cleaning it and makeing the school heathley.

My paragraphs contain:

- ☑ A clear statement of my reason
- ☑ Examples and/or evidence
- ☐ Transitional language such as:
  - ☑ Another
  - ☑ For example
  - ☐ This is important because
  - ☑ As you can see
- ☐ Elaboration strategies such as:
  - ☑ Short stories
  - ☐ Purposeful repetition
  - ☐ Twin sentences

Reason or Idea 3 **:** Mr. Michand is always willing to help.

- He always help clean a mess in the caferteria.
- He helps vacume our classroom.
- He helped carry the book order box to the classroom with nobody sayin to.
-

Mr. Michand is always willing to help. For example he helped bring the bookorder box without anyone telling him to. Another example is he helps vacume our classroom everyday. As you can see Mr. Michand is always willing to help because he always help neaten the school. This important because he always help in a good way and he always cleans a mess.

My paragraphs contain:

- [ ] A clear statement of my reason
- [ ] Examples and/or evidence
- [ ] Transitional language such as:
  - [x] Another
  - [x] For example
  - [x] This is important because
  - [x] As you can see
- [ ] Elaboration strategies such as:
  - [ ] Short stories
  - [ ] Purposeful repetition
  - [ ] Twin sentences

When we duplicate this process with students, they grasp the abstract concept that we have to stay focused within our argument, avoiding redundancy and maintaining organization. Sometimes within this process, I have had students say to each other, "That's part of my paragraph." This leads to important conversations that help them to understand overlapping reasons and the importance of structure.

Another way students benefit from shared opinion writing is that they create pieces of writing that need introductions and conclusions, and we can isolate those skills. Returning to the progressions from Chapter 3, we can hold up various levels of introductions (or conclusions) and challenge students to create ones for the pieces they've written collaboratively.

The bridges we provide our striving writers may need to be placed in different parts of the process.

Chaining is a technique used in behavioral analysis in which complex tasks are broken down into discrete steps (Cooper, Heron, & Heward, 2019). Applied behavior analysts do a complete task analysis, breaking the overall task down so that they identify each teachable unit into a behavior chain. Slocum and Tiger (2011) explain backward chaining as a system in which we teach the final step of the task analysis initially and progressively teach early components. Universal Design for Learning suggests "setting up prioritization, sequences, and schedules of steps" (CAST, n.d.). We can break these steps down within the order they come, but we can also break these steps down and prioritize them or work from different stages of the process. When we think about these steps and we break them down, we can invite students into the process on different sequences and schedules. While we don't necessarily think of writing as a "behavior," we can think of it as a series of discrete steps that students need to understand and progress through. In other words, we can place a bridge into the writing process and help a student to master a specific step. Then, once they incorporate it into their writing repertoire, we show them how that step fits into the chain so they can start to complete the chain of steps independently.

Let's look at what this could look like within writing. Typically, when we introduce a new writing unit, we generate excitement, immerse the class into the genre, present one or two anchor charts, and we're off. Sometimes we show students a process chart of the steps early on, and mostly, we move sequentially. We move through the steps, first to final, expecting experimentation, approximation, and mastery.

THINKING OUT LOUD

Striving writers are often striving readers and striving mathematicians. Therefore, they may have gaps in their understanding of the writing process because they are pulled for interventions for reading or math during writing time. Since they already miss enough instructional minutes, do *not* allow any sort of non-emergency excursions during direct instruction! Striving writers can hold off on trips to the bathroom, water fountain, or nurse for the ten minutes or so that direct instruction is happening.

Sometimes it helps our strivers to start in the middle of task, as opposed to the beginning, borrowing some of the thinking of backward chaining. In order to be more intentional about using backward chaining in writing instruction, I first create a task analysis (refer back to Chapter 3). Once we know the discrete steps of the process, it is much easier to *identify* the place where a child becomes stuck. Sometimes, beginning at the beginning plays over and over again into the stuckness, but beginning at a different point can provide a bridge over the mud for a writer whose wheels seem to spin.

BACKWARD CHAINING IN NARRATIVE WRITING

Over and over, I hear from striving writers that they can't come up with an idea for a story. Sometimes, necessity is the mother of invention, and one day, while working with a writer who struggled to think up an idea, I sketched a story across three pages representing beginning, middle, and end. On the first page, I sketched someone trying to think of a story. On the second page, the person came up with an idea, and on the third page, the person looked happy to have written a story.

"Write this," I said.

The child wrote their interpretation of the story, and seeing the success of this strategy, I sketched out a few more stories. While your stories could be ones you create, mine included the following:

- A child has a loose tooth, wiggles it until it falls out, and then gets a prize for it the next day.
- A child walks into a shoe store with a plan to get a new pair of sneakers. It's hard to decide because there are so many choices, but the child picks out a pair and seems happy with their choice.
- A pet hamster disappears while playing in its walker, and the child looks all over until the hamster is found and returned to its home.

(All of these and more are included on the companion website, resources.corwin.com/everychildcanwrite, ready for you to download and print for your students.)

These incomplete stories remove the task of thinking of an idea and planning how events will unfold. These stories are scaffolds, invitations into the complicated process of writing. "Sometimes it helps to get the hang of storytelling by having someone else's story to tell," I say. Some students benefit from using only one of my shared stories, while others choose to use two or three. Rarely have I had a student write more than that before wanting to generate their own idea and create their own plan. I celebrate and point out to them that while they're writing *my* stories, they're practicing some of their own important skills. (See how this is similar to the draw-think-write strategy from Chapter 3, as well? This time, though, the teacher is providing the bridge from thinking of an idea to writing it.)

THINKING OUT LOUD

Backward chaining is a form of a scaffold, so if you're going to try it, make sure you're planning for its removal. In this narrative work, students move from using my story starters to creating their own. Because I am thinking about the sequence of learning, sometimes I challenge them to think of an idea with me, then draw it on their own so they are one step closer to independence. Often, they make the jump straight to independence after writing out a couple of mine, though.

BACKWARD CHAINING IN INFORMATION WRITING

As students progress through the grades, we expect them to complete increasingly complex tasks that require the understanding and integration of information. These skills are new or developing for many students. The Common Core's eighth writing standard addresses the integration of information through digital and print resources, and it asks fourth graders to "recall relevant information from experiences or gather relevant information from print and digital sources; take notes and categorize information, and provide a list of sources" (CCSS, 2019). For students who already face challenges with reading as well as writing, we are asking them to reach for grade-level information writing standards, and at the same time, learn and integrate *unfamiliar content*. Thinking back to Cecily as a new driver, I would not want her to learn how to turn on and adjust her windshield wipers on a new street; I'd want her to be in well-known territory. So how do we balance the content and context of what students are learning and writing about in an informational writing class?

One of the first issues we run into when striving writers head out into the Internet jungle is that they find very little information and spend an inordinate amount of time doing so. Therefore, one of the first things I do is, within a unit, anticipate topics of curiosity, and collect some digital and print resources about them.

TIP!

Padlet has been a great tool for curating resources. Basically, it serves as a digital bulletin board. You can choose various set-ups and then digitally pin resources. When I use the "Grid" format, resources appear in columns.

Photo 4.5 The link to this Padlet is https://padlet.com/meehanmelanie/jr8hkqcbhcpv

TIP!

When I create Padlets, I work hard to keep more accessible information toward the top. This helps striving writers develop their background knowledge before trying to navigate more complex texts.

Sometimes collecting and curating resources still leaves striving writers with too difficult a task, and students get stuck in the notetaking phase. Therefore, I have created some sets of notes for topics that I anticipate are ones striving writers will choose or accept a nudge toward. To do this, I sit with the texts and take bulleted notes on cardstock that I've cut into squares. My notes are not complex—they are usually between ten to fifteen words each, with the name of the resource in the corner—and I try to create twelve to fifteen of them. As I create the notes, I intentionally try to find different but related information that can be sorted in more than one way. That way, students experience sorting information into logical categories or sections. When I am working in classrooms, I try to have sets for at least three topics in order to offer students choice, and I use different colored cardstock in order to easily sort them.

TIP!

Remember, you can reuse many of these tools year to year, so the up-front work of creating some of these scaffolds now will pay off in the long run.

With the elements of research and notetaking removed from the mix, I can turn the power back over to students. I can do one of a few things:

1. I can give students a few of the cards to sort and continue to give them notes as they are successful in sorting.
2. I can give students all of the cards and challenge them to sort them.
3. I can encourage students to generate questions about the topic and then write the questions that seem the most like topics or subtopics on separate pieces of paper. Then, they can use the cards to answer the questions.

Returning to the concept of backward chaining, we have now taken out two to three beginning steps in the process, and we can continue along the series of tasks, depending on what the students' entry points are. What is crucial is that we know what those entry points are, and the student goes through another process, beginning at an earlier point. Remember, striving writers should write *more* pieces than other students in your classroom because volume supports pathways toward mastery. Students who use my notes gain an understanding and appreciation for what notes could and should look like, and they can begin to approximate the work in subsequent pieces. When I engage in this chaining process with students, I constantly communicate where students are in the process and what goals they could be setting as learners.

PAUSE FOR PD

Let's make a couple of sets of information card sets.

1. Set up a Padlet (www.padlet.com), if you haven't already. When you select your board, you'll want to choose the grid style.
2. Think of three topics you know would interest striving writers in your classroom.
3. YouTube is a great resource for short topic-oriented videos. Find a three- to five-minute video to put at the top of your resources. Just a video overview of a topic helps orient students, and they are able to understand subsequent reading selections.
4. Find three to four additional resources that provide different or increasingly complex information about the subject.
5. Take notes on cardstock squares, using a different color for each topic. (Note: if you use cardstock, these tools are more durable, and your initial time investment seems more worthwhile. You can also create digital sticky notes, which I'll talk about more in Chapter 7.)

BACKWARD CHAINING IN OPINION WRITING

By the time students hit fifth grade, they are expected to write research-based essays. Thinking through the steps in the process of writing a solid essay, students must not only write, but also read and integrate information. Take a look at the steps listed in Photo 4.6 for writing a research-based essay.

As I worked with a group of striving writers in a fifth-grade writing class, they struggled with accessing information from research in order to write their opinion essays. In fact, they were spending all their time reading about their topics—vaguely understanding the ideas and taking ineffective notes. They couldn't get through the reading and information-collecting process, so there was no way they were getting to their essay writing.

Photo 4.6 I created this list of tasks as I thought about the unit for research-based essays. When I use this chart with students, I emphasize to them that Step 6 involves making some sort of a plan.

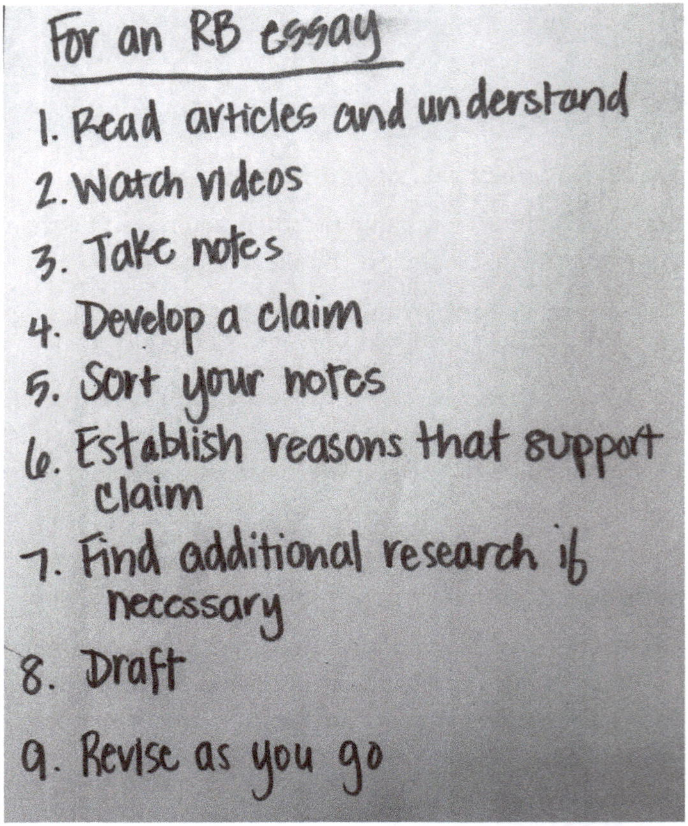

Within the principles of backward chaining, I *started* our strivers with writing an essay, offering *concrete* topics as choices. To do this, I thought about student interests and created collections of pictures of cars, of dogs, of sneakers, and of flowers. The students chose a picture-topic and wrote essays about their favorite, their least favorite, or the best in specific situations. Working progressively through the task analysis, the first couple of essays emphasized the importance of setting up a structure, and I taught the students how to make themselves a set of boxes and bullets. Each striver wrote three to four essays using the picture sets, developing their ability to plan, use transitional language, and add more and more details and evidence to their thinking. The students weren't trying to learn *all* of the skills for essay writing in one piece; they were building on a developing foundation.

Our backward chaining system allowed striving students to start from a position of strength, although it may have been from a position far from the regular starting point, since the regular starting point was reading through text sets and taking notes. Once they had developed intact skills later along the writing pathway, they were able to bridge to the other learning pieces—such as note-taking and organizing new information—and experience success, adding in elements of research.

In order to complete the initial skills of reading, note-taking, and integrating information, we went through a similar process we'd used for information writing, gathering text sets, and creating sets of notes. That way, students could enter the overall task at different points in the process without becoming stuck and nonproductive.

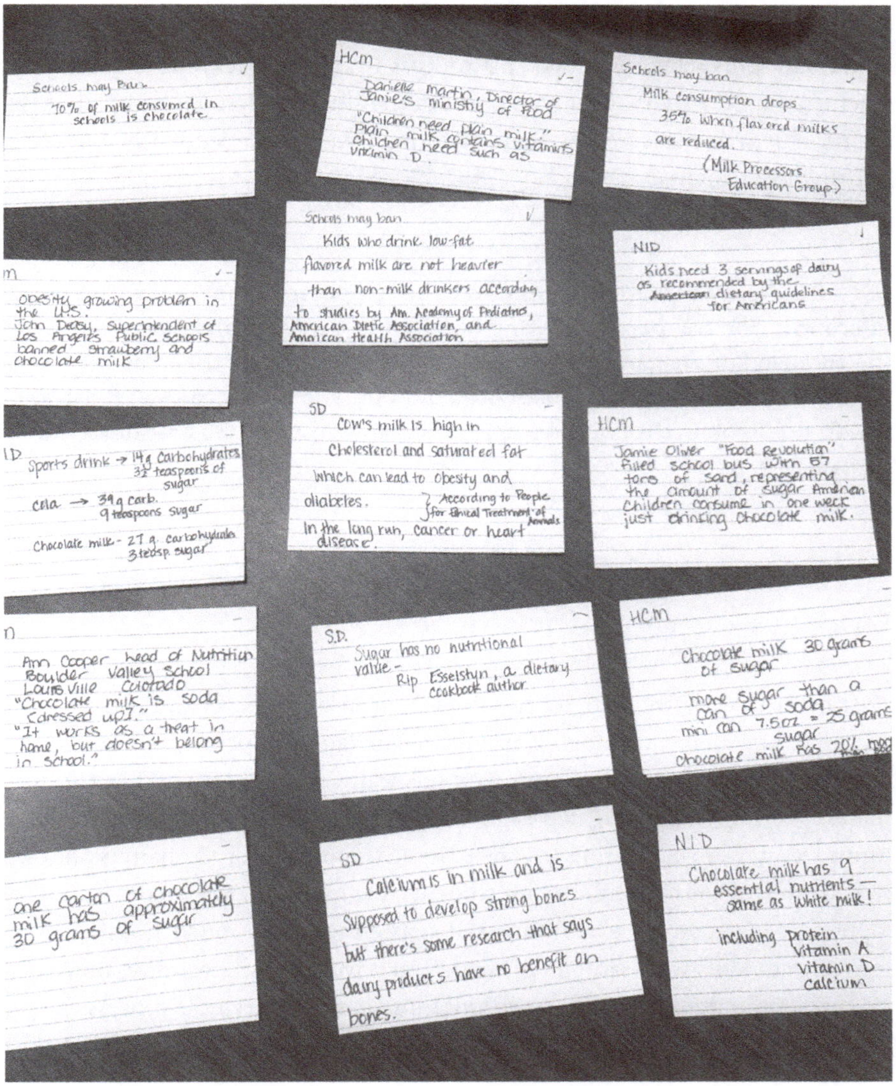

Photo 4.7 In our district, we follow the *Units of Study in Opinion, Information, and Narrative Writing* (Calkins, 2016), so many students research and write about whether or not schools should serve chocolate milk. The set of notes above are from the articles that support or refute serving chocolate milk in school.

TIP!

If you decide to create your own set of note cards for an issue, make sure you take the time to sort them yourself, making sure that there's enough evidence to create at least two reasons for both sides of an issue.

As in most endeavors, success inspires learners. Our students did not have to compliantly wait for an adult to walk them through each step; instead, they had pathways that empowered them to practice more intentionally toward mastery or targets that were within their realm of possibility. Their self-assessment and final outcomes were testimony of their growth as learners. In the classrooms where we used this process involving backward chaining and increased productivity, over 85 percent of the students demonstrated increased achievement as measured by their performances on independently completed writing assessments.

THINKING OUT LOUD

A scaffold is, by definition, supposed to be temporary. Whenever we introduce a scaffold for any part of writing, we should be able to explain how it will be removed. If we can't think of a plan for its removal, then the task we're asking students to do is probably too difficult and well into their frustration level. Remember that no one enjoys working in their frustration level. It's exhausting.

Sometimes isolating skills is an effective way to improve overall performance.

Just before Cecily went to get her driver's license, we knew she had to spend time on the highway moving from lane to lane. Therefore, we worked on smaller roads with multiple lanes and less traffic, isolating the skill of shifting lanes. We can isolate targeted skills with student writers in order for them to improve and grow. Writing involves the juxtaposition of so many skills, and when students, especially striving students, begin drafting, sometimes they are approximating almost everything and mastering pretty much nothing. If we provide students with samples of writing that we write strategically, they allow for practice and mastery of *just one targeted skill,* then the whole process can feel less overwhelming; students can feel more success; and learning gates can open wider. Let's look closer at how this can play out as targeted revision in narrative, information, and opinion writing.

TARGETED REVISION IN NARRATIVE

In the backward chaining section within this chapter, I shared some of the stories I give students when they are stuck. While I can use these stories to offer opportunities for students to write, I can also use these stories to target specific skills during revision. For example, I see many striving writers who overuse dialogue to the point where they don't know who is doing the talking and what the trajectory of the story even is. Sometimes, I intentionally write pieces that contain this same issue. This way, when I sit down with students, we can work together to revise first *my* writing and then their own. This targeted revision allows students to see the type of trouble writers can get into, as well as pathways to *fix* that trouble. So often we show students good writing and expect them to create it when, sometimes, they really need to see how to revise writing that contains pitfalls.

Other predictable pitfalls and problems I see in striving students' narrative writing include (but isn't limited to!) the following:

- Shifts in tense
- Shifts in who is telling the story (first person versus third person)
- No establishment of setting or minimal details about it
- Run-on sentences
- Lack of transition words

Keeping these issues in mind, I have created several versions of the same story, each one leaving out a skill that we can work on together. Once students have seen and talked through the trouble writers can get into and how we can *fix* it on *someone else's* writing, then they can take that knowledge and skill to their own writing with more confidence and subsequent success.

STRATEGIC WRITING IN INFORMATION AND OPINION

Just as I described in narrative writing, predictable problems show up in information and opinion writing when we look over the shoulders of striving writers. For example, lists show up in information writing. One of my favorite pages in my chartbook shows students how they can make list-like writing turn into more interesting text, and I have created a short sample of what list-like writing tends to look like (see Photo 4.8):

Photo 4.8 My sample of writing provides students with practice of ways they can improve list-like information writing.

The rest of the page offers students choices of how to improve *my* writing.

Using the same sort of thinking, I might look over a shoulder and find a student working on an opinion paragraph that has no clear link to the overall claim. For this commonly seen issue, I share a paragraph I've written that doesn't have a clear link to the claim, and we revise my paragraph together. This targeted practice enables and empowers students to head into their own writing, identify a similar issue, and then understand how to fix it.

We don't want these bridges to be permanent, as our goal should stay focused on creating independent, competent writers, but if striving writers need them to feel success and gain the courage and momentum to write further down the writing highway, then on subsequent pieces they are likely to find success and entry points without bridges we provide.

The process of making the work, challenges, and goals visible for students is powerful in that they truly become invested in their own pathway toward learning and mastery. Within the Universal Design for Learning is the importance of maintaining a focus on what we want students to know and what the barriers are; the strategies in this chapter can build bridges over the barriers, so we can help them maximize their learning. Bridges grant students access to the curriculum, which gives them opportunities to practice and engage in tasks, even if not in a concrete sequential order.

End-of-Chapter Questions

1. How can we use shared writing to change the mindsets of striving writers from "I can't get started" to "I am able to participate in the writing process?"
2. How can backward chaining offer students opportunities into the process that they weren't able to access through more sequentially oriented instruction?
3. When using any of these methods—shared writing, backward chaining, or strategic writing—how do we plan for transference to increasingly higher levels of work?

Take Action!

1. Sit down with a group of students—not necessarily a group of striving writers—and create a sample of shared writing. Sometimes it helps other students to see a finished product, and it will help you to see how the process can work with a group of enthusiastic writers.
2. Decide on a genre of writing and create a few "sets" that you can use for implementation of backward chaining.
3. Think about specific skills or learning targets that you know impact your striving writers. Create a strategic piece of writing that intentionally leaves out just that one—maybe two—skills.

Part 3

Providing Pathways

CHAPTER FIVE

THE POWER OF PAPER— DON'T UNDERESTIMATE IT!

How can we leverage paper choice to inspire our writers who face instructional obstacles?

The first parts of this book have focused on creating a productive environment, finding entry points, and building bridges. At this point, we are moving into providing pathways for progress. While the strategies in this book are aimed specifically for our striving writers, the ideas in this chapter may help any other writers in our classrooms. Our pathways begin with low-tech tools, and paper would be one of the most basic tools we can provide. Maybe because paper is so foundational, we don't think about its power in the lives of writers.

I have clear memories of paper from my own elementary school days, and I was in elementary school in the 1970s. The rough yellow paper was for drafting, and the white paper was for final products. I remember thinking that the drafting wasn't that important because the paper was ugly. I also rushed through the drafting because I didn't like the kinesthetic feel of the yellow paper. It even had a distinct smell. And I didn't like it! I don't remember the spacing of the lines, but I do remember that some paper made me feel like a writer, while other paper did not.

Paper has the power to both intimidate and inspire. When we give students a set amount of lines, we communicate an expectation. Our expectation could be above a student's ability or below it. Additionally, when we mandate a specific template (such as "write a how-to on this paper with the pre-numbered five steps . . . "), then we are limiting the students' choices, conforming *their* ideas and writing to *our* predetermined standards.

Let's think about the message that paper can send: Pieces have only one draft, final copies are worth more, we need final copies that are perfect—I'm not sure those are messages we want to send to our writers. In this chapter, we'll focus on how paper can send positive messages about writing to young writers. We'll also think about how we can use paper as a scaffold and also as a tool. Tools make any task easier and more efficient, whether a home-improvement project or a writing assignment. Once we've determined a striving writer's entry points to writing and built bridges through the process, paper choice can offer striving writers a way forward on the pathway to success.

THINKING OUT LOUD

While I will address some ideas about technology, I do think that striving writers make more growth when they begin their drafting on paper as opposed to on computers, at least until they become proficient on the keyboard, which usually doesn't happen until fifth or sixth grade. That being said, for students with severe dysgraphia and IEPs that specify the use of keyboards, you can read many of the ideas about paper with the lens of how they can be set up within a digital folder.

THE BIG IDEAS

1. **Paper has the power to communicate what is important—neatness or content?** Some types of paper even send strong messages about letter formation and handwriting. Writing instruction should be about ideas and the sharing of them.
2. **Paper choice communicates our expectations and helps students set expectations for themselves.** Without realizing it, we communicate expectations through our paper choices and options. Let's take a closer look at what paper says to our striving writers—and how we might change the messaging.
3. **Paper can be one of your most powerful scaffolds for focus and organization.** I'll say over and over that scaffolds should come with a plan for removal, and paper differentiation is a straight-forward scaffold to create and to plan for elimination.

Paper has the power to communicate what is important—neatness or content?

Sometimes I look at a piece of writing that is neat and has easy-to-understand spelling, and I am lured into the belief that the content will be great. Many times, however, those beautiful looking pieces are missing great *ideas*. Bobby, a fifth grader, has handwriting worse than my father's was—my father was a doctor, and he was testimony to the widespread belief that doctors have terrible handwriting. Since first grade, Bobby's work has been an aesthetic disaster, but his stories and the ideas that live within his lines are amazing. If someone had handcuffed Bobby with expectations of neatness, we would be missing out on some great work—and worse, Bobby would be saddled with the self-concept that he's not a good writer. How can we help kids, especially our strivers, to understand the value of their ideas over the neatness of their handwriting or presentation style? Let's start by thinking about something so simple it's often overlooked: the lines on the paper in front of our kids.

THINK ABOUT THE LINES

"Do you use the three-lined paper?" a teacher asked at her new teacher orientation. I was working with the new teachers, going over basic structures and components of our writing instruction.

"What do you mean?" I asked, legitimately not understanding her question.

"The kind with the dashed line in the middle," she explained. She had to draw it for me. Although I realize this paper is used quite often in elementary schools, I've repressed it.

"Why would you use that?" I asked.

I had meant the question to inspire reflection on her part, but she must have sensed my disdain for the paper. My point to this new teacher—and I did try to soften my delivery—was that those lines add a significant element of cognitive demand to an already challenging process. If you have a student who is focused on making the perfect letter—or even less than perfect but with a lot of effort—then that student isn't going to be thinking as hard about the content of the ideas. For the most part, this type of paper shows up in early primary classrooms when children are first learning letter formation, but if you are using it with your older students, please consider getting rid of it.

In Chapter 3, we discussed cognitive task analysis, and for young and striving writers, we can add letter formation to the list of tasks required. Not only are we asking students to think of and remember ideas, they are also learning fundamental skills within the writing process—letter formation, sentencing, spaces between words, letter–sound correlations. The last thing we want to do is paralyze students with paper that implies that perfect letter formation is necessary. Whenever we can lessen the cognitive demand, we should! In this

Pause for PD

Go ahead and try to use this type of paper. Write about what you had for breakfast this morning, and make sure that you keep your lower-case letters just at the lower line. Upper case letters should go to the top line. Use all you know about handwriting to keep those letters perfect. Then, write about what you had for lunch on less restrictive paper. Pay attention to the cognitive work you are doing, and think about that work from the perspective of our young writers, especially ones with poor fine motor skills.

Partnering with Caregivers

Many caregivers are understandably concerned with their child's handwriting. The more we can explain the cognitive demands of the writing process, the better we can engage caregivers as partners. Yes, writing involves letter formation, but writing also involves the generation of ideas, planning, and drafting. Additionally, we can suggest activities that build fine motor strength and coordination. Children can develop fine motor skills through activities such as cutting paper or materials, tearing paper, using clay or Play-Doh, coloring, or drawing. We can even teach parents about the benefits of different positions for improving fine motor strength and control—some children have a much easier time writing, for instance, if they lie on their stomachs on the floor.

case, we can remove the expectation that letter parts *have to be* one size and not another, so that the thinking energy can streamline straight to the process of getting ideas down on paper.

THINK ABOUT FONT SIZE AND PERSONAL COMFORT ZONES FOR STUDENTS

At the beginning of a writing class, Aaron, a third grader, took his papers—a story he'd been working on over the course of a few days (and one with a clear beginning, middle, and end and a lot of voice, as well)—and he ripped it up.

When I talked to him about why he did that, he explained that it was too messy.

"Messy doesn't matter," I said. "The ideas matter."

We debated that point; he was stuck on the idea that handwriting and spelling were the hallmarks of good writing. I worked on building Aaron's courage as a writer.

"Your bedroom should be neat," I joked with him. "But I can handle messiness in your writing, as long as your beautiful ideas are shining through."

TIP!

I see many tools, such as pencil grips and slant boards, for students with poor fine motor skills when I am in classrooms. Sometimes those tools provide distractions. Try having students lie on their bellies to write. It works and sometimes offers a quicker, less distracting fix.

Aaron has fine motor challenges, as many striving writers do. Originally, he had been working on basic composition paper. The lines are tight, and Aaron had to work hard to fit his writing within those spaces. When his writing didn't fit in those spaces, he became frustrated with the "messiness." When we moved him to specially designed paper with wider lines, he was able to concentrate more on his *story* and less on his handwriting.

Line size is complicated, and we have to respond to and differentiate between the writing we see. For some students, wider lines will cause them to write larger, sometimes with just a few words on a line when they are capable of more than that. Those students might benefit with more narrowly spaced lines.

My toolkit travels with me from classroom to classroom, and I have an entire folder for paper choices. (You can download some of the paper choices I offer kids directly from the companion website, resources.corwin.com/everychildcanwrite.) I am constantly giving these to teachers and refilling this folder. Line size and numbers matter in terms of the comfort that writers feel as they do something as basic within the writing process as making letters. Your writers, especially your striving writers, will grow more as writers when they have paper that feels comfortable to them.

THINKING OUT LOUD

I'm not saying that handwriting doesn't matter, but the most important aspect of it is that students are able to read their own writing. Truth—every now and then I get whirling on an idea in my notebook, and I can't read my own writing. Just saying. Students can (and should) continue to work on handwriting and fine motor skills, but not in conjunction with the complexity of writing original texts.

Paper choice communicates our expectations and helps students set expectations for themselves.

Lincoln, a first grader, was staring into space when I sat down next to him. His paper was full of erasures next to the steps for a how-to page.

"What are you working on?" I asked.

"I'm trying to figure out what step to leave out," he answered.

"What do you mean?" I asked.

He explained that getting ready for soccer practice had six steps, but his paper only had *five* spaces. Even when I showed him that we could add a number and a line, he was too committed to his issue of eliminating a step rather than writing an extra one.

Thinking back, I realize that if I'd given him a blank piece of paper and taught Lincoln to make his own lines for however many number of steps he'd need, then he would be taking charge of his own writing in a much more authentic way.

The number of lines sends a subtle but strong message to writers, in terms of writing standards. Ten lines could mean that the expectation is for that page to be about ten lines long. For striving writers, a piece of paper with lots of lines might feel overwhelming—the more lines, the more overwhelming. Even the size of paper is something to consider as we think about striving writers and what gets in their way. I want my writers to think "Yes, I can fill up those pages!" I don't want them to think, "There's no way I can write that much." Additionally, I don't want them to write bigger to fill the lines or create entire lines of exclamation points—which I've seen!

Let's think about some of the ways we can communicate our expectations of our writers—and help them set clear expectations for themselves—with the paper choices we offer.

SET UP AND TEACH INTO PAPER STATIONS

The more students can have choice within their independent writing lives, the better, and paper is an opportunity for choice. Sometimes, I'll pull out three options of paper with varying line numbers for a student, as shown in Photo 5.1. I make this paper myself by creating a text box and adding lines below it. That way, I am always able to customize my paper choices.

"What one do you think you're ready for?" I'll ask.

Photo 5.1 You may download any of these options for paper choices from the companion website, resources.corwin.com/everychildcanwrite. Feel free to print these or create your own.

I actually love watching students process this question. They really do understand that their choice represents a commitment on their part.

While I keep my paper choices in a folder within the traveling bag that comes with me into classrooms, many teachers set up paper stations where a number of paper options are readily available in bins or folders. They teach into these stations by talking to students about the options available and the responsibility of writers to make decisions as to what choices work optimally for themselves. Every now and then, a writer will need a nudge to move along the number of lines continuum, but mostly, children make great paper choices for themselves.

TIP!

Some students may need more guidance than others about the choices they make. You can think about individual conferences or small group meetings to talk about the rationales and decision-making process.

LESSON PLAN: *Teaching Students How to Choose Paper*

Materials Needed: Several different choices of paper with varying numbers of lines

Teaching Point: We can choose paper in order to support the work we are doing as writers, making sure that we

- Have the right amount of space for our ideas
- Set ourselves up to move to different pages for different parts of our writing (a different scene in narrative, a new idea in opinion, a different section in information)

Additionally, we can use paper to

- Create reminders on the pages about what belongs within each part
- Leave space for revision

Demonstration: Teacher can share their own writing plan and model thinking about what will go on each page, making intentional decisions about the number of lines that are anticipated, as well as the plan for each page.

We can also teach students to design their own paper and sometimes nudge students toward paper with just a few more lines that they might have been using.

CLOSURE: Whenever we are writing something, we can envision how much we have to say and make decisions about paper. We can also push ourselves to write more by choosing paper with more lines, and if we feel like we need reminders, we can even choose paper that includes small checklists on the paper itself. It's up to us to decide what we need as writers.

TAP INTO THE POWER OF PAPER STRIPS AND STICKY NOTES AS REVISION TOOLS

Writers—all writers, and especially striving writers—struggle with the revision process. And yet, revision is **the way** we become better writers. For striving writers, the idea of revisiting their work—reading through it and trying to think about what should be added or taken away—presents its own set of challenges, but additionally, sometimes the words don't physically fit on a page.

Paper strips and sticky notes are playful and less intimidating ways that we can use paper to encourage the revision process. Photo 5.2 shows what this looks like in practice. We had a small group of students who hadn't stated their opinions, and because we had paper strips, they were open to writing an opinion statement and taping or stapling it where it belonged on their piece. Writing pieces can look like a construction zone with different colors and sizes of paper strips, and students enjoy using them.

Paper strips offer huge amounts of flexibility in a classroom. We can change up the size of them to accommodate for various scales of revision. We can also change up the colors for various types of revision. For example, I have seen one teacher use four different colors of revision strips during her narrative writing unit. One color is for dialogue, another is for description, another for action, and one more for inner thinking. Many of her students loved switching up the colors, and they were making intentional decisions about the types of elaboration they were using in their narrative work.

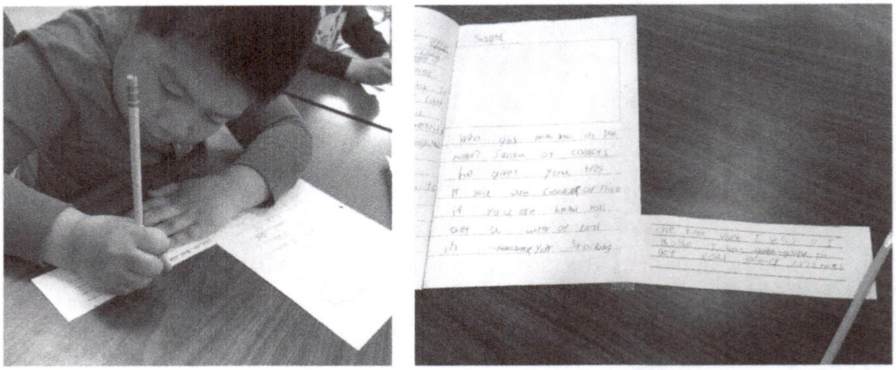

Photo 5.2(a&b) Paper strips offer students more space to revise and can provide a playful feeling to the revision process.

Paper can be one of your most powerful scaffolds for focus and organization.

At some point, all writers struggle with structure. We write and write, and then we read what we've created and it makes no sense. Organization is challenging for many striving writers, and writers tend to dump all of their ideas in as little space as possible, making it difficult to read and nearly impossible to revise. We can use paper to scaffold writers as they work to organize their thoughts and develop their ideas.

One of my favorite strategies for using paper as a scaffold is to provide students a packet of three pages and ask them to write a beginning on the first page, the middle of their story on the second page, and the end of the story on the third page. That's it! Even if there are only a few lines on each page, a three-page packet is going to help a striving second grader—or even older students—to think about and write through a sequence of events.

We can also use paper to serve as a planning tool. For example, Madison has struggled to remember her ideas, even though she has some lists in her writer's notebook. We took her ideas out of her notebook and had her write notes for herself, just in terms of beginning, middle, and end. Now, with those cards stapled to the front of her paper packet, she is set up to write. She has three stories ready to go: one about getting a shot, one about losing her phone, and one about getting a special present for Christmas (Photo 5.3 shows Madison's story planning).

PAUSE FOR PD

Take some time and draft a story across first three and then five pages. Try to write different versions of the same story that meet the various grade-level expectations below. Pay attention also to how the paper supports your understanding and creation of organization and structure.

Grade 1	Grade 2	Grade 3	Grade 4
Three pages with enough room/lines to describe some details, include temporal words and have a sense of closure. Students will understand the separateness of events if they learn to switch their page for a new event and for their end to their story.	Three to five pages with enough room/lines to describe actions, thoughts, and feelings. Again, students will learn to distinguish between events if they are physically writing on a separate piece of paper.	Three to five pages with enough room/lines to describe actions, thoughts, and feelings. Again, students will learn to distinguish, recognize, and produce written work with more details when they are physically writing on a separate piece of paper.	Three to five pages with enough room for actions, thoughts, and feelings, as well as sensory details. When given a few extra lines than in third grade, students will see the physical evidence of more sensory details.

My message to Madison and other students like her is this: "When you get to the middle of your story—past the beginning—then you turn the page. If you need more space, you can use the back, or we can add a page. When you are starting a new event in your story, you turn the page. If your event doesn't take up much room, it's okay. We can still understand that it's an event." I cannot tell you enough how much this helps story-tellers develop and internalize the structures of story. Sequence is such a critical understanding.

Another benefit of these paper packets is that once we get these students to *spread out* their ideas, then they have space, and they can see what they need

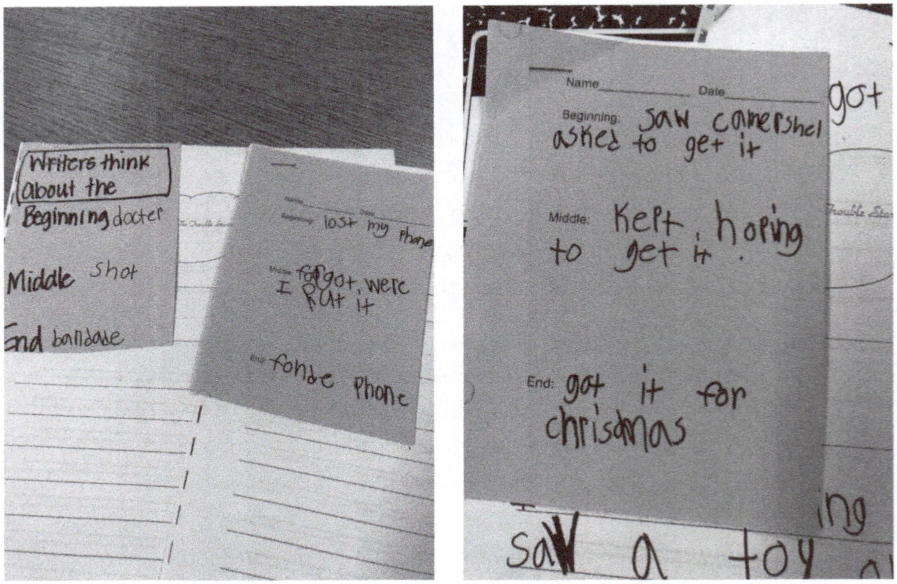

Photo 5.3(a&b) Madison first plans the beginning, middle, and ending on cards. And when she begins drafting, Madison knows to turn the page when she moves from one section of her story to another.

more of. Madison saw that there was room for dialogue, description, and inner thinking, so she started to include those elaboration strategies, and she started to create much more developed stories.

If structure and elaboration aren't enough rationale for teaching students to write across pages—even if they are not filling those pages up—packets also make it clearer to students when and how to use transitional words. The separation of events onto pages divides stories and thoughts into clear sequences of events—sequences with beginnings, middles, and ends. Just as students can think of *stories* in terms of beginnings, middles, and ends, they can think of transitional words coinciding with beginnings, middles, and ends. Photo 5.4 shows a chart I've provided students that cues these transitional phrases for narrative.

When students have these charts in front of them, then I can say to them, "Make it a goal for yourself to include at least one of these words in each of your sections. You might even come up with words of your own." And then I let them in on a secret: Although it's not a 100 percent guarantee, when you use one of these words, you are almost always beginning a new sentence. This realization, explicitly linked to the paper scaffold, gives students a solid footing on the path to understanding what a sentence is and where they should use end punctuation and capital letters.

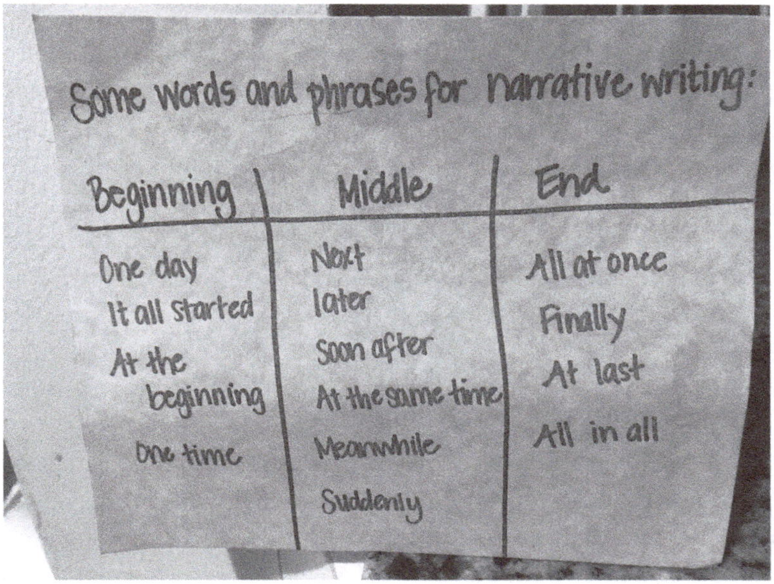

Photo 5.4 This chart of transition words offer choices of words and phrases for students to try to incorporate within the separate parts of a narrative text.

THINKING OUT LOUD

My youngest daughter, Cecily, keeps her closet very organized. She has shelves, so she keeps her shirts on one shelf, shorts on another, long pants on another—you get the idea. Even if there's extra space on the shorts shelf, the pants need to occupy their own space. "That way," she once told me, "you can tell what I really need more of."

Cecily's comment has stayed with me when I've thought about paper and space, especially for striving writers. Just as Cecily spots wardrobe needs through her closet organization system, paper systems reveal places where stories should be developed. So often, striving writers compress and compact their stories and writing pieces, getting everything they have to say down as quickly as possible in one space. Without room to spread, it's hard to find physical space to add the sort of details that are often a part of the revision process—and these are writers who don't love revision anyway.

PAPER SCAFFOLDS IN OTHER GENRES OF WRITING

Just as narrative writing has a beginning, middle, and end, it's helpful for writers to recognize that other genres have this sort of structure as well. We just call them slightly different terms. We can use paper as a scaffold to help students think in terms of beginning, sections, and conclusion. Similarly, we can use paper to help students see the separation of ideas within information and opinion papers. "When you are writing about this part of your topic, you're on this page," I tell students as they are working on an information text. "This reason and everything that supports it stays on this piece of paper," becomes a visible reminder of idea separation when it comes to opinion writing.

As in narrative writing, we can also teach students to categorize transitional words for information and opinion writing, as shown in Photos 5.5 and 5.6. When they have already established that a section is part of an introduction or of a specific section or idea, then it's easier for them to identify where they have incorporated transitional words or where they still need to do some work.

In narrative writing, if a student has written across pages and they have the structure of events, then they can add action, thoughts, and feelings about those events in the space that remains on the page. Extra space in informational pieces allows for explanation of facts and details, an important element of information writing. Likewise, when working through an opinion text, students sometimes struggle to differentiate between reasons and examples. Separating reasons onto separate papers sends a strong message that those reasons need explanation, and it's that explanation that has the potential to lift the level of the writing.

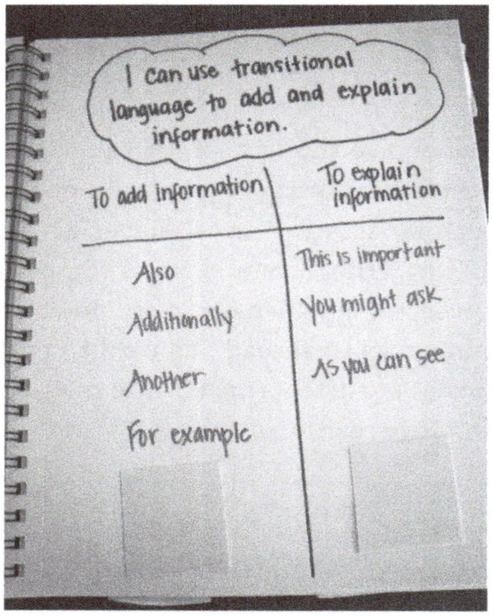

Photo 5.5 shows transition words writers can use in information pieces.

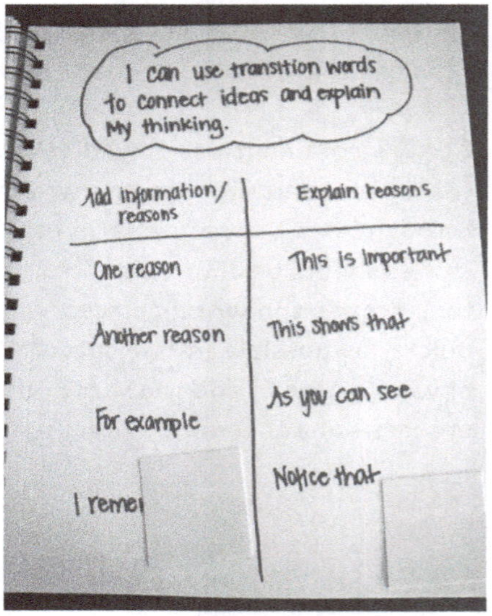

Photo 5.6 shows transition words writers can use in opinion pieces.

Whenever possible, it helps students regardless of their writing ability to have visible tools for teaching and learning. When writers are using paper that is *set up* in those sections, the instruction and the learning becomes more visible, and internalization happens more quickly.

THINKING OUT LOUD

When we use paper to communicate to students when to shift from section to section, we have provided them with a scaffold. Scaffolds should be temporary, so as soon as students seem to have internalized the structure of beginning, middle, and end, then challenge them to set up their own paper. "You no longer need my writing on the page," I say to students. "You can remind yourself to move from section to section."

Honor was a third-grade student who wrote very little when I first started working with her. In fact, she wrote nothing. We had no way to even evaluate the standards she was achieving or not achieving, since her production was so low, as was her belief in herself as a writer. Her fine motor skills were not a problem, so I offered Honor sticky notes to write her story. She looked at me as if I were joking. "I can fill those up," she said.

We had to come up with ideas together, but over the course of a few days, Honor wrote stories that looked about like Photo 5.7.

My celebrations? She was getting words down on paper! She had a clear sequence of events with an intentional beginning, middle, and end. Although there's not much

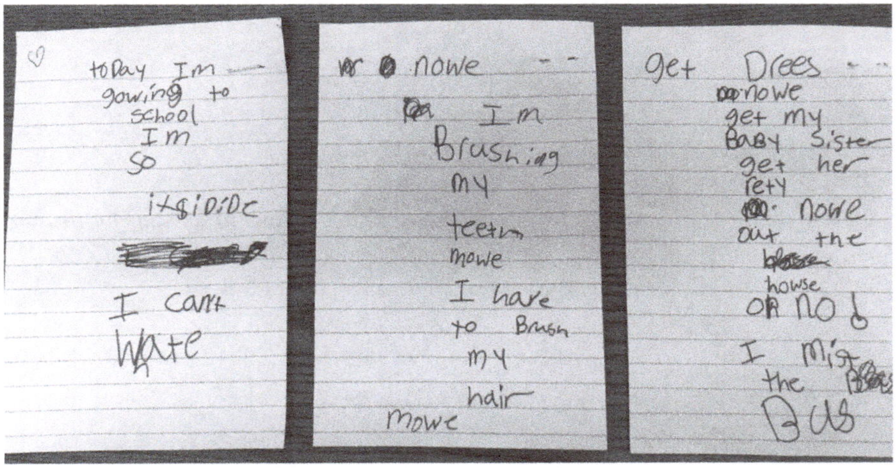

Photo 5.7 Honor's sticky note story: *Today I'm going to school. I'm so excited. I can't wait. Now I'm brushing my teeth. Now I have to brush my hair. Now get dressed. Now get my baby sister ready. Now out of the house. Oh no! I missed the bus!*

in the way of conventions, Honor's story has voice and humor with the ending. I could celebrate her writing with her in ways I couldn't when she spent the whole writing period out of the class or crumpling up paper that felt overwhelming to her.

Her classroom teacher had a rainbow pad that Honor loved, and after the success with the sticky notes, we let Honor use the rainbow pad. Independently, Honor stapled three-page packets together and she wrote story after story, coming up with ideas on her own.

Photo 5.8 shows Honor's second story which she wrote across three pages with a clear beginning, middle, and end.

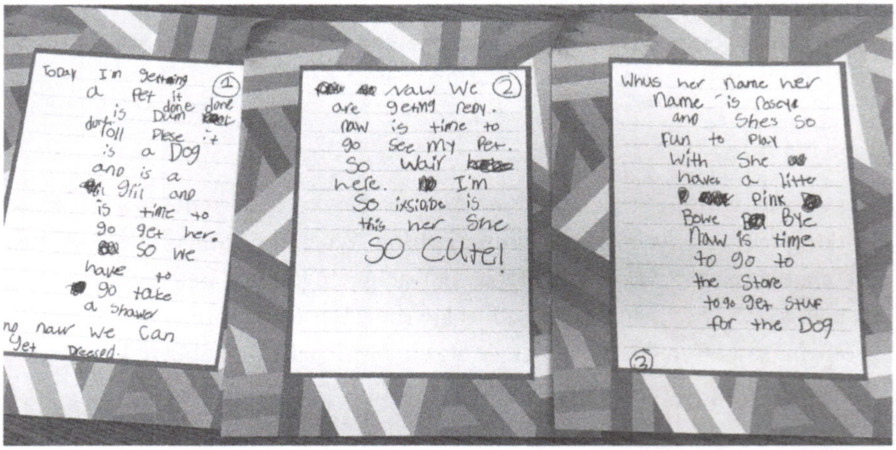

After about two weeks, she wrote the following story:

Today I'm getting a pet. "Is it done, done, done? Please?" It is a dog and it is a girl and it is time to go get her. So we have to go take a shower and now we can get dressed. Now we are getting ready. Now it is time to go see my pet. We're here. I'm so excited. "Is this her? She is so cute!"

"What's her name?"

"Her name is Rosy, and she's so fun to play with."

She has a little pink bow. Bye. Now it's time to go to the store to get stuff for the dog.

So here's how Honor grew as a writer, thanks to paper choice:

- She more than doubled the volume of her story (43–104 words) while her story stayed focused.

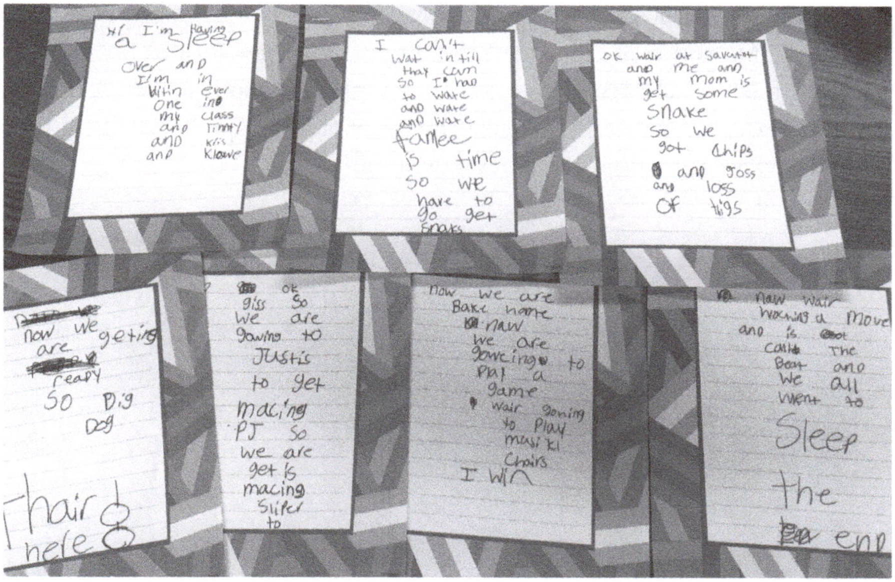

Photo 5.9 shows Honor's third story, which she wanted to write across several pages.

- She generated ideas and initiated the task of writing on her own.
- She increased her time on task from less than 2 minutes to over 10 minute intervals.
- She began to think about the dialogue and thinking that would develop her stories.

Clearly, we still have work to do, especially in the area of conventions, and yes, I'd love to see Honor write even more. But she is a braver writer and she gets words down on a page, a huge leap in progress compared to a child who used to write almost nothing. Now her teacher can see the areas of strength and challenge in Honor's writing too, so she can make instructional decisions. Changing up Honor's paper changed up her mindset, and Honor went from flat-out refusal of writing to a willingness to try out ideas, and then to an engaged student during her independent writing.

THINKING OUT LOUD

We'd go broke if we tried to provide all students with this kind of paper, but Honor is not representative of all kinds of students. If we have a pad lying around that has the potential to jumpstart a nonwriter into a more prolific one then by all means, use it.

Choice and self-efficacy are so important to learners, and paper can become a comfortable and easily established pathway for writers. Just as my husband picks through, examines, and makes careful choices about his wrenches and screwdrivers, students can also make choices about their paper that help them grow and develop skills in all genres of writing.

End-of-Chapter Questions

1. How does paper deliver messages to writers in terms of neatness, volume, and expectations?
2. How can we use paper to help students internalize concepts of structure, development, and even conventions?
3. How do we introduce paper choices to students, and how do we encourage students to create their own structure within their choices, thereby reducing or removing the scaffold?

Take Action!

1. If you have any paper in your room with dashed lines in between the lines, get rid of it.
2. Create a digital folder of paper choices, customizing paper with lines and blank boxes to look however you want. Manipulate the number of lines on a page and even the space between those lines in order to accommodate for productivity and fine motor issues. Add blank text boxes to allow for pictures.
3. Set up a paper station as part of your writing center and teach into the various options that exist within it. Include paper strips of various colors and sizes to encourage revision.

CHAPTER SIX

CO-CREATE CLASSROOM CHARTS AS PATHWAYS TOWARD INDEPENDENCE

How can we use charts to develop students' independence within our writing classrooms?

Classroom charts provide students with visual access to learning and are an important component of UDL. Chapter 6 talks about the importance of making classroom charts in front of and with students, providing specific and actionable strategies for increasing students' awareness and use of them.

When Cecily, my youngest daughter, was learning to cook, we spent time making a chart of the terms, conversions, and tools she kept reading in recipes and asking me about. While I still had to supervise some of her kitchen projects, this chart allowed her to do more with greater independence, and she appreciated that—so did I! As Cecily cooked more, she needed the chart less and less. Eventually, we took it down since she knew the information without having to look.

The classroom environment has to be full of reasons for students to ***want*** to write, but it also has to show ways for them to learn ***how*** to write (Smith, 1994). Charts do just this, which is why it's important for me to dedicate an entire chapter to charts as a pathway to independence for striving writers.

By providing visual reminders, charts scaffold the independence for writers of all different levels. Furthermore, charts maintain a focus on the goal of learning and provide tailored assistance when learners need them within their own individual process, two critical elements of scaffolded instruction (Hogan & Pressley, 1997). Advanced writers may use charts in place of lessons; sometimes they only need reminders of expectations or strategies in order to incorporate them into writing, and they may lean on those charts for only a short period of time before internalizing the lessons. On the other hand, striving writers might not be as productive as some of their classmates. Therefore, they may not be ready for some of the strategies that we teach on a particular day, but they may be ready for those strategies a few days later. Our striving writers may need reminders and scaffolds of strategies they've learned but haven't yet assimilated as their own. Charts remind students of their options, of lessons they experienced but didn't really get a chance to try—yet. Additionally, some strivers may have executive functioning struggles or attention issues. Charts have the power to aid those challenges as well. As teachers, our goals should always include providing pathways toward independence and transfer. To that end, charts are important and effective tools. Photo 6.1 shows how I think about students' pathways to independence. It's important to think about the balance of direction and scaffolding we are providing with the amount of learning and transfer we are expecting.

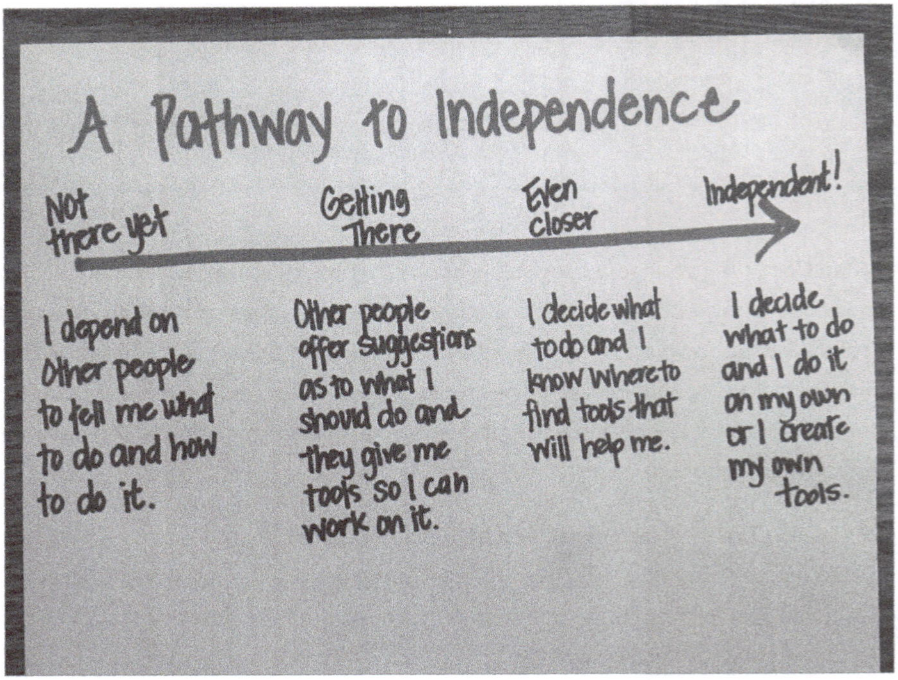

Photo 6.1 As we think about the pathway to independence, charts fit into all of the steps except for the final one since they are tools we design with students and keep available for them until no longer needed.

THE BIG IDEAS

1. **It's important to be confident about the types and purposes of various charts.** When we have clarity as to what our chart is for and what our chart will look like, then it's much easier to begin its creation.
2. **We need to address what gets in the way of relevant, responsive charts—and know what we can do about it.** Not every class needs the same chart, and whatever we create should contain useful and usable information to the class of writers here and now.
3. **More than anything else, classroom charts are there for students to use.** We need to do *whatever we can* so that students recognize these tools as useful scaffolds, playing the role of substitute teacher when you are unavailable.

It's important to be confident about the types and purposes of various charts.

Before delving into the challenges we face around making charts and then getting students to use them, let's establish some categories and terms by which to think about charts. Photo 6.2 shows some of my big recommendations when I think about charts. As you read about the different types and purposes, keep in mind that charts don't have to be perfect or even beautiful. They should be present within the instructional environment so that students have access and can use them with intention and independence.

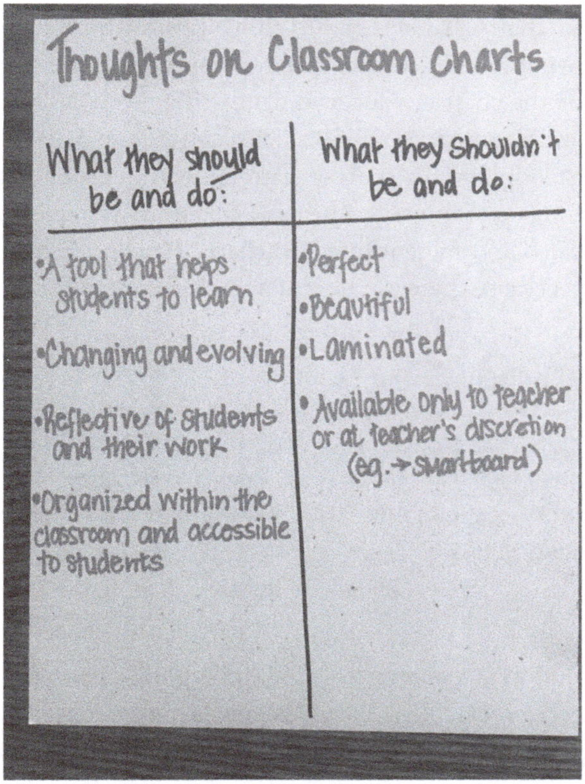

Photo 6.2 This photo contains some key elements that guide my thinking about classroom charts.

Before we go any further, I want to address store-bought or laminated charts. Please don't use these at all. My recommendation? Throw them out. When we lean on store-bought charts, we run the risk of not fully understanding the intention behind creating them. Likewise, when we use laminated charts created in front of previous groups of learners, we run the risk of our current learners not understanding and integrating the intention and meaning that exists behind the product. Puntambekar and Hubscher (2005) analyzed important attributes of instructional scaffolds. One of their four key features involves intersubjectivity and the joint ownership of the task between student(s) and teacher. When we create charts with students, students share the relevance and the understanding of process. When we present charts as finished products or just point to them on the walls, students do not share the journey, understanding, or ownership.

Whenever I am creating a chart, I think about both the purpose and the structure of the chart. Therefore, if I keep in mind the various types and categories of charts, I have more clarity as to what I want to put on them. Once we move beyond store-bought charts, we have the choice of teacher-created charts or co-constructed charts. It helps me to think within those two categories and then break down the various types within them. Keep in mind, too, that even if you're creating the chart in your own handwriting, you're doing so in front of the class and with student input. This helps create shared ownership, as well as shared understanding of the goals of learning, both research-based elements of effective learning environments. The table below shows a quick-reference guide of teacher-created and student-involved charts. (You'll notice inquiry charts in both columns because these can be either teacher-created or student-involved.)

Quick-Reference Guide to Classroom Charts

Teacher-Created Charts	Student-Involved Charts
Anchor charts—explain how to complete an entire task	**Who has tried it? charts**—contain strategies and include a place for students to write their names or initials when they've tried it
Procedural chart—names how to go through a process	**Tallying attempts charts**—contain strategies and include a place for students to tally when they've tried that strategy in their writing
Strategy charts—offer choices for a particular skill	**Co-created charts**—include student writing and ideas since they are created cooperatively with the class
Inquiry charts—begin with a question and then contain a series of possible answers or ideas	**Inquiry charts**—begin with a question and then contain a series of possible answers or ideas

TEACHER-CREATED CHARTS

As the name implies, teacher-created charts are ones made by teachers. Sometimes, you might make these charts over the course of several days, adding to them as you teach through a unit. Other times, you might make an entire chart in one teaching session. Within the teacher-created charts, there are a few different types, and categorizing them provides a helpful framework for feeling more comfortable about making them. Knowing and understanding the different types of charts helps when we are trying to decide not only how to structure a chart, but also what sort of information to put on it. Is this chart going to serve as a procedural resource, a revisiting of instructional points, or a reminder of options for a learning target? Once that decision is in place, it's clearer as to what to include on the chart.

Anchor Charts

Anchor charts are aptly named because they contain the overall skills necessary for an overall task. If we are teaching to the *what* of the task, we are generally creating the bullets for an effective anchor chart. Photo 6.3 shows an anchor chart of third-grade narrative writing. Notice that the CCSS narrative writing standards are translated into statements most students can more easily understand, and the statements reflect the expectations for the overall task of narrative writing.

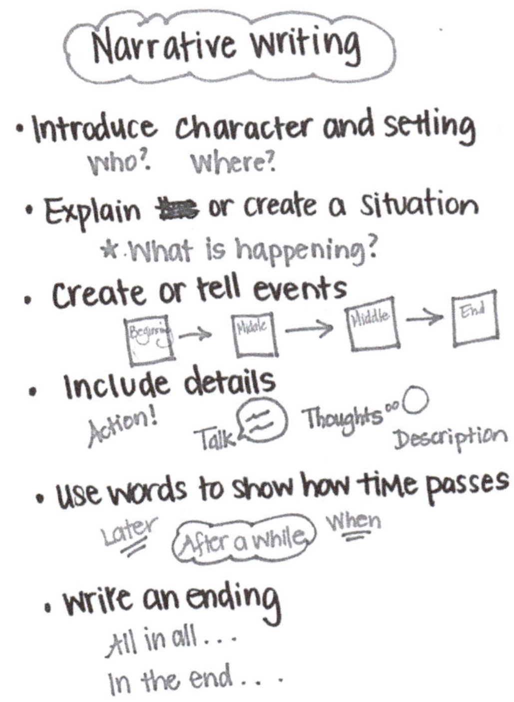

Photo 6.3 This narrative anchor chart provides exactly what is expected for students working toward third-grade expectations.

Using a similar process, we can create grade-level anchor charts of the various genres of writing. This series of charts helps to differentiate tools and resources, providing accessible pathways for striving writers to learn. For example, using these charts, we can create checklists with students that reflect and interact with their ZPDs (zone of proximal development). That way, expectations, standards, and learning targets align—and students learn and grow with confidence as opposed to frustration.

Procedural Charts

Procedural charts are closely related to anchor charts in that they enumerate the steps of a process. However, they tend to encompass the *steps of a process* rather than the *components of* a piece of writing. For example, a procedural chart may contain the steps of writing a narrative text. A procedural chart may also describe the expectations of a writing class. Or a procedural chart could list the student and teacher roles within the writing class. In other words, procedural charts explain how to break down a larger thing into its component tasks. Photo 6.4 shows a procedural chart for researching before opinion writing.

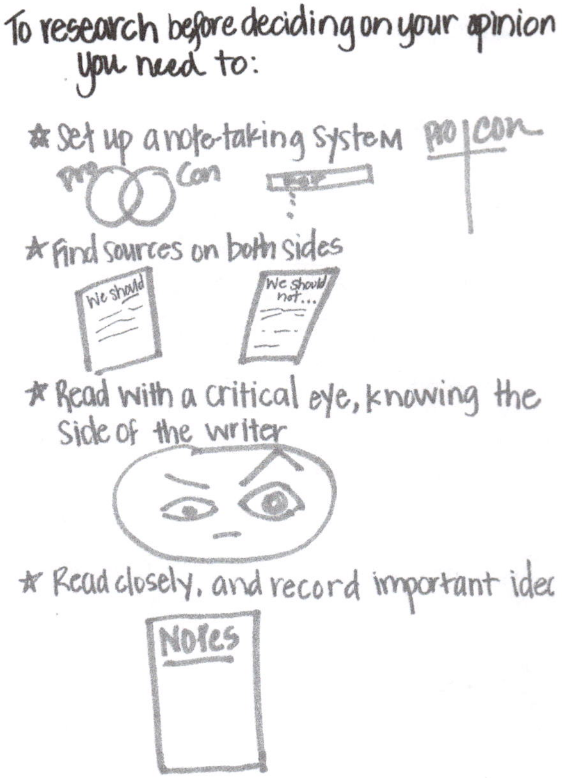

Photo 6.4 This procedural chart reminds students of how to research and take notes before drafting an opinion/argument piece of writing.

Strategy Charts

Strategy charts offer students choices for a particular skill. These choices can be written on the chart, either as bullets below the goal or on sticky notes as we share them. For instance, if we are teaching students how to write a beginning for a narrative story, we would write something such as "Writers introduce readers to the world of their story and want to make sure readers are interested. We can do this by:" Then, there are several choices we can offer through our bullets or on the sticky notes:

- Dialogue that lets readers know what's going on with the character
- A noise or sudden action that gets the readers' attention
- A description of the setting

Other useful strategy charts that explain how to do something might include the following:

- Hook readers (in any genre)
- Create citations
- Use transitional words
- Remember punctuation

As an example, Photo 6.5 offers various strategies for the different ways to begin an informational piece of writing. Additionally, the chart in Photo 6.6 provides strategies writers can use when spelling unfamiliar words. And the chart in Photo 6.7 shows a combination procedural-strategy chart—it's okay to mix it up to meet your students' needs!

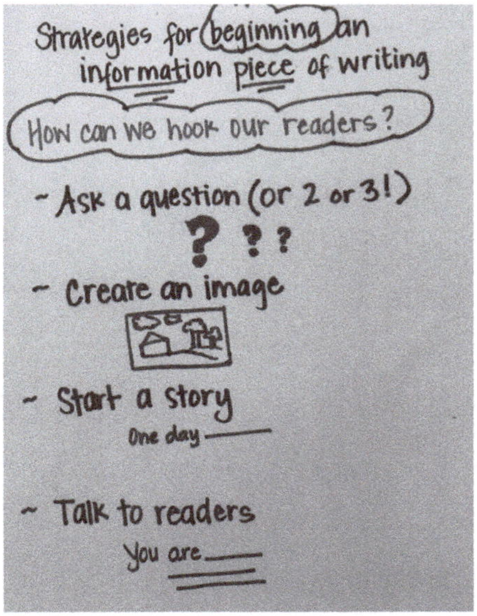

Photo 6.5 This strategy chart shows various choices writers have for beginning a piece of information writing.

Photo 6.6 This is an example of a strategy chart of various ways to spell words.

Photo 6.7 This chart is somewhat of a hybrid of a procedural and strategy chart. While it tells how to use a quote in a piece of writing, it also offers choices of different ways to do that.

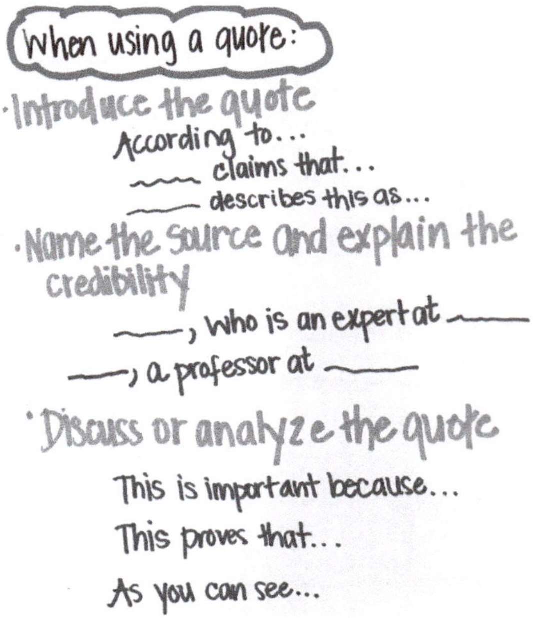

STUDENT-INVOLVED CHARTS

Unlike teacher-created charts, student-involved charts will include some student writing on them—or at least evidence of student interaction with them. They may also include pictures of students themselves or student work.

Who Has Tried It? Charts

One of my favorite ways to inspire students to interact with a chart is to include a "Who has tried it?" column on a strategy chart. Students love to add their initials or names to a chart, especially when there are different colored markers. Once their names are on that chart, we can ask them about their use of the strategy. Having their name on public display is an organic form of accountability. The "Who has tried it?" column also serves as meaningful formative assessment for teachers.

The chart pictured in Photo 6.8 was created during a third-grade inquiry lesson about the different ways to begin information books. In this instance, the teacher and I selected a few titles, the students named the strategy used to begin the book, and then we challenged them to try out some of these strategies in their own writing. You can see from the initials in the far right column that many students were eager to try them out!

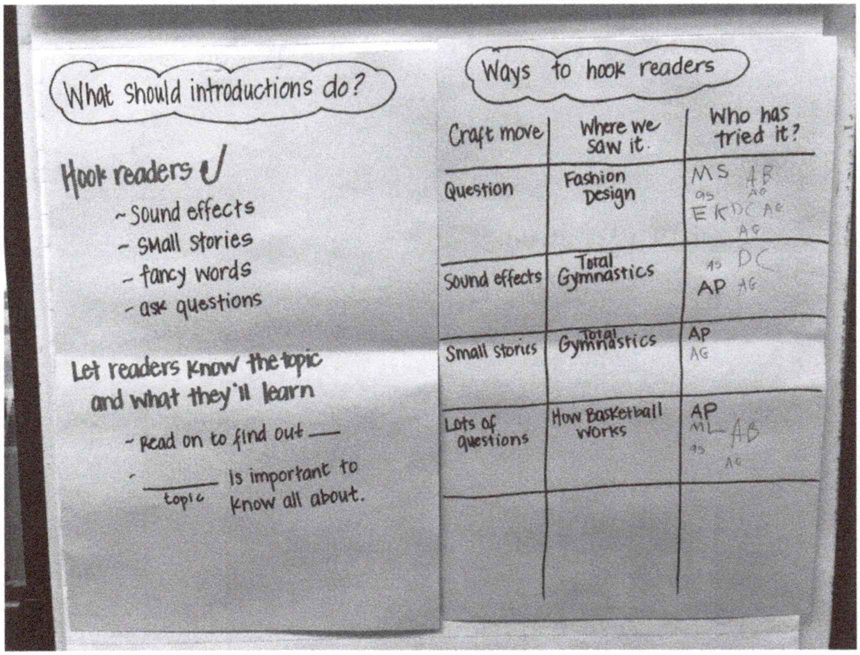

Photo 6.8 This chart lists some of the strategies writers can use in order to introduce topics, identifies where those strategies can be found, and invites students to indicate that they've also tried out the strategy in their own writing.

This type of chart works with older grade levels, as well. In this chart, the middle column is where we found the strategy, but the middle column can also be about what the strategy looks like. Either way, it's a powerful way to incorporate ownership of classroom charts.

Thinking about our strivers, we don't need those initials to go up *right away*. Striving writers may get to parts of the process at different times, and that's okay—the goal is that they get there! Students don't have to add their initials on the same day that we create the chart; the chart can remain as an interactive element within the classroom environment, a resource that reminds and supports students as they work through their own writing process. We can wait until striving writers are ready, until they're at that part of the process.

Tallying Attempts Chart

Invite students to tally when they have used a strategy. Tallies could be used on many different strategy charts in order to encourage students to recognize the importance of variety and experimentation in their writing. For example, if you noticed that many students were beginning opinion paragraphs with a question, you could create a tallying chart with other options for beginning a paragraph (i.e., telling a quick story, creating an image, giving an interesting fact

Photo 6.9 This chart was created during a fourth-grade informational writing unit in order to inspire, remind, and support writers to use transitional language throughout their texts. The tallies represent students' use of that word or phrase.

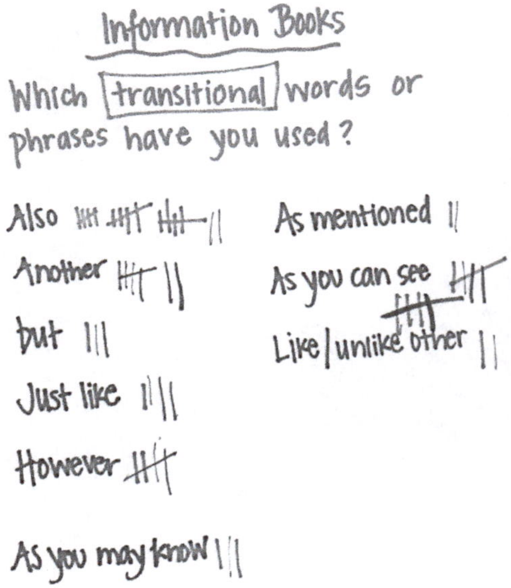

are other options), and then the tallies, or lack thereof, could stimulate some experimentation, variety, and voice in student writing.

You'll notice in the chart shown in Photo 6.9, the teacher presented the students with a list of the words he'd like to see in their writing, and they put a tally mark next to the words they used. (What a great graphing lesson this could be!) This chart increased students' awareness of transitional language and inspired many of the students to try to vary the words and phrases they used in their own writing.

TIP!

Some of our striving writers look for things to do during writing time other than write, and the tallying chart *could* become a source of productive distraction in the same category as sharpening pencils, erasing, or going to the bathroom. One way to manage the need to get up and down in order to tally transition words or any other skill you're looking for is to create individualized charts for students. That way, they don't have to leave their desk in order to tally their work. Students can tally their use of the strategy without leaving their workspace. In Photo 6.10, I created a simple sticky note chart for a student to keep tallies on.

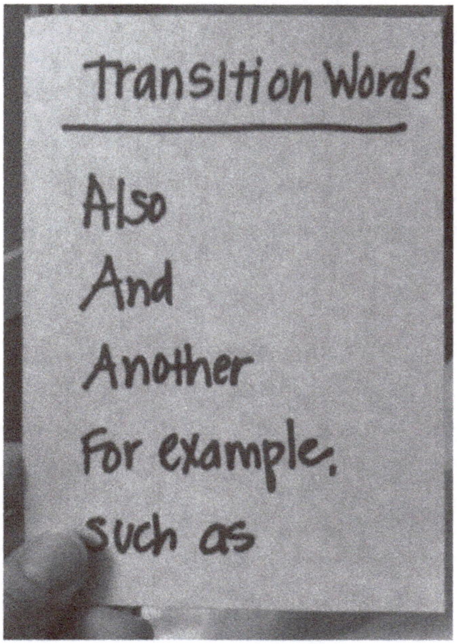

Photo 6.10 This smaller version of a chart serves as an individual tool for a student to tally the transition words in a piece of writing.

Co-Created Anchor Charts

While *all* charts should be created in front of students and are all co-created in that sense, some charts actually have *student writing* on them. These charts tend to really inspire students because of that inarguable thrill of having your words up there in the front of the room and that pen in your hand. When students help to *write* the chart, they *remember* it. Make sure that what they write is important, even if it's not neat and spelled correctly, and you have a powerful teaching tool!

TIP!

As suggested in the above section, some of us are not comfortable as artists. Another opportunity for co-ownership of charts between teachers and students is to invite students to become a "Chart Art Team." If students provide illustration for charts, it serves two purposes: Students feel greater ownership of charts, and teachers feel less pressure to create beautiful pictures.

THINKING OUT LOUD

Co-created charts require relinquishing control.

- Not every word will be spelled correctly.
- Not every letter will be neat and perfectly formed.

We have to really embrace the thinking that charts don't have to be perfect if we're going to allow students to share the pen and write on our charts.

Co-created anchor charts work especially well when students have a writing sample that contains clear examples of the strategies and techniques you want everyone to be trying. Students also need to know what they are looking for, so a list of standards, expectations, or checklists will help them notice and name the components the piece of writing demonstrates. We can increase access for striving writers throughout this task with a few strategies such as the following:

- Provide them with a shorter list of expectations to focus on as opposed to the entire list all at once.
- Give them an individual copy of the reading selection in order to minimize the vulnerability they may feel.
- Partner them with peers so that the work feels more collaborative and interactive.

The chart shown in Photo 6.11 supported a fifth-grade lesson at the very beginning of our narrative writing unit. We enlarged the text of a narrative story and gave students charts and checklists so that they could notice and note the craft moves used by the author.

Photo 6.11 Students worked to annotate a narrative piece of writing, underlining and labeling the places in the text that demonstrate a specific trait of writing.

Inquiry Charts

An inquiry chart can be teacher created or student involved because it is built around a question. For example, "What are the different ways to end a story?" could be a question that students investigate and answer. When we teach an inquiry lesson asking students to supply some of the responses for the teaching point, we can put their initials on the chart, crediting them for their contribution. That way, students are interacting with the chart, and whether they realize it right away or not, they become more accountable. How great is it to be able to say, "Look, you were the one who suggested ______. You *must* be the classroom expert. I can't wait to see how you do _____ in your writing!"

The chart in Photo 6.12 focused on conventions and helped students see that they could name the expectations of conventions, making it seem a little less

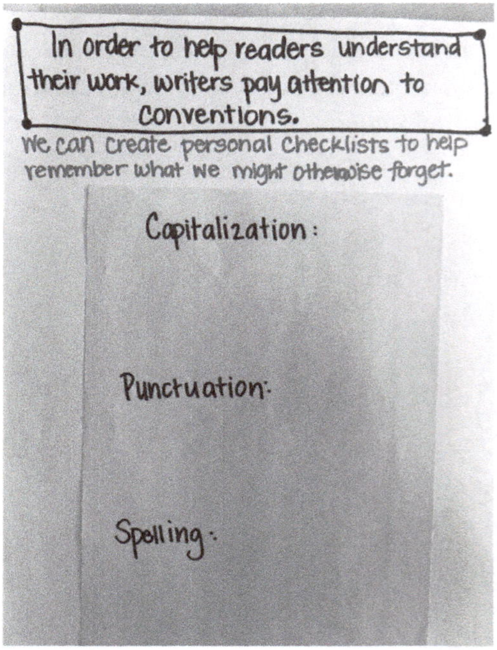

Photo 6.12 The chart shown here, co-created with a class of third-graders, began with just the top statement—when writers write *anything*, they want their readers to be able to read it!—and the three boxes for capitalization, punctuation, and spelling. We asked students what conventions they should be including in their writing as an inquiry lesson.

PAUSE FOR PD

Take some time and think about an upcoming unit. Try designing and/or planning for some charts that you can use. Work on the following:

- An anchor chart that enumerates the specific skills and standards that you expect to see in final pieces of writing from that unit
- A procedural chart that lists the steps involved in the successful creation of that specific type of writing
- A strategy chart that addresses one of those skills and offers specific choices and options for addressing it

Remember that when you're ready to share your chart with students, you should be co-creating it with them, as opposed to presenting your already created product. The charts that you design or plan ahead of time should only serve as inspiration or a planning tool—like a rough draft.

overwhelming to transfer that knowledge into their own writing. All writers, especially striving writers, benefit from having these sorts of visual reminders.

THINKING OUT LOUD

Chapter 2 emphasizes the importance of the environment and an organized, clutter-free space for learning. As we think about charts, we have to think about the available space in our classrooms. We don't want to have too many charts, or they will begin to feel like wallpaper. To manage charts, consider taking them down when students aren't using them. Also, consider using different colored construction paper to create charts. Not only does this practice take less room than traditional chart paper, but also we can refer to charts by color when we are directing students to use one of them.

We need to address what gets in the way of relevant, responsive charts—and know what we can do about it.

What gets in the way of producing relevant, responsive charts—and what can we do about it? Even when we believe in the importance of charts and we have clarity about the different types of charts, there are still some obstacles to overcome. Three questions surface over and over again as I work with teachers about creating charts in front of students.

1. I'm not sure what to put on it.
2. My writing is so messy, and I'll have to have cross-outs.
3. I have to turn my back on the group, and there's liable to be behavior problems.

The following sections address these issues and provide some ideas for what to do about these concerns.

I'M NOT SURE WHAT TO PUT ON IT.

Once we have clarity as to the different types of charts, then we can think about what information should go on them and where we can look to find that information when we're not sure. My hope is that once teachers think about their charts in categories, it's easier to think about how to structure their charts and what sort of information should go on them. Thinking about our striving writers, we can also think about how we can differentiate our charts so that all students can access them without becoming overwhelmed by too much information or concepts that are above current functioning levels. Here are three possible ways to think about the content of anchor charts.

Use Your Understanding of Standards and Progressions.

For an anchor chart, it's helpful to have resources such as the Common Core State Standards. What exactly are the expectations for the grade level? With the standards in front of us, we can enumerate the expectations of a unit, or we can create a roadmap for a specific strategy. For example, the fourth-grade narrative standards are as follows (CCSI, 2019):

Write narratives to develop real or imagined experiences or events using effective technique, descriptive details, and clear event sequences.

- *Orient the reader by establishing a situation and introducing a narrator and/or characters; organize an event sequence that unfolds naturally.*
- *Use dialogue and description to develop experiences and events or show the responses of characters to situations.*
- *Use a variety of transitional words and phrases to manage the sequence of events.*
- *Use concrete words and phrases and sensory details to convey experiences and events precisely.*
- *Provide a conclusion that follows from the narrated experiences or events.*

We can translate these standards into more student-friendly language—maybe even some pictures—and create a standards-based anchor chart, as shown in the first section of this chapter in Photo 6.3. Appendix E contains two additional examples of anchor charts as well.

In Chapter 3, we thought about learning progressions, and those progressions can also serve as inspiration for differentiating anchor charts. If students aren't ready to write a full-out introduction, as suggested by the Grade 4 standards, then we can look toward the Grade 3 or Grade 2 standards for what seems to be within students' zone of proximal development. For striving writers, we might even consider creating a continuum of anchor charts. Photo 6.13 shows a sequence of opinion charts moving in complexity from a second- to a fifth-grade level.

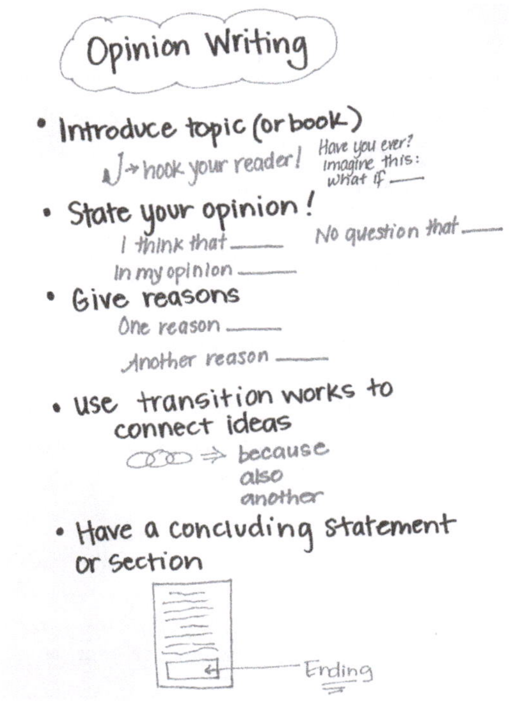

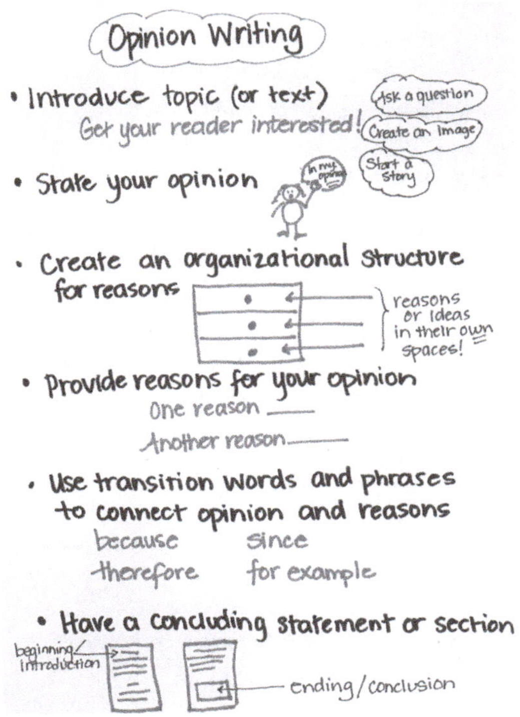

Photo 6.13(a-d) These charts form a progression of expectations that are representative of second- through fifth-grade opinion writing standards.

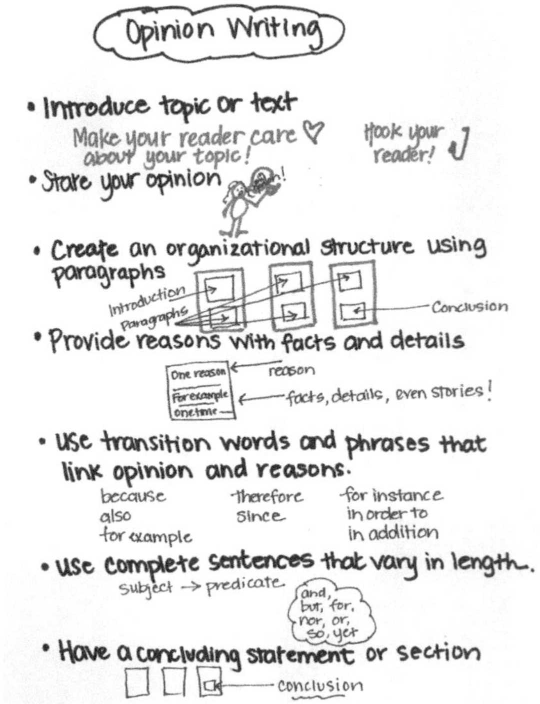
Opinion Writing
• Introduce topic or text
Make your reader care about your topic!
Hook your reader!
• State your opinion
• Create an organizational structure using paragraphs
Introduction
Paragraphs
Conclusion
• Provide reasons with facts and details
One reason
For example
one time
reason
facts, details, even stories!
• Use transition words and phrases that link opinion and reasons.
because
also
for example
therefore
since
for instance
in order to
in addition
• Use complete sentences that vary in length.
subject → predicate
and, but, for, nor, or, so, yet
• Have a concluding statement or section
conclusion

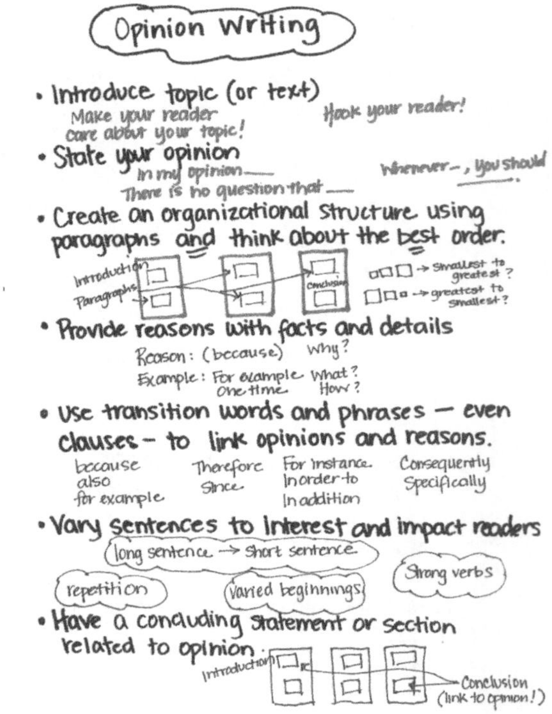
Opinion Writing
• Introduce topic (or text)
Make your reader care about your topic!
Hook your reader!
• State your opinion
In my opinion___
There is no question that___
Whenever__, you should
• Create an organizational structure using paragraphs and think about the best order.
Introduction
Paragraphs
Conclusion
→ smallest to greatest?
→ greatest to smallest?
• Provide reasons with facts and details
Reason: (because) Why?
Example: For example What?
One time How?
• Use transition words and phrases — even clauses — to link opinions and reasons.
because
also
for example
Therefore
Since
For instance
In order to
In addition
Consequently
Specifically
• Vary sentences to interest and impact readers
long sentence → short sentence
repetition
Varied beginnings
Strong verbs
• Have a concluding statement or section related to opinion.
Introduction
Conclusion (link to opinion!)

When I work with striving writers one on one, I share three of these charts, in much the same way as I share progressions of writing samples that I described in Chapter 3. If I know where students are functioning, I present them with a chart that is just *below* where they are, *at* their current functioning level, and just *above* that level. "Which chart do you think will help you as you try to bring your writing to a slightly higher level?" is a question that I pose to students. If they choose the chart that is below or at their level, I emphasize that the chart will serve as a great reminding tool for them. On the other hand, if they opt for the higher-level chart, then I teach them how to use the chart as a scaffold that supports their learning.

If You Use Checklists, Consider Making a Chart Out of Them.

Checklists can go hand in glove with anchor charts. If you have created a checklist or have access to one for your unit, then those items on your checklist can match up with your anchor chart. For example, consider the narrative anchor chart shown in Photo 6.3. We could make that into a student-facing checklist. If you can create a checklist, you can create a chart, and vice-versa.

Translate Student Learning Objectives Into Anchor Charts, Which Helps Maintain Instruction Focus and Fidelity to the Unit.

One other place you can potentially find ideas for your anchor chart is from your unit or curriculum map, depending on how it's written. Many units list the goals and objectives; whatever students are expected to know and be able to do as a result of the curriculum and instruction makes sense to have on an anchor chart.

Strategy charts require a little more understanding on the part of teachers of the possibilities within writing processes. For example, if we are teaching students the different ways to begin an opinion essay, we have to *know* some possibilities. Our overall statement is something such as, ***"Writers work hard to engage their readers at the beginning of an opinion essay, and there are different ways to do that. We can . . . "*** From there, we need to offer students choices for writing their introduction.

Teachers run into trouble with strategy charts when they are not sure themselves of what some choices are, so the trick to this type of chart is to be sure to have some strategies ready to go beforehand. We can even have some strategies already named and some *examples* of those strategies already written on sticky notes.

MY WRITING IS SO MESSY, AND I'LL HAVE TO HAVE CROSS-OUTS.

Sometimes, I look at charts I've made in front of students, and I'm struck by how messy they are. The writing isn't perfect and there are cross-outs. However, if I watch students—and if I talk to them—students are *using* those charts. More than anything else, students' use should be our gauge for the effectiveness of our charts. The value of charts is not in their beauty; the value is in the engagement and the understanding. Students don't care about the neatness of the chart. In fact, sometimes I think students appreciate messy writing from teachers because it communicates the all-important message that the quality is in the message itself, and not in the aesthetic appearance. Regardless, many teachers are not comfortable creating charts on the spot in front of their students. I get it. But charts don't need to be perfect. The writing on them doesn't need to be beautiful. Students don't need perfect or beautiful—they need tools that help them learn. There are, however, two simple ideas for addressing the aesthetic components of charts.

TIP!

Don't let perfect get in the way of the good. Charts should not be perfect—they should be tools that students recognize, access, and use.

Use Color Strategically.

One relatively simple way to feel better about charts and their aesthetic value is to use color. Discipline yourself to make certain parts of your charts be certain colors. For example, the big idea—whether it's the overall task or overall strategy—can always be one certain color, and then the supporting ideas be a different color. As simple as this idea sounds, it will help students recognize the information on the chart that will help them. We can also add interest to charts simply by boxing out or making swirls around key terms, using a different color than the text. A box or circle around important terms draws students' eyes to the major points, which may be especially important for our strivers who have attention or sensory challenges. Again, this step does not require extensive artistic training—only an understanding of what the important words are and a decent set of markers.

Use Sticky Notes

I know there are still instances where you might not feel comfortable writing on your chartpad in front of students. Sticky notes might be the answer for you!

TIP!

Sometimes, teachers feel less self-conscious about their handwriting if they have access to different colors of markers. Invest in markers you like to write with. Try some out. Different types of pens feel different. I travel with my own set of Sharpies. Don't forget that many of our striving writers feel self-conscious and even paralyzed by their own messy handwriting. When teachers play the role of lead learner and risk-taker, our students are empowered to take more risks. Content is more important than handwriting.

You can add a sticky note to an overall chartpad during instruction, and you can have that sticky note prepared ahead of time. Sticky notes come in all different sizes, so you can write your teaching point or strategy on a large sticky note and present it to students during your lesson. You can also write demonstration pieces ahead of time and share them as you read them. That way, if you make a mistake that you can't live with on a chart in your classroom (I don't think that's possible, but some people do!), then you can simply start over on a fresh sticky note.

THINKING OUT LOUD

We all make mistakes, which is another significant message to offer students. Communicating that we don't have to be perfect and we can still move on is especially important for striving writers to see and understand!

I HAVE TO TURN MY BACK ON THE GROUP, AND THERE'S LIKELY TO BE BEHAVIOR PROBLEMS.

Sometimes, it feels uncomfortable to turn your back on a group of students, and if you are making a chart in front of them, then yes, you do have to write on the chart and probably have your eyes there instead of on the students. Consider, whenever this is a challenge, how much you are trying to teach students in one lesson. Attention spans are short, and instruction should take ten minutes or less. After that, students should have a chance to write, trying out new and developing skills and strategies. If the chart is taking too long to make in front of students, then it's likely that the instruction is taking too long as well. Charts can be *in process,* meaning that we add to them over the course of several days. This can be a great solution if you find that you are spending too much time standing in front of your students and they are disengaging in your lesson.

Just as sticky notes can help with the challenge of feeling self-conscious about messiness and mistakes in front of students, sticky notes can also streamline instruction. Almost everyone can read faster than they can write, so again, consider pre-writing your chart on a note and then presenting it. That technique minimizes the amount of time your back is turned, and it maximizes instructional minutes. Sticky notes are especially effective when you are creating demonstration snippets of writing since those can be presented right away.

An added bonus of using sticky notes is how easy they are to pull off and copy for striving students, who often have attentional issues or visual processing challenges. If, instead of having an example on a chart across the room, you can move that example to *right in front of them,* you will oftentimes see strivers interacting, using, and benefitting from the resource more.

More than anything else, classroom charts are there for students to use.

Getting students to actually *use* the charts that hang in your room should always be at the forefront of chart development and presentation. At the beginning of the chapter, I reviewed different types of student-created charts. The more we can encourage students to interact with the charts, either through tallies, adding initials, co-creating, or any other way, the greater the possibility that students will use the tools.

More and more, another way we've been making sure that charts become access points along our writers' pathways is to create individual ones that are either the same as the ones on the wall or close enough that they don't require instruction for students to access. This strategy has helped many of our students with both executive functioning and with attention issues because students choose what they need *when they need it* and then they can have it *right in front of them.* Here are some ways we've been doing this:

PERSONAL-SIZED CHARTS FROM THE BULLETIN BOARDS

"I keep making the same charts over and over again when I confer with students," a fourth-grade teacher said to me. "I taught the lesson, and I've hung the chart, but it's like they have to have it right in front of them."

The next day, we created an interactive bulletin board for students to access, and we taught them to take a chart when they needed it and return it when they were finished. Mostly, these charts were smaller versions of the ones the teacher had made in front of the whole class. As students learned how to access them, we added a few additional charts of specific skills or ones we'd used with individual or small groups of students. All of a sudden, we dramatically increased the number of students we could reach during independent writing time, albeit not necessarily with either of us physically sitting with them. If someone had a question about how to start an introduction, we could direct them to a specific chart.

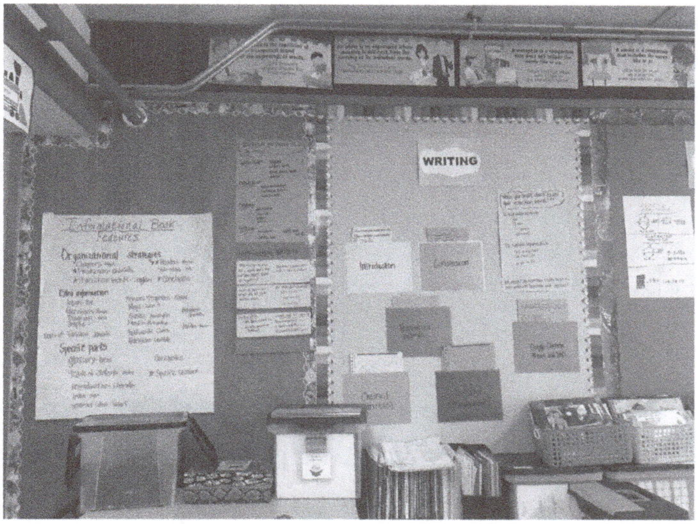

Photo 6.14 A third-grade teacher offered specific tools as well as small charts for her students to take.

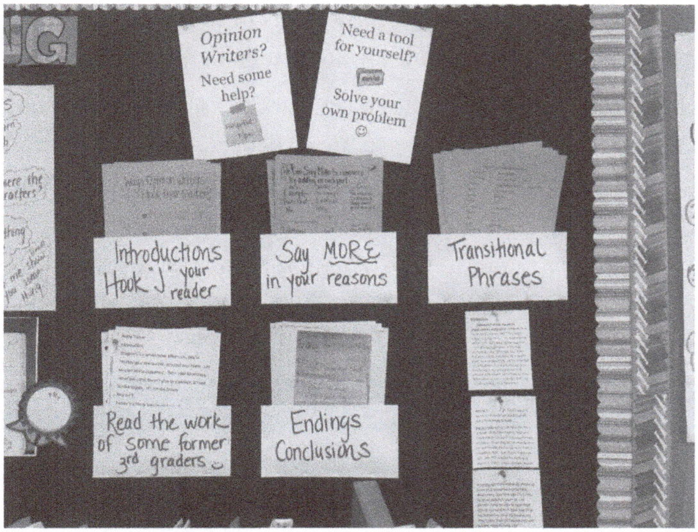

Photo 6.15 This interactive bulletin board provides individual-sized charts that students can borrow and use as they need.

Other teachers have created similar systems in their classrooms. In addition to charts, we can also include mentor texts, checklists, or other tools. While students have the choice of many different charts, teachers may also suggest a specific chart for a student, and having those available is helpful for striving writers because so often they are at different places in their process as well as their level than other students in the room. These systems support a spectrum of learners in the classroom because students can review as they need and even differentiate for themselves. Furthermore, having the chart right there in front of them filters out many of the distractions of other charts or bulletin board features so the focus stays right there on the intended goal for that writing session.

TIP!

Make sure to take the time to teach into *how* to use these interactive bulletin boards. Students will not use them if they don't understand how to problem-solve and build intention for themselves.

LESSON PLAN: *Building Independence With Charts and Resources*

MATERIALS NEEDED: Demonstration writing, small versions of classroom charts, checklists

TEACHING POINT: When we pay attention to our own independent writing processes, we identify goals that we're working on. With those goals in mind, we can seek out materials and resources that will help us work toward achieving those goals.

DEMONSTRATION: Teacher introduces some of the charts, checklists, and other resources that are available in the classroom for students to use. Teacher shares demonstration writing, talks about goals, and models how to choose a resource, use the resource, and then replace it when feeling more confident about the work.

CLOSURE: No matter what type of writing we are working on, we can set goals for ourselves as writers, and we can use any and all of the resources we have available to us within our classroom.

TRIPOD STANDS AND PLASTIC FRAMES

Tripod stands can hold three charts, so these are great if you have a student who you want to manage more closely but still offer choice. I have constructed tripod stands out of cardstock and mailing tape, but cardboard would work as well. Students' choices then become one of three, as opposed to all of the options in the writing center or on a chart. Small charts can be clipped right onto the stand with paper clips or binder clips.

Photo 6.16 A student uses a tripod, having made the decision to have a specific chart to reference during her independent writing time.

One other way I've coached teachers to provide individual charts is through the use of plastic frames. If you invest in frames, I highly recommend the type that restaurants use to display menus that stand up straight as opposed to slant. Teachers *or* students can decide what charts should go into their frame, and again, having that reminder standing right there in front of a student helps them focus on goal, intention, and production.

Photo 6.17 Plastic menu frames are a great way to display charts, offering the possibility of students taking them to their work space on an as-needed basis.

The second principle of UDL involves providing multiple means of representation, and an important goal of all instruction is independence and transfer. Thinking about Cecily in the kitchen, I could have availed myself anytime she was tackling a recipe and directly answered her questions about teaspoons and tablespoons. However, her chart allowed her to function more independently. Now, she just knows the symbols and amounts associated with measuring spoons. Our classroom charts have similar potential for minimizing students' dependency, maximizing our instructional time, and providing pathways of independence for all of our learners from the striving ones to the exceeding ones.

End-of-Chapter Questions

1. What are the different types of charts we can create, and what ones are the easiest to make? The hardest?
2. How can we make the charts in our classrooms feel co-created and co-owned by the students in the room?
3. What are some ways to encourage use and increase accessibility of the charts we create?

Take Action!

1. Learn or create a cheat sheet for yourself of the various types of charts. Our brains function best when we have structures and categories in place.
2. Equip yourself if you haven't already. Get some pens you like to write with, as well as an easel and/or a chartpad. If making mistakes is a concern for you, get some sticky notes of various sizes.
3. Begin with an anchor chart and create one for each genre for your grade level. Again, if making mistakes is a concern, write the features or learning targets of the genre on separate sticky notes and present those as part of your instruction over the course of a couple—or even several—days.

CHAPTER SEVEN

VENTURE FORTH ON HIGHER-TECH PATHWAYS . . . WITH INTENTION AND FORETHOUGHT

How can we leverage technology to find entry points and build bridges or pathways for our writers who face instructional obstacles?

> Technology has the power to increase options and possibilities within all three UDL principles. This chapter provides ideas within engagement, representation, and action/expression so that students have additional bridges and pathways for growth and achievement within their writing processes.

My mother has a binder for all of her recipes. To the rest of us, that binder has minimal organization, yet she can find anything in her binder; we can't.

Once Cecily and I turned the pages of the binder in a frustrating and unsuccessful search for our favorite lemon bar recipe. When my mother walked in, she flipped right to it. While my mother's system works for her—for reasons the rest of us don't fully understand—her physical binder challenges others, and my daughter, Julia, has been threatening to digitize my mother's recipes for a while now. Julia's system could provide higher-tech pathways for the rest of us to access my mother's recipes, although my mother doesn't need it.

If my mother were the only one using the recipe binder, there would be no need for a change, which is an important point to think about as we introduce technology into our classrooms. If technology has the potential to improve or increase accessibility, then by all means, we should implement it. However, if lower-tech pathways are serving the same purpose, then we have to evaluate whether the time it takes to learn how to use a different system enhances or detracts from learning.

The SAMR model, presented by Ruben R. Puentedura in 2009, offers categories to think within when it comes to technology (see Photo 7.1). Those categories include substitution, augmentation, modification, and redefinition. Thinking about my mother's recipe binder, Julia would like to *augment* it; if she were to digitize those recipes, we would still have the recipes all in one place, but we could search more successfully for that elusive lemon bar recipe. Knowing Julia, she'd probably write some sort of computer program to create menu ideas, and then she would start *modifying* or even *redefining*, as we could categorize and search for recipes in ways that were previously unavailable.

Photo 7.1 This chart shows a technology progression based on Puentedura's work.

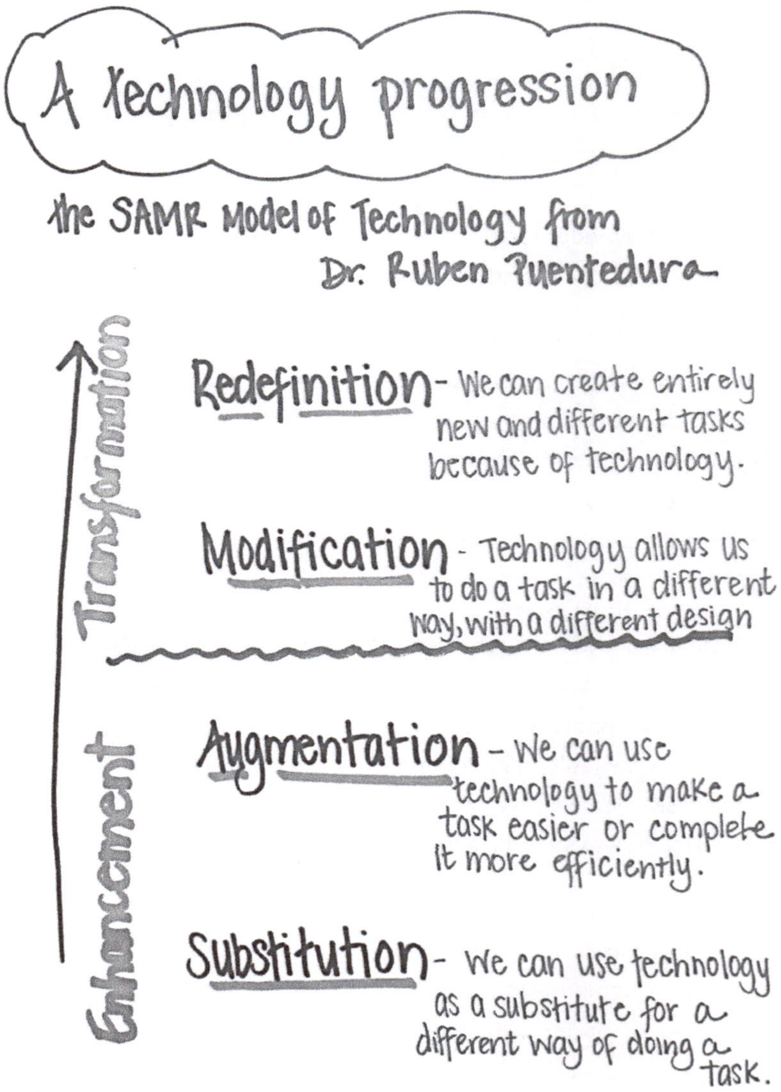

Source: Adapted from Ruben R. Puentedura, *As We May Teach: Educational Technology, From Theory Into Practice* © 2009.

Puentedura's model works for many fields, and he did not envision it solely for education. However, when we apply the concepts as we think about teaching and learning, we definitely can categorize many of the ways we implement technology in our classrooms. Regardless of how we use technology and the category under which it falls, technology should be serving the purpose of allowing us or our students to work or learn better—with greater efficiency and higher quality results. Maybe we substitute keyboarding with talk-to-text programs. Maybe we incorporate videos into lessons, augmenting or modifying teaching and learning experiences. With principles of Universal Design for Learning (UDL) in mind, we can think about how we increase engagement, representation, and action/expression for our striving writers.

My school district uses the Google platform for many functions. Therefore, most of the technology I use is Google oriented, and many of the suggestions in this chapter are based on Google platforms. However, please keep this in mind: The platform does not matter as much as the mindset. As you read about the concepts within this chapter, envision them with whatever platform, application, or program you're most comfortable with, keeping in mind the principles of UDL and the progression from enhancement to transformation.

THE BIG IDEAS

1. **Technology has the power to impact students, and it has the power to impact teachers.** Remembering the first principle of UDL (engagement) and the importance of providing students with opportunities for success, we can leverage tools and resources in order to identify instruction and entry points for our striving writers.
2. **Technology enables us to provide access to students so that tools, charts, and other resources can be easily accessed at points in the process where and when students need them.** In other words, technology can provide a bridge or a pathway toward independence for kids who otherwise struggle with writing.
3. **It's important to pay attention to the reason we are using any digital device, modification, or tool with students—and make sure it fits a students' needs.** The third principle of UDL involves action and expression. Sometimes students spend more time learning or initiating the implementation of technology than they do actually producing any meaningful work, but when we think about the bridges and pathways we can provide through technology, we can improve their ability to communicate and contribute, participating in the writing process.

Technology has the power to impact students, and it has the power to impact teachers.

When we think about incorporating technology tools into our teaching, we have to remember that technology has the power to impact students as well as teachers. When I was working in a fourth-grade classroom, the teacher and I had a conversation about the concepts of the zone of proximal development (ZPD) and how they fit within writing classrooms. She recognized that her instruction was too high for many of the learners in her classroom, but she made an important point.

"There's so much I need to know," she said. "I'm trying to keep track of grade-level standards for all of my content areas, and now I have to know standards from other grade levels as well, in order to really meet these needs."

Her comment stayed with me. I'd given her hard copies of progressions for written expression, but there's a lot of print on those pages. How could I make previous grade-level standards easier for her to access so that she could identify instruction and entry points for our striving writers?

What I have since created are grade-level progressions and teaching points that teachers can access in Google forms. Teachers can use these forms as they confer or have small group instruction with their writers. They can check off who they are working with, and then they can decide which grade-level standards to use in order to focus their instruction. These forms allow teachers to think about the UDL principle of engagement more intentionally because the forms enable teachers to quickly access instructional objectives and standards that are within students' optimal challenges. This increases the emphasis on effort, improvement, and achieving a standard rather than on relative performance, a tenet of the principle of engagement. For example, if a fifth-grade teacher is working with a student who is functioning a year or two below grade level, then the teacher may want to pull up the third-grade standards in order to decide what to compliment and teach that student (see Photo 7.2). This way the instruction is within the student's ZPD, standards based, and following a learning progression that will lead to higher levels of writing.

resources.corwin.com/everychildcanwrite

You are welcome to use the form I have created (linked from the QR code here), or you can follow the directions in the Pause for PD box to create your own. If you commit—truly commit—to using it whenever you confer with students, you will love the information and insights you gain about your teaching and student learning!

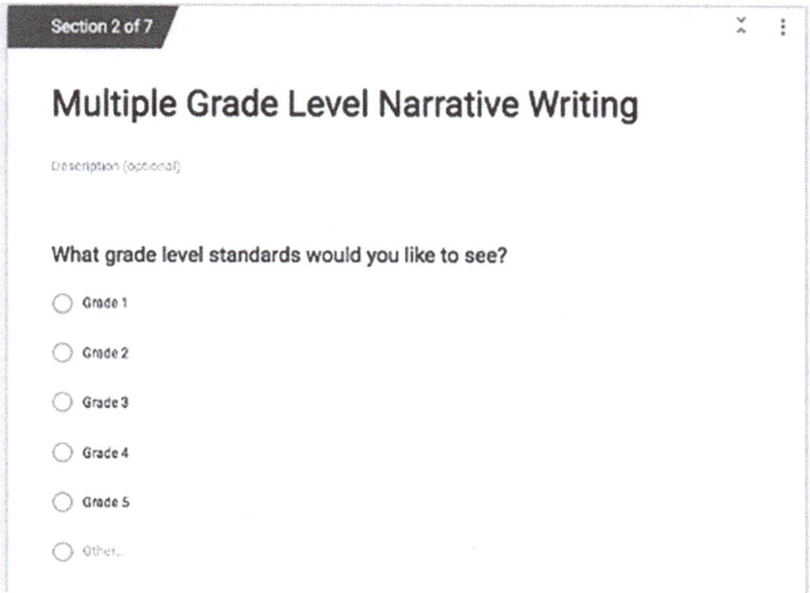
Section 2 of 7

Multiple Grade Level Narrative Writing

Description (optional)

What grade level standards would you like to see?

- Grade 1
- Grade 2
- Grade 3
- Grade 4
- Grade 5
- Other...

Photo 7.2 The first section of the form allows teachers to select a specific grade level.

THINKING OUT LOUD

If a teacher uses these forms with fidelity as they confer with students, then they will generate a spreadsheet with a clear record of what and how the students have been taught. Additionally, using this spreadsheet, teachers can see who they are spending their individualized teaching time with and hold students and themselves accountable for retaining and transferring the instruction.

PARTNERING WITH CAREGIVERS

Spreadsheets offer the power to sort data. Therefore, it becomes possible to isolate just one child's history of conferences and small-group instruction to enrich the conversation and communication with caregivers. When we have the clarity of what we've taught *right there* in front of us as we talk to caregivers, it's easier for them to understand how to support the work we're doing at home with their child.

HOW TO MAKE A GOOGLE FORM FOR WRITING PROGRESSIONS

1. **Go to your Google Drive and make a new form.** To make a form, you will have to go to the "More" button as "forms" appears just after "slides."
2. **Give your form a name and enter in your students' names as checklist items for the first question.**
3. **The second question should be "What grade level are you looking for?"** Depending on your level of students, you will enter in three to five grade levels. Because the focus of this book is on striving writers, I recommend two to three grades below your class's actual grade. If you want to be able to use the form for students who are also exceeding, then consider also including teaching points for one or two grades *above* your grade level. For example, if you are in a fifth-grade class, you may want to have Grade 3, Grade 4, Grade 5, and Grade 6.
4. **Create separate sections for each grade's teaching points.** You can create a section using the icon that looks like an equals sign on the right side of the screen, as shown in Photo 7.3.

5. **Once this new section is in place, then you can list the teaching points that address the specific grade-level standard.** (See Appendix F for grade-level standards of the three genres.) Repeat this process, creating different sections for each grade level that you want to be able to select from.

6. **Return to Section 1,** where you choose the grade level you want to see. You will want to create pathways based on responses. When the responses to the questions are in multiple choice mode, the program offers the choice of going to different sections based on answers, as shown in Photo 7.4.

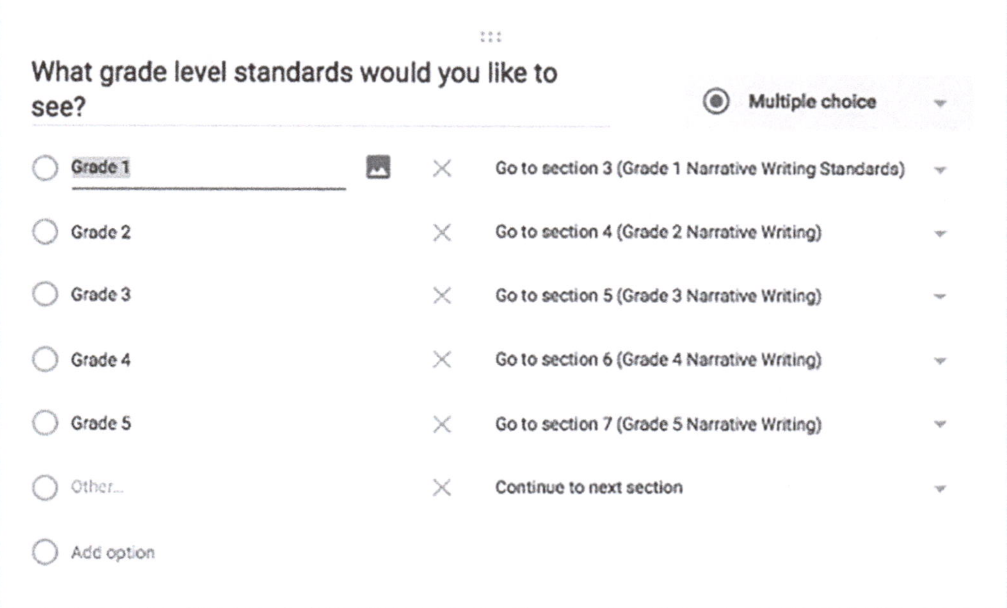

7. **Send yourself the form and start using it in your classroom!** Use this form every day when conferring with writers to see how it can transform your teaching and their learning.

> Technology enables us to provide access to students so that tools, charts, and other resources can be easily accessed at points in the process where and when students need them.

Moving into the second principle of UDL, representation, technology offers us ways to provide multiple means for students to access information. This may include the timing of presentation as well as the sensory option, as we think about auditory, visual, and combined presentations. Two ways to increase representation for students include bringing charts closer to them and using the power of videos.

BRING DIGITAL CHARTS CLOSER TO STUDENTS

Throughout our district, teachers use Google Classroom to manage classrooms, assigning and managing student work through this platform. In addition to assignments, teacher also have the ability to upload documents and pictures, which is how it's so powerful for striving writers. Using this platform, students are able to access resources when they need them within their own process.

Reviewing the concepts of Chapter 6 and the importance of charts, we can create both classroom-sized charts as well as personal-sized charts. This way, students have the power to make decisions about their own need for a tool. For any of us, there are times when it is helpful to have a tool right in front of us as opposed to hanging on a wall, where we have to keep looking up at it. When we teach students to use a split screen, we have that same effect, only within a digital context (see Photo 7.5).

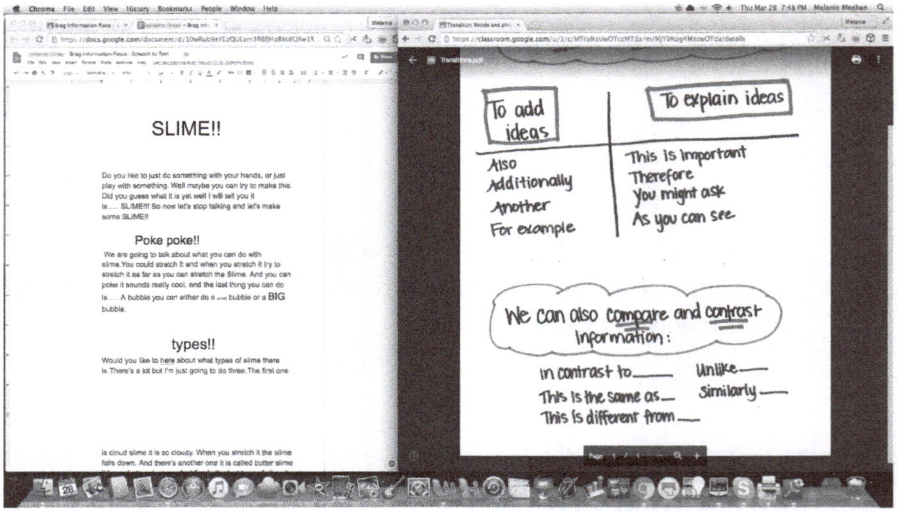

Photo 7.5 In this picture, I've taken a chart from a Google Classroom, I've split the screen, and I've opened a document to work on a story. As such, this chart is right in front of me on the computer screen, if I were to begin my story.

Teachers can create digital folders of charts, checklists, or other tools that have the potential to increase students' ability to complete work independently. Students can make intentional decisions about tools that will help them with their work, and they can access and utilize those tools. While we use Google Classroom, other platforms may work as well, too, depending on your comfort level and your school or district's commitment to technology.

EXPAND YOUR OWN PRESENCE WITH VIDEOS LESSONS

Sometimes necessity is the mother of invention. A few years ago, I was coaching in a second-grade classroom, and our most vulnerable writers were also our most vulnerable readers and mathematicians, so guess what? They kept being pulled out for intervention, missing writing instruction! In an effort to provide them with missed lessons, I created videos of myself delivering shortened versions of the teacher's lessons. We had to teach these young learners how to interact and *learn* from a video, but it worked, and I have expanded the practice, creating a progression of lessons across genres and levels.

For example, here are some videos I have created to support the narrative writing process. The first folder teaches students how to think about the structure of a story in terms of beginning, middle, and end. The digital folder contains a chart, as well as a video of me teaching the lesson.

Once students can independently structure a story in terms of beginning, middle, and end, then they are ready to think about what the story is really about. The next digital lesson contains a chart, as well as a short video of myself teaching the concept of what the story is really about.

resources.corwin.com/everychildcanwrite

UDL emphasizes the importance of having multiple means of representation so that students can gain access to information in a variety of ways. While UDL is focused on visual and auditory systems of representation—sort of the *hows* of what is being taught—we can also think about the *whens* in terms not only of our striving writers, but also all writers in our classroom. I've said before that most of us teach writing in a sequential form; we have our sets of lessons or a curriculum map, and those lessons can—and mostly *should*—guide us. However, when students are working on their own pieces of writing and they are setting goals for themselves, sometimes they need lessons that are out of order or have already been given. Or they just need to hear a lesson again, which is often the case with striving writers. We can use video lessons to address these situations.

Just as we can add charts and checklists into our digital classrooms, we can also add videos. My colleague, Lisa Jacobs, has a series of videos for her narrative writing unit created in a classwork folder within Google Classroom (see Photo 7.6). Each of these videos is between three and four minutes long, and they each target a particular skill within narrative writing. Again, this is something you can replicate with your own school's technology platform.

Photo 7.6 The narrative writing tutorials show up for students in a classroom folder within Google Classroom.

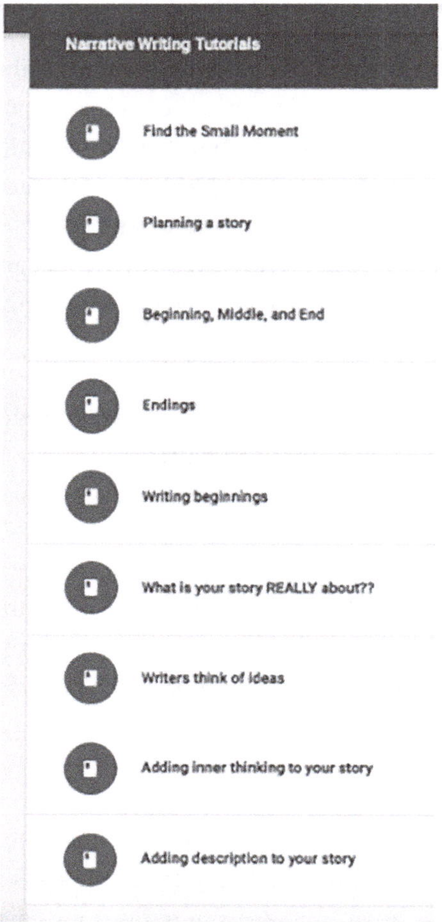

THINKING OUT LOUD

When we first introduce these videos to students, there's a newness factor to overcome—almost everyone wants to watch one. The first couple of videos kids watch may or may not impact their writing. However, if you *teach* into how to use the videos, modeling how we as writers determine next steps and goals, then students begin to become more intentional, selecting videos that really are relevant for the work they are doing right then and there.

Google Classroom is free to educators at the time of this writing, but if for some reason you are not using it or do not have access to it, there are other ways to make tools and videos accessible to students:

1. A private YouTube video series that is accessed through a QR code
2. A folder on a shared drive within your district that students could access through their desktops

HOW TO CREATE A SERIES OF VIDEO LESSON

1. Determine high-priority lessons. Most of our video lessons are about structure, as opposed to development. In all three genres, lessons about language and specific transitional words/phrases were also high priority lessons since so many of these students struggle with basic grammatical concepts.
2. Create charts that coincide with the high-priority lessons. Each chart should coincide to a teaching point. The teaching point is clearly written at the top of each chart, with additional steps of ideas included in the chart as well.
3. Use a device to video yourself teaching the lesson. Each lesson should be between three to four minutes, or you won't maintain students' engagement. Make sure you state the teaching point, demonstrate how to do it on a piece of your own writing, and give students a chance to pause the video and try out the strategy on their own.
4. Give your video a name, and upload the video to wherever you have decided to store them. Within my Google Drive, I create folders for each lesson. Within each folder, there is the video, a picture of the chart, and the sample of work from my writer's notebook.

In our school, because this resource is on Google Drive, I can share it with teachers as I work with them. Besides just reteaching a lesson to students, these videos have also helped teachers visualize how to teach a concept, capitalize on the adult resources in their classrooms, or offer yet-to-be-taught strategies to students who are ready for them. Some teachers are even thinking about sharing some of the lessons with parents and caretakers in order to involve them in our work.

Partnering With Caregivers

Digital charts and videos of lesson provide great platforms for communicating and partnering with caregivers. Many caregivers welcome the opportunity to have charts available to their children at home. Some caregivers will even take the time to review lessons with their children if those lessons are accessible. Keep your videos short and simple, and you have the potential to engage caregivers in a really positive way!

It's important to pay attention to the reason we are using any digital device, modification, or tool with students—and make sure it fits a student's needs.

Action and expression are the focus of the third principle of UDL, and talk-to-text programs are common within writing instruction as we work to provide alternatives for expression and communication. Maybe because talk-to-text programs are so prevalent and such a go-to strategy within the realm of modifications and accommodations, I see their misuse more than with other technology tools. Without question, talk-to-text programs have the potential to open gateways for our striving writers. However, these programs can also lead to misuse, frustration, and dead ends if not implemented with thought and intention.

Several years ago, I worked with a student, Matt, who had been diagnosed with dysgraphia. Talk-to-text programs were beginning to emerge, and we tried to use them with Matt. However, he had a hard time speaking clearly enough for the technology to capture his ideas. Over and over again, the computer "heard" different words than the ones Matt wanted it to. Therefore, most of his sentences made little or no sense. Furthermore, like many striving writers, Matt was not a fluent reader, so finding and correcting the mistakes was as challenging as writing them in the first place. He spent a lot of time creating what amounted to very little, and his most used button on the keyboard was delete. Matt's classroom teacher and I had many conversations about how his technology served more as a tool for task-avoidance than as a productive accommodation for his learning and achievement; we had to work to find a different pathway for Matt.

More recently, I have watched other students sit in front of a talk-to-text program and just start spouting off a story. While voice recognition and prediction have come a long way since Matt's struggles, students still ramble and wind without any sort of focus or organization. Additionally, students may repeat a phrase, verbally try to fix a sentence, or stutter over a word, creating text that lacks fluency or coherence. And then there's the issue of punctuation, which remains a serious challenge. Talk-to-text has the potential to create nonsense unless the user is constantly checking that what they said is what the technology "heard" and created. Even when the computer "reads it back," no one—including the student—understands what was meant. Students become understandably frustrated when the program doesn't create what they expect, and these tools do not serve the purpose of building bridges or providing pathways for better expression.

So what can we do? This is where we have to pay attention to the reason for using the accommodation. For most striving writers, we want to remove the obstacles that get in the way of their written production. If those obstacles include the fine motor skills involved with writing, spelling, and fluency—and frequently they do—then we can initiate the use of a talk-to-text program. However, we have to take the time to instruct students as to its productive and purposeful use.

PAUSE FOR PD

Take some time using a talk-to-text program to compose a piece of your own writing that is in progress. Try it first without any sort of verbal rehearsal. What were some of obstacles you noticed? Did anything frustrate you? Did anything become simpler?

Then try composing with a talk-to-text program using the "How to Use the Talk to Text Program" chart (following), making checks after you work through each step. Spy on yourself as a learner and as a thinker. How does the verbal rehearsal help you? What revisions do you make within your piece? How difficult is it to revise and remember to state your punctuation at the same time?

Lucas has been one of the greatest success stories I have ever seen with a talk-to-text program because we worked together to plan his writing first. When I first started working in Lucas's classroom, he produced very little informational writing. However, when he spoke, he could tell me a lot about his subject. His language reflected an understanding of sentence structure, as well as a sense of transition words and clauses that provided fluency. He knew and understood his topic, so he was able to include facts and explanations around content-specific vocabulary and other elaboration strategies. He was verbal; his language just didn't translate to the written or typed page.

With the help of our district's technology specialist, his teacher and I introduced Lucas to Google Read and Write, a talk-to-text add-on for the Google toolbar, available free of charge to educators and students. So that Lucas would not misuse the program by beginning to dictate without a plan or organizational structure, we created a procedural chart for him to help him plan and rehearse his writing. This chart has helped many students since.

How to Use the Talk-to-Text Program

Plan what you are going to say.

Write yourself a script either with notes or sentences.

Practice saying your ideas until you can say them smoothly and accurately. This might take three to four times.

Practice saying your ideas and include the punctuation that should be there, including the following:

- End punctuation—periods, question marks, or exclamation points
- Commas

Say one to two sentences at a time, including the punctuation.

With this chart in place, this talk-to-text program moves from a replacement category up into the realm of augmentation and possibly even modification. Lucas was able to communicate his ideas through written expression more effectively than he ever had before. Through this platform, Lucas learned the power of verbal rehearsal, how to use conventions, and the importance of revision. With the words in front of him, the idea of making changes, deletions, or additions was less overwhelming for him than it had been with a blank sheet or screen in front of him. He wrote several pieces over the course of our six-week unit, and at the end of the unit, he was able to write an on-demand piece that not only met but exceeded grade-level standards in some areas. Lucas himself would tell you that the tool allowed him to become more independently productive. By practicing it and using it often, he learned the importance of diction, and an unintended and welcome consequence was that he began to speak more clearly in other areas, as well as when he was transposing his words to the computer screen.

Ultimately, talk-to-text programs can empower students, but we have to remember that the goal of students using this program is for them to be able to communicate their ideas clearly. We have to be able to think before we can talk, and we have to be able to talk before we can write. If these foundational processes are not in place, then the speaking will not turn into legible, coherent text.

Lucas worked with this talk-to-text program, along with a few other students in the classroom, and we created another chart all together, as well, shown in Photo 7.7. The chart helped students to remember how to speak clearly as well as the importance of using conventions as they envision their writing. It also reminded them that everything did *not* have to be spoken; they could use the keyboard if they needed to insert a new paragraph or use special punctuation that the computer did not understand.

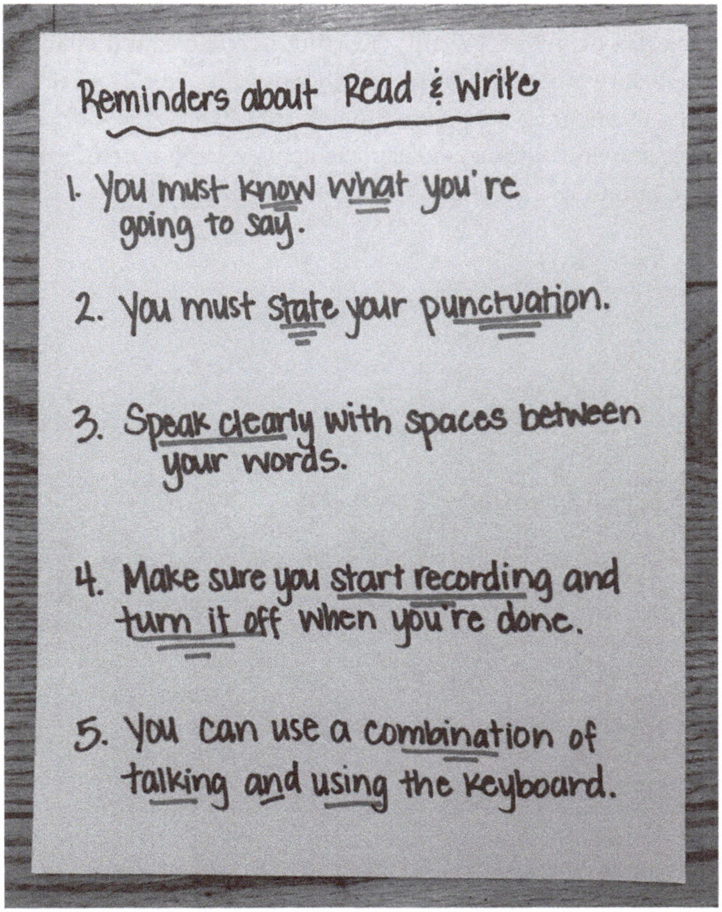

Photo 7.7 Students use this chart as they are beginning to use our talk-to-text program. This way they have a visual reminder of what they need to remember.

Talk-to-text is an example of a technology that requires us to ensure that students benefit from the additional options for action and expression—and that the benefit outweighs any frustration. Some considerations for any alternative include the following:

- Does it move students toward more independence?
- Can students implement it themselves—if not immediately, then in the foreseeable future?

If we can answer these questions affirmatively, then our accommodation or modification has the power to build bridges and pathways for our striving writers.

Digital recipe books are probably not in my mother's near future since she is functional without taking the time to learn and implement higher-tech representations of her recipes. She is independent within her cooking and baking, and it would be a while before she could implement the use of digital devices herself. However, whenever we can make the complex tasks and hierarchies of the writing process more relevant, engaging, accessible, and attainable for our learners, we should do so. In our rapidly changing world of technology and availability, we should pay attention to how we can leverage tools and resources to optimize student learning and achievement—as well as to optimize our own instruction and time.

End-of-Chapter Questions

1. How can technology make it easier for us to understand and implement entry points and high-level instruction in our writing classrooms?
2. What are some ways to use digital resources so that students have alternatives and options for the integration of new and developing skills?
3. When considering alternatives for action and expression, how can we evaluate the costs and benefits of any accommodation or modification?

Take Action!

1. Create a form that is grade and/or genre specific that enhances your ability to access and know standards from adjacent grade levels. This way, you can tailor your instruction to the ZPDs of your students.
2. Upload digital resources so that students can access them as they work through their own writing processes.
3. Create a checklist or list of considerations that you can use when you implement any form of technology into the learning lives of your students.

CHAPTER EIGHT

SPELLING AND CONVENTIONS— THE PITFALLS AND POTHOLES ALONG THE TRAIL

How can we address the skills involved with spelling and conventions while not losing momentum with the overall writing process?

Over and over, I see striving writers avoid writing altogether because of spelling and their fear of making mistakes. Furthermore, many people consider spelling and conventions to be the hallmarks of good writers. To some extent, this is true, although there's so much more to being a good writer! In this chapter, I talk about how we can think about these skills as separate categories, as well as address ways to teach them more effectively to striving writers.

My brother-in-law, Paul, began teaching my nephew to fish as soon as Tuck could walk. Now that Tuck's a teenager, he catches dinner on a regular basis—all by himself. On the other hand, his mom and I occasionally go out on the boat to fish with Paul, and we are constantly asking for help. "Bait the line, cast the rod, is that a fish?" Amy and I say throughout our expeditions. We've been at it for as long as Tuck, but we've never had to solve our own fishing problems.

In many ways, Amy and I on the fishing boat remind me of many striving writers in a classroom, and those writers are often tripped up because of spelling. Early on, students learn to seek out a more competent speller—ideally an adult, although a peer who can spell works as well. Then, all thought flow around planning or ideas is placed on pause as they receive coaching on how to spell or sound out a word.

Frank Smith, a psycholinguist, describes two processes within writing: Composition involves generating ideas, planning, and drafting, while transcription accounts for neatness, spelling, and conventions (Smith, 1994). While Smith envisions grammar within the composition process, I think of grammar as the component that straddles both sides; for fluency, writers need their subjects and predicates to match, but we can also use grammar to increase interest and enjoyment for our readers.

Compositional Skills	Transcriptive Skills
• Generating ideas • Organizing ideas and sections • Creating structure for any type of text • Using techniques and craft moves for development and elaboration • Using grammar and sentence structure for impact	• Spelling • Conventions • Subject/verb agreement • Pronoun/antecedent agreement • Neatness

Whenever I meet with teachers about striving writers, whenever I talk to parents about striving writers, and whenever I work with striving writers themselves, they bring up the transcriptive side of writing, and I bet that as you've read this book, it's been the elephant in the room. So often, striving writers struggle with conventions. More importantly, they think of themselves as *bad* writers because people can't read their writing. However, a lot of times, these students really do have strong ideas as well as clear voices behind the curtain of conventions. Many striving writers *know* the rules about conventions to *say* but just not to *do*.

I have a complicated relationship with handwriting, spelling, and conventions; they matter—that's for sure. However, students are much more likely to retain and transfer skills when those skills are in the context of their own writing (Graham et al., 2012). But if students are nonproductive because they are frozen by the idea of having correct spelling, neat handwriting, and proper conventions, then we don't have contextual writing. It's a conundrum. Therefore, I emphasize and prioritize the compositional side of writing *before* engaging in too much instruction about the transcriptive components. Transcriptive elements matter both for readability and for craft. It's admittedly tough to translate random letters. Additionally, writers have the power to control readers with well-placed punctuation. However, brains are only wired with a limited amount of capacity for new material (Miller, 1956, as cited by Fisher & Frey, 2010), and as teachers, we have to balance the number of cognitive tasks we expect students to juggle. The more that we can transfer processes to long-term memory and incorporate their practice into automaticity, then the more success students can feel about using them (Ericsson & Kintsch, 1995).

Writing is a complicated process, and there are a lot of plates to spin. Metaphorically, when students can keep their compositional plates spinning, we can start to add more spelling and punctuation plates to the mix. In this chapter, we'll focus on some strategies for teaching and learning the transcriptive elements of spelling and punctuation, with an emphasis on application and transfer in students' own writing.

THINKING OUT LOUD

I've admittedly left out handwriting. Truthfully, I very rarely ever teach handwriting when I am working in writing classrooms. In Chapter 5, I talked about getting rid of paper with the dashed center line that is for handwriting instruction because of the cognitive distraction it could create. I also talked about providing wider lines, which is an accommodation that could also help students with messy handwriting. Sometimes something as simple as having a child write while lying on their stomach (even in upper elementary school) or with a different pen can make a positive difference. I am not planning to say anything more about handwriting in this chapter, but if you have a student who really struggles to write legibly, consider consulting with the occupational therapist in your building or district for further ideas for interventions. For some students, handwriting is a serious impediment, and specialists may be able to provide pathways I don't know about. Richard Gentry is a researcher and educational consultant who cites recent studies that indicate the importance of handwriting instruction, both in early grades and in upper elementary grades (Gentry, 2016). If you want to learn more about this topic, I recommend starting with some of his work.

THE BIG IDEAS

1. **Striving writers—no, all writers—need to see conventions and spelling done correctly.** It doesn't help young writers to see incorrect examples on worksheets or examples that they are asked to correct. Whenever we can have their eyes on correct usages, we should.
2. **As we teach the transcriptive elements of spelling and punctuation, our instruction must be within students' realm of possibility and transference—within their ZPD.** In an earlier chapter about entry points, we talked about how difficult—often even impossible—it is to learn something that is miles over our heads. We have to apply this same understanding to students when it comes to spelling and conventions.
3. **We can improve correct usage by finding ways to embed conventions across the day, increasing the level of intention, and infusing elements of play during students' independent writing time.** For as much time as we spend teaching and reminding students to use conventions and good spelling, they spend a lot of time *not using* them. We have to overcompensate for that discrepancy however and whenever we can.

PARTNERING WITH CAREGIVERS

Because spelling and punctuation are important to many caregivers, consider how you can communicate some of the concepts within this chapter to them. For example, you might want to reinforce the following ideas in your conversations and conferences with caregivers:

- Writing involves the integration of many different skills, and we will work on specific skills during specific parts of the writing process as students demonstrate readiness.
- We want to balance our instruction of spelling and punctuation with our instruction of idea generation, planning, and drafting.
- Like many activities, we can sometimes show mastery of skills in isolation, but the transfer of those skills to more authentic work may tend to lag.

Striving writers—no, all writers—need to see conventions and spelling done correctly.

I have not had many struggles with spelling and conventions in my life. But there are a couple of words I know are hard for me. *Embarrass* is one of them. With most words, if I have any question at all, I can write them, eyeball them, and accurately recognize that it "looks right." With that one word, the *e*-word, my eyeball trick doesn't work. If you lined up three different versions with varying *r*'s and *s*'s, I wouldn't be able to tell you the right spelling without consulting my other strategy of remembering two sets of doubles. All I know from the visual choices is that spelling the *e*-word is tricky, not what the right choice is.

I share this example because I see young writers have similar experiences on worksheets and even on teacher-created examples. "Find the mistakes" or "circle the correct examples" are cues that there are some wrong examples in the mix. But here's the deal: Showing a couple of wrong ways and one right way may not get the brain to remember the right way. The brain may choose instead to remember only that it's complicated, especially if the brain is working on integrating and approximating other new information and skills at the same time. Brains have their limitations. For instance, Miller (1956) found that we can only work with about seven new and previously unassociated bits of information at a time. To minimize cognitive demand and increase the potential for integration and transfer to working memory, my recommendation to teachers is to give students as much exposure to *correctness* as possible when teaching students transcriptive skills. I emphasize this idea when it comes to both spelling and grammar, discouraging any use of worksheets or exercises that ask students to choose the correct spelling or usage from options of incorrect ones.

So how could it look if we were only going to provide students with *correct* examples to work on? The chart below shows some alternatives for spelling skill builders. The difference may seem subtle, but it has strong implications for learners.

Instead of	Try this
Choose the correct word: (They're, their) going to (there, their) cousins' house for dinner.	Write in the correct they're, there, or their: ________ going to ________ cousins' house for dinner.
Which sentence is correctly punctuated? "I love meatballs", she said. "I love meatballs," she said.	Explain why the following sentence is correctly punctuated. "I love meatballs," she said.

Another way to build this "see it the right way" framework is to set up centers for writers. When I set up convention-/spelling-oriented centers, I keep a couple factors in mind:

1. The activity should be short and students should be able to independently complete it.
2. The examples should be *correct* examples, as opposed to choices of correct and incorrect.
3. Students should have to create or produce something as a result of the centers.

Remember that you don't want to have students looking at incorrect examples and choosing between them, so try to keep it positive. Photo 8.1 shows pictures of some of the stations I have created. Depending on the resources in the classroom and the functioning level of the students, I may even make a chart that supports the skill of the center. For example, I may make a chart to accompany the second example about the reasons we use commas. That way, when students work at the center, they have three experiences: They see a correct example, they review the rules about the skill, and they create something of their own. (Additional examples of stations can be found in Appendix G.)

Photo 8.1 This series of cardstock "centers" targets some of the skills we have been working on in a fourth-grade classroom. Teachers have used them not only as a pre-writing activity but also as choices when students arrive or find themselves with pockets of time during the day.

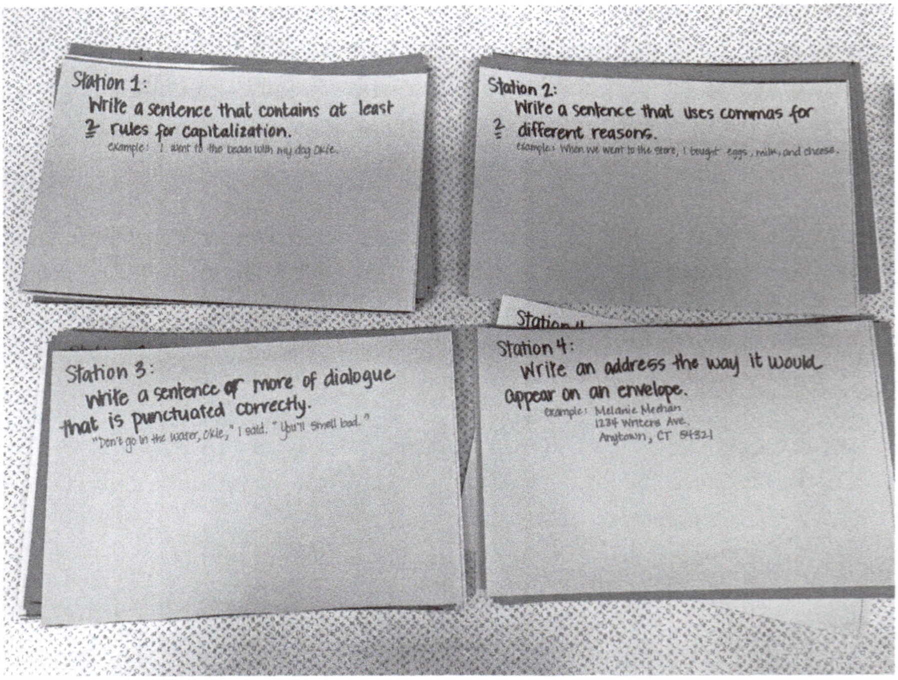

PAUSE FOR PD

Lets Make a Few Centers

1. List a few conventions and spelling-related skills that your students are working on. These skills could align with your word study program, as well as relate to mistakes you've been seeing within students' drafts.
2. Label the station and create a task that addresses one of the skills. Include an example.
3. As you feel necessary, make accompanying charts that students can refer to as they complete the task of the center.

As we teach the transcriptive elements of spelling and punctuation, our instruction must be within students' realm of possibility and transference—within their ZPD.

"How do you spell responsibility?" I heard Jamal ask the other day. He's a current third grader who has not been meeting grade-level expectations in writing.

The adult in the room began to sound it out for him, syllable by syllable, and he played the guessing game, letter by letter. This process took an inordinate amount of time until I couldn't stand it anymore, and I interrupted.

"Just write the rest of it the best you can," I said. "That way you won't forget about the ideas you were planning to write."

THINKING OUT LOUD

Try sounding out a word for even a minute—that's a long time to spend on a few syllables! Furthermore, let's think about what Jamal has just learned. More than anything else, I think he's learned that he can't spell long words without an adult. Remember my e-word? If every word I had to write had the equivalent of the cognitive challenge that one has for me, I'd *never* get through a page, yet that's the experience for many of our striving writers.

It's critical to remember that students tend to replicate what adults do in a conference or whenever they work together. If an adult spends a long time breaking down and prioritizing a single word, then the child is going to get the message that this process matters; many children will attempt to do it (unsuccessfully) on their own . . . and that's the best case scenario. The more likely event is that the writer will just find some reason not to write.

The goal of learning should always be transfer. If what we are teaching today has no chance of being integrated or approximated in tomorrow's writing, then we're not teaching the right thing. If we sit with them and spell out words, all we're really teaching them is that they can't do it themselves. Spelling a six syllable word was a long, long way from Jamal's ZPD (zone of proximal development)—but providing bridges to independence will help our strivers experience success. Let's think about some ways we can head back into that critical zone, both in regards to spelling and conventions of language.

GENERATE WORD LISTS FROM STUDENTS' WRITING AND ADD THOSE WORDS TO DIFFERENTIATED LISTS THROUGHOUT THE YEAR

This could be done a number of ways, but I would suggest word cards. I use cardstock, and I write one word on each card. By studying students' process writing, we can identify spelling errors or inconsistencies, thinking about priority words. Priority words could come from a list, or they could be words you know represent the student's spelling level. They could also be words you know are likely to show up in future writing pieces. Then, choose three to five words to be the focus for that student for a set interval of time. That interval may vary, but should be long enough for the student to feel confident with spelling those words *without the cards*. You can tell students that you expect them to work on *all* words—but especially those.

You can even weave in the element of choice by asking students where and on what they'd like those words written for them—an index card taped to the desk, a sticky note that stays in the folder, separate pieces of cardstock . . . whatever works for you and the student. However, what happens is this: Teach students to let you know when they no longer need the words in front of them; once this happens, the word goes into a zipper storage bag as a student's own personal word collection.

THINKING OUT LOUD

> This word collection may need to be fluid because sometimes some words may need to be "taken out" and revisited. Sometimes students slip back to old spelling habits with words they'd felt they'd mastered. We can emphasize that this isn't a big deal—just something to address with another round of studying—and probably a shorter round of studying, at that!

PROVIDE CHOICE AND OWNERSHIP OF SPELLING AND CONVENTION STRATEGIES BY CREATING INDIVIDUALIZED TOOLS

In all likelihood, you've been teaching from a spelling program, and probably most of your students are learning to spell fairly successfully. However, many spelling programs are developmental, and they rely on learners having mastered previously taught concepts. That might not have happened. Whenever I discover gaps in learning, I revisit curriculum, lessons, and resources from earlier grades.

Sometimes process/strategy charts that enumerate some of the steps involved in encoding words help our older striving writers.

I returned to Jamal later that week, and we talked about the different ways he could tackle a word like responsibility in the future—without having to track down the nearest adult. "But what if it's not right?" he wanted to know. I assured him that his spelling didn't have to be perfect; it had to contain enough sounds so that he and his intended audience could figure out what he was trying to say.

Students like Jamal benefit from choice and ownership, so oftentimes I will create a chart of options with students (see Photo 8.2) or even have them make their own tool for strategies they feel will work best for them.

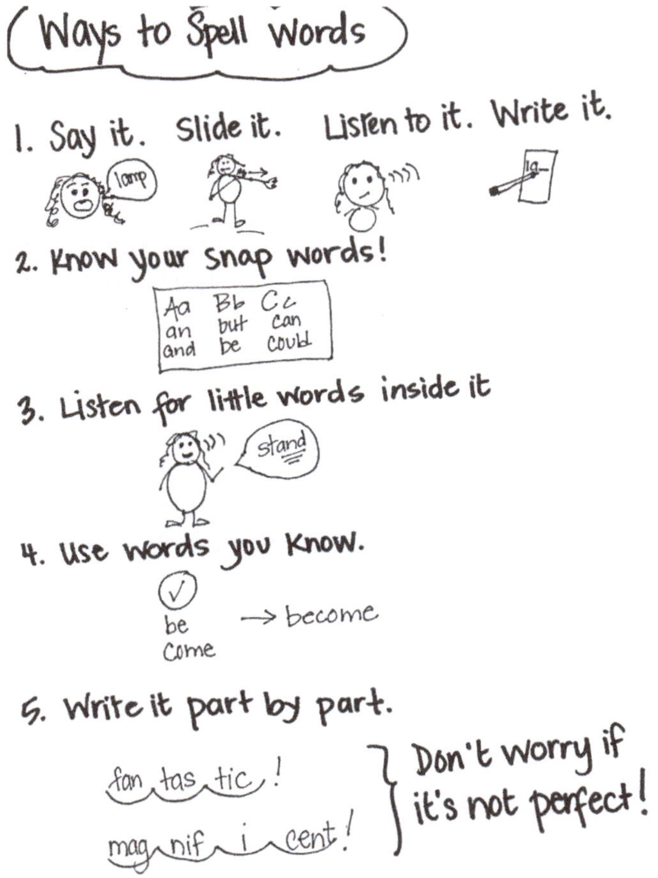

Photo 8.2 This spelling strategies chart is a helpful tool for many upper elementary students who struggle with spelling.

"You're working on spelling a long-ish word," I may say. "Which strategy do you think could help you? There's not a right or wrong answer—it really has more to do with what you think would help you."

This sort of conversation empowers students, honoring their own learning process and shifting the responsibility of learning from us to them.

Sometimes, spelling really has the potential to freeze striving writers. Therefore, in addition to teaching them some strategies for trying out spelling on their own or beginning a personalized word collection, it's also important to teach them some strategies for trying it out and moving along. Basically, we let students know that we give tricky words our best try, but we don't let them take over our writing progress. We want to help strivers make a note that they recognize the word might not be spelled correctly, but they also should recognize it's time to move on and get their ideas down on paper or on the computer screen. Some strategies include but aren't limited to the following:

- Circling the word and continuing along
- Writing *sp?* next to the word
- Underline or star the word

THINKING OUT LOUD

When students are drafting on the computer, I have them turn spelling notifications off. That way, they aren't distracted by every red line or computer-generated suggestion that comes along. Those notifications can derail the flow of ideas, and students can do a spell-check at other points in their writing process.

Pause for PD

Let's look at Will's writing together.

When I started working in Will's classroom, he wrote almost nothing. He spent independent writing time going to the bathroom, sharpening his pencil, trying to think of ideas, and staring off into space. Now, because we've worked through some of the composition challenges he faced—the ideas part of the process—Will thinks of and writes stories with clear beginnings, middles, and ends. He is fairly productive during writing time, and he's excited to share his writing with others, but his spelling and conventions are still lagging. Let's take a look at the beginning of a recent piece, in Photo 8.3. (So you're not in suspense, the main character starts a mystery team, and they find his missing earphones in his sister's room.)

Photo 8.3 Will's first page contains some spelling mistakes, but a solid structural beginning for a narrative story.

Let's first think about what is intact for Will as a speller:

- Some basic sight words: one, was, start, will
- Endings/suffixes: -ed, -ing
- Medial sounds and vowels: mistery

What could we offer him to work on? Just from this page, we can see that *could*, *watch*, and *thought* are misspelled. Those three words are ones that will show up in other pieces, so we could offer Will those words—and maybe *just* those words—as ones to work on. I would give him those words to keep somewhere in front of him when he's drafting. We could also teach him to mark a word like *mystery* so that he can come back to it later, after he's completed his draft.

Some important ideas to keep in mind when we work with students like Will include the following:

- Have them focus on just a few words at a time
- Have them concentrate on specific spelling patterns or rules that align to other lessons

Empower them by letting them know that while you care about spelling, your more important concern is that they get their thoughts out.

Take some time to go through this process with one or two of your own striving writers' work, just as we analyzed Will's spelling strengths and growth opportunities.

In addition to teacher-created charts, we can also address conventions by having students create their own individualized convention cards, and most students really enjoy this task. Depending on the levels and ages of students, we might start with something like the yellow card (see Photo 8.4).

Photo 8.4 This chart offers space for students to fill in what they are personally working on as well as strategies insofar as convention skills are concerned.

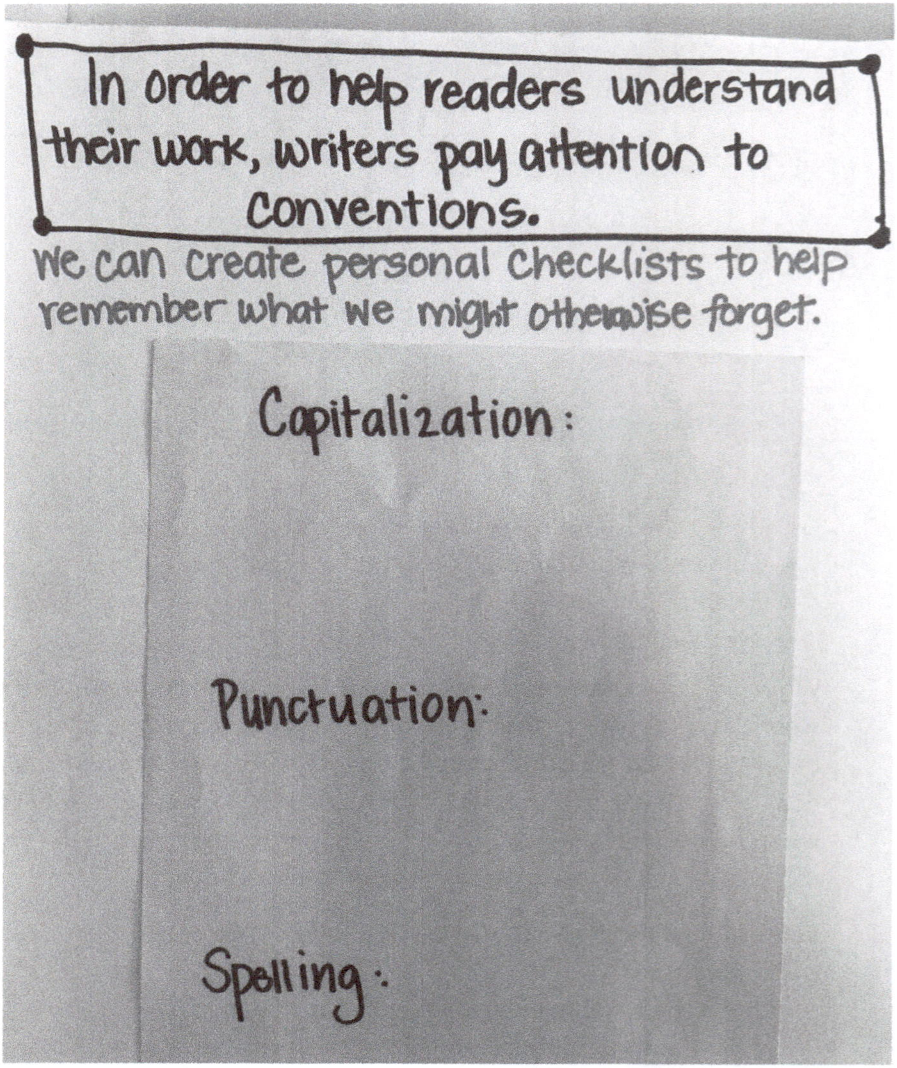

From there, students go "convention shopping." I give them convention charts from various grade levels, and I have them fill out three to five skills for each category (see Photo 8.5).

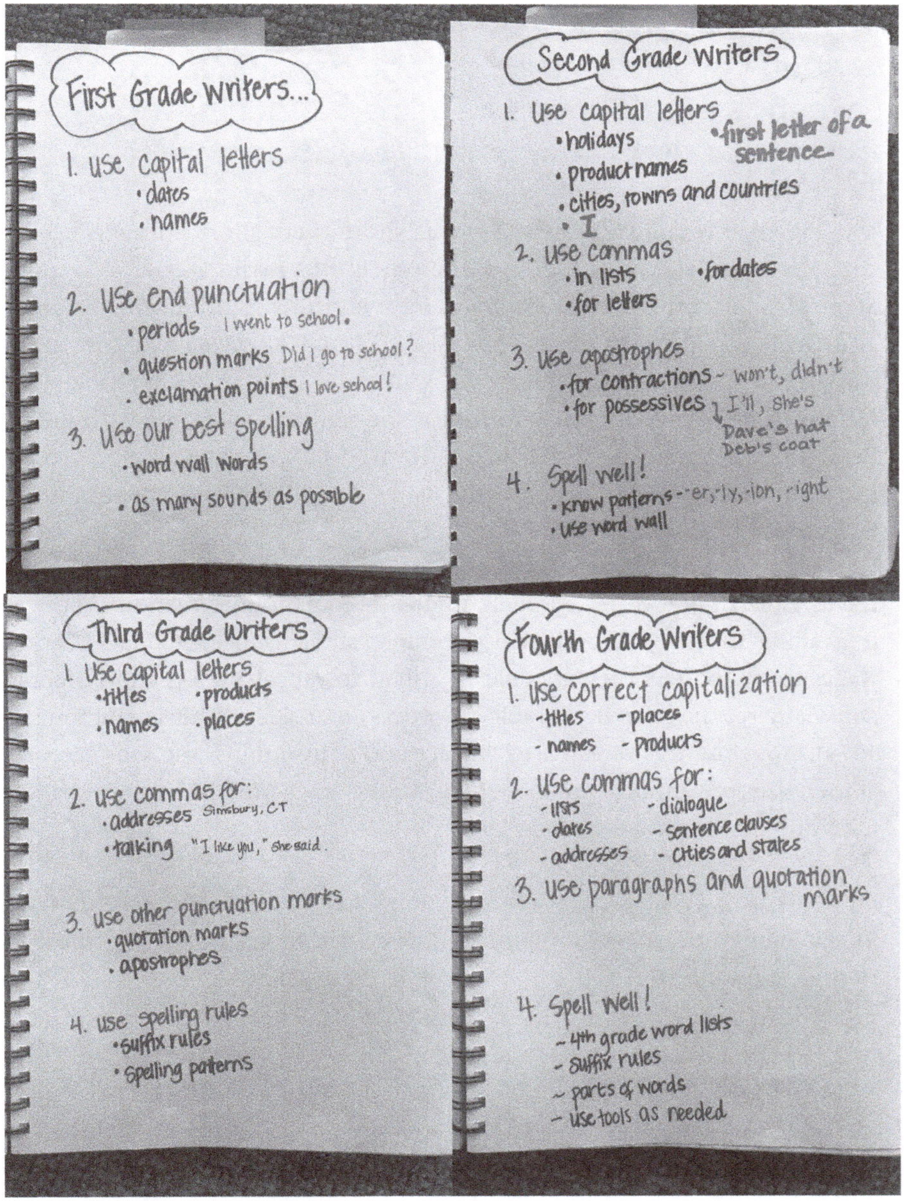

Photo 8.5 These charts align with the Common Core Language Standards, listing the specific skills expected for students as they move through grades.

The skills students choose should be the ones that they are trying to remember but aren't perfect about. The skills should *not* be ones the students are just hearing about for the first time. Again, think about ZPDs. What skills are developing, but need a little extra scaffolding or nudging along the trail of mastery?

We can improve correct usage by finding ways to embed conventions across the day, increasing the level of intention, and infusing elements of play during students' independent writing time.

My dog Okie is almost perfect. He falls short—very short—though when it comes to approaching other dogs when he is on a leash. I spoke to a trainer about it. She complimented me on doing everything right insofar as training and working with him on it. However, her advice was to take him to the walking trail at least five times a week in order to change Okie's behavior. "It has to be part of his daily routine," she said. It's the same with people; before any behavior becomes habit, we need to work at making it part of our daily routine. The same can be said for students and conventions of language.

David LaBerge and S. Jay Samuels studied automatic information processing in reading in 1974, finding that the more students need to pay attention to accuracy, the less they are able to attend to processing. As they approach automaticity, they are better able to process as readers (LaBerge & Samuels, 1974). Applying this research to writing and conventions, the more students automatize conventions, the more they are able to dedicate their energy toward ideas and drafting.

But how can we do that? One important way is to make conventions an integrated part of the writing process, as opposed to a separate step within it. Here are a few ideas.

ALLOCATE A FEW MINUTES EACH DAY TO WORK ON JUST SPELLING AND CONVENTIONS

Students have to understand that working on spelling and conventions is not a separate step in the writing process. This can be done in conjunction with a personalized "Convention Card." What I like to say is something along the lines of, "Writers, pause for a moment in your drafting process. I want you to take about a minute, maybe less, and just reread what you've been writing, making sure that you are using everything you know about spelling, capitalization, and punctuation as you are drafting. Once you've done that, get back into your writing."

When I speak to them, I assume positive intention: *Of course they are working on their conventions as they draft!* Students usually react favorably to that approach!

1. **Expect spelling and conventions in all types of written expression, regardless of content area.**

Often I will see reading responses or math explanations with little or no regard to the conventions students have been working on in their independent writing. Remember the idea of showing students only correct examples of spelling and grammar? The same sort of thinking applies here; if students are capitalizing first words of sentences for an hour a day, but are ignoring that rule for all other writing done throughout the day, then they are less likely to internalize the skill and shift into mastery. When I stop in during other times of the day and students are writing something, I might ask, "Is there a reason you're not using ________?" Without exception, they laugh at this question . . . then they head into their writing and fix it!

2. **Try inserting punctuation into your oral language when speaking with students and ask them to try it as well.**

For example, comma, when you ask students to line up, comma, state the period at the end of the sentence, period. Have you ever tried, this question mark? Students think it's really funny, exclamation point!

But if students can't think it, they can't talk it. And if they can't talk it, it's highly unlikely they can write it. Verbal rehearsal is powerful, and it helps with conventions, as well as other components of the writing process.

3. **Incorporate play into learning about transcriptive skills.**

In addition to more intentional daily practice, purpose and play also contribute to improving conventions. Roy Peter Clark (2006) suggests transforming the rules of punctuation into useful tools, and that there are two main reasons for punctuation: to set the pace of reading and to divide words, phrases, and ideas into groupings. He writes, "Punctuate with power and purpose when you begin to consider pace and space" (p. 46).

Consider having students illustrate or create analogies for punctuation. For adults, traffic signs work well, but give your students a chance to think about the creative representation they can come up with for punctuation marks. One child drew dog pictures to represent end punctuation marks. The sitting dog represented a period. The dog cookie represented a question mark since his dog always looked so interested when a cookie was in the near future. The picture of the door, which represented the exclamation point, had to do with his dog barking excitedly when a guest arrived. These representations may seem far-fetched, but they help increase students' awareness of punctuation in the world or writing.

Another idea that I've modified from Roy Peter Clark involves re-punctuating sentences. Students need to practice this at first, but once they realize what is being asked of them, they love it. Challenge them to make readers go fast in some places and slow down in others. I recommend starting with one fairly simple sentence and then play with all the different ways to punctuate it, such as the following:

We saw the ducks.

We saw the ducks!

We saw the ducks?

We saw the . . . ducks!

We saw the . . . ducks?

We—saw the ducks.

We saw the ducks . . .

You get the idea. . . . The ultimate example has to do with grandma and eating. I'm not sure who originally shared it on the Internet, but these two sentences have dramatically different meanings!

Let's eat Grandma.

Let's eat, Grandma.

Students love to talk about the different scenarios that could be happening when the punctuation is different, and it really helps them realize the importance of punctuation as an author's tool. We really can control readers with dots and lines!

Once students see this on a demonstration sentence, then you can challenge them to change the punctuation of sentences within their own writing. As we assume positive intention when it comes to our few minutes of daily convention checks during independent writing, we also assume that students are using punctuation in the first place when we ask them to change it. Whether they are or are not, our request for a change reminds them of our expectation and increases their awareness and eventual usage.

TIP!

If you decide to shift your approach from rules to tools, you might want to change your wording about rules. Instead, use the word *purpose*: "The purpose of punctuation and grammar is to make your writing available to readers and even control your readers' experience of your writing." You could also emphasize that while we are talking about conventions as tools, there are also rules that involve punctuation, and people expect to see them in certain places. Here are some ways you can emphasize purpose when conferring about spelling and conventions.

Instead of	Try
Where does the period go?	Where do you want readers to slow down and take a breath?
Here's how to spell a word . . .	Write the sounds you hear and move on.
Let's work on fixing your spelling and punctuation.	Let's just circle the words you want to check later, so now we can talk about the structure of your story/what you're teaching readers about/the opinion you're expressing to the world.

Maybe more than anything else, students need to understand the importance of spelling and punctuation within the context of audience and purpose. However, they also benefit from hearing about the two sides of writing—composition and transcription. In a recent conference with a fourth grader, I shared this thinking with Micah, a striving writer with a belief that he couldn't write because he couldn't spell. I wasn't sure he believed me when I told him that his composition skills were strong and important, but since that conference, he has called me over to read his pieces with pride I hadn't seen before our conversation.

Just as teachers need to know and understand the balancing act between composition and transcription, students benefit from this metacognitive knowledge as well. So many striving writers do not think or believe they have something to say in the world that matters—they do! Just as much as anyone else in their community, our striving writers need to believe in the importance of entertaining, informing, and persuading through written expression. Teach them about conventions, give them tools for spelling, and praise their bravery for getting their words out into the world!

End-of-Chapter Questions

1. How does thinking about writing in categories of composition and of transcription guide and/or change your practice?
2. How can Vygotsky's theory about ZPD relate to the transcriptive elements of writing?
3. How can you make spelling and conventions a more regular part of the academic day for your students?

Take Action!

1. Eradicate any materials in your teaching world that ask students to choose from incorrect versions of skills or spelling.
2. Consider the ZPDs of your striving writers. Just as we worked to find entry points for them into the process of writing, help them find entry points into spelling and conventions with intention and correctness.
3. Establish some ways to increase the presence of spelling and conventions throughout the days of all your writers.

CHAPTER NINE

EVERY CHILD CAN WRITE—A CASE STUDY

What does it look like in a real classroom when we merge entry points, bridges, and pathways?

If, for students, writing is like spinning plates, for teachers, writing instruction is like spinning heavier plates, faster, and standing on one foot. Throughout this book, we have thought about the environment, routines, structures, and various strategies that have the potential to expand the access points for our striving writers, and I have provided many different ideas and strategies. As an instructional coach, I work in classrooms for up to six-week cycles. Although there's no way that I can implement everything from this book during one coaching cycle, in this chapter, I will share how several components came together in a third-grade classroom—and students who had not experienced much success with writing changed their course and grew into much more confident and competent communicators of their ideas and stories.

An important component of my work involves working with teachers when they have concerns about their student writers. Typically, we study student work, patterns, and trends in order to target and name specific learning goals for written expression. Our work aligns with units of study, so those goals are usually genre specific, but ultimately, students need to transfer their skills and learning to any type of writing. As I work with both teachers and students, I emphasize that even though narrative, information, and opinion writing may seem different, there are common elements in terms of structure, development, and conventions. Furthermore, as confidence grows in one genre, striving writers meet with more success, and success builds on success in other genres, as well.

This chapter is about merging the strategies and ideas together so that striving students grow as writers. I am sharing the experiences we used in one third-grade class so you can see not only the complexity of the work, but also the possibilities and the positive outcomes for students and learning.

Increasing Volume as a Crucial First Step

Lisa reached out to me after scoring her third graders' fall narrative prompt. "They're not writers," she said, as we talked about her students.

Based on their assessment data, Lisa was right. Of her twenty-three students, only eight met grade-level standards for our district's narrative writing prompt. Of the other fifteen, four scored in the below range and eleven were in our approaching range. When I probed about their issues and what seemed to be getting in their way, Lisa said that they just didn't write anything.

"They sit there," Lisa said. "It's almost like they don't know how to do school. Some of them wrote almost nothing on the personal narrative assessment."

When I looked at some of their writing samples, I saw what she meant. There were several writing samples that contained hardly any writing, and the samples contained very few conventions and learned spelling rules or sight words. We agreed that part of the challenge would be to just increase the volume of writing production for many of these students.

Establishing Routines

One of the first things Lisa and I did was reestablish routines for her writing class. Lisa teaches within the framework of a writing workshop, so we taught an inquiry lesson about what the teacher's role should be, as well as the students' roles. Photo 9.1 shows a chart we created with the students to clarify these roles and establish routines.

Photo 9.1 This chart was created in response to the question, What are the roles of teachers and students during a lesson? The initials show who supplied the response.

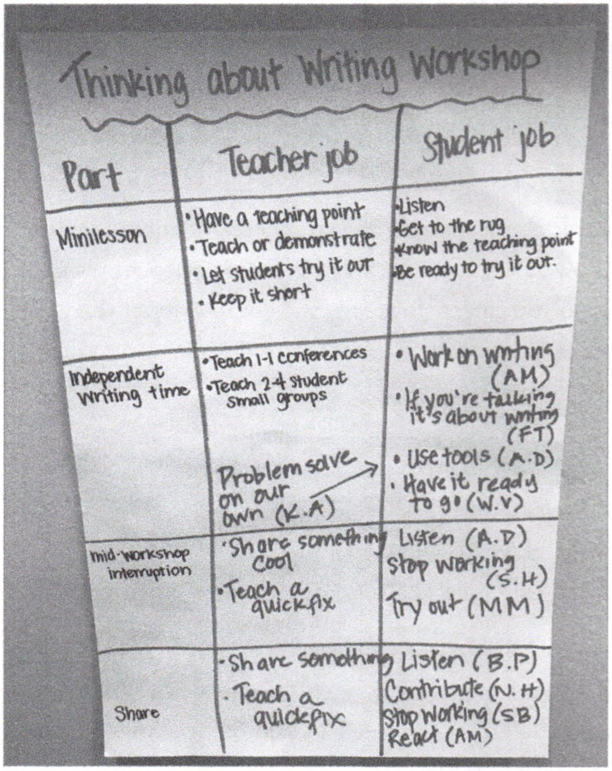

Lisa's point about her students not knowing how to "do school" had some validity. The first time I asked them to come to the rug, several students debated over who sat where, and others sat in places where they could not see either the smart board or the easel with a chart pad. Thinking about some of the concepts noted in Chapter 2 that have to do with behaviors and learning readiness, we spent some time going over basic transition expectations. We had students demonstrate what great transitions looked like, we challenged other students to notice and name the transitional behavior, and until transitions became much more intentional, we had only a few students move at once.

In addition to reestablishing transition behaviors, we also taught into what attending to instruction really means. Learning is not something that should happen *to* students; it's something that should happen *with* them. Over the next few days, Lisa and I took turns teaching minilessons, and if we watched students not paying attention, we pulled them aside and talked to them about what was getting in their way and what they could do about it. During these meetings, we had students fill out Green Greatness forms. We used an engagement inventory to observe and record behavior during instruction, and after a week, 21 out of 23 students were paying attention to our minilessons, as determined by our observations.

TIP!

You can find all of these ideas in Chapter 2:

- Transitions minilesson (p. 30)
- Strategies for smoother transitions (p. 29)
- Green Greatness Forms (p. 33)
- Engagement inventory (p. 48)

Providing Charts for Independence

As part of our commitment to increasing the tools available to the students within the classroom environment, we created several different types of charts over the course of the unit. We had the overall process chart, enumerating the steps in the process of writing a realistic fiction story as shown in Photo 9.2, as well as an anchor chart, shown in Photo 9.3, which echoed the CCSS but in student-friendly language—with exactly what their narrative writing should include.

Photo 9.2 This chart lists the possible steps for writing a realistic fiction story.

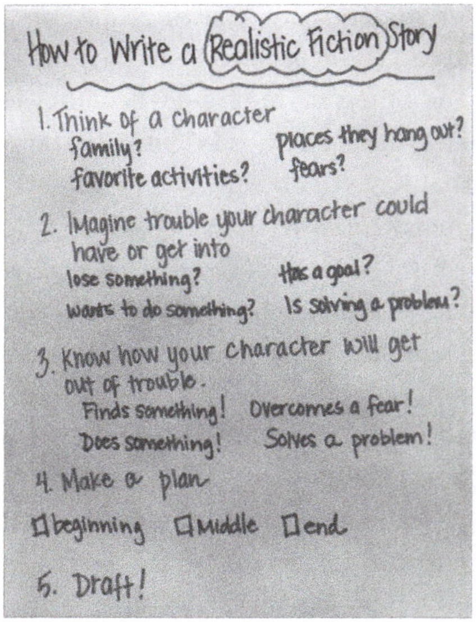

Photo 9.3 This chart lists the qualities of a third-grade narrative piece of writing in student-friendly language.

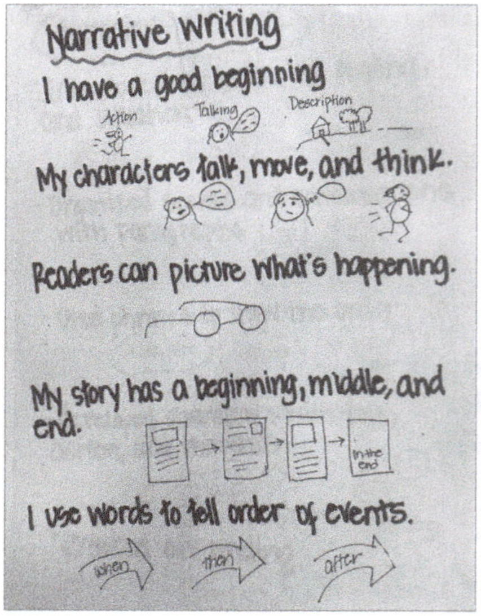

We also had a strategy chart that developed over the course of a few days that offered students various ways to think of stories. Because this skill had been an issue for many of the students in the previous unit, we used sticky notes on that chart; this way, we could "borrow" a sticky note for a student when there seemed to be a strategy that would particularly help them get going with idea generating.

Most of our strategy charts were created on 11 x 16 colored paper. This type of paper took up less space on Lisa's available bulletin board space; if we used regular-sized chart paper, we would not have been able to fit as many resources.

These charts went on display as we taught them, and they even rotated in with other charts. This way, we didn't have too much on the bulletin board at any one time, which could overwhelm students and undermine our plan that they would use these charts to build independence.

As we co-created the charts during instruction, we also created smaller versions of the charts so that students could access different teaching points as they needed. Those charts are in the small envelopes on the bulletin boards. Students accessed these charts regularly, either on their own or because we suggested that they take a look at a specific one. We taught students to borrow and return the small charts so that they used them with intention and so that the charts didn't get buried in student folders, a common tendency.

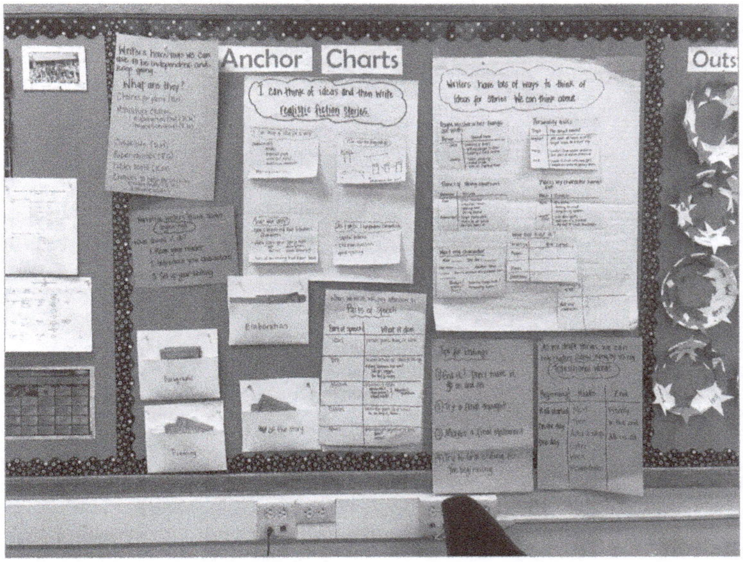

Photo 9.4 This bulletin board developed over the course of the unit. The larger charts have sticky notes that can be "borrowed," while the smaller charts on construction paper enabled us to refer students to the charts by color. Additionally, individual-sized charts are in the four white envelopes. Technically, all of these charts are not "anchor charts," as the title of the bulletin board suggests. (See Chapter 6 about charts.)

As I look at the bulletin board from Lisa's room now, I am struck by its imperfection. For instance, the overall title of the bulletin board, *Anchor Charts,* is technically not correct, since many of the charts are not anchor charts. Furthermore, some of the charts are crooked, and not everything fits like a Tetris game or art gallery wall. However, as we think about concepts from Chapter 6, the best charts are the ones that are *used by students,* and perfect should never get in the way of the good. As students started to understand the resources available to them on this bulletin board, they not only responded to our cues to check out the blue endings chart or take an orange elaboration tool, but they also accessed the board on their own when they were working on a specific part of writing. That spoke to the growing self-efficacy and intention in the room.

TIP!

All of these ideas for charts can be found in Chapter 6, including strategies for individualizing charts for strivers' use. Refer to Chapter 1, as well, for suggestions about maximizing your classroom environment, including walls and bulletin boards.

Finding Different Entry Points

Looking at the data and the writing samples from the most recent independently created samples, we knew we had six students who needed extra work on basic story structure. With two of us in the room, we made the decision that Lisa would coach that group of students in a shared writing project. With the students, Lisa followed the progression of gradual release. First, as a group, they developed a character (described in Photo 9.5).

Photo 9.5 This document shows how Lisa and her students brainstormed about their character.

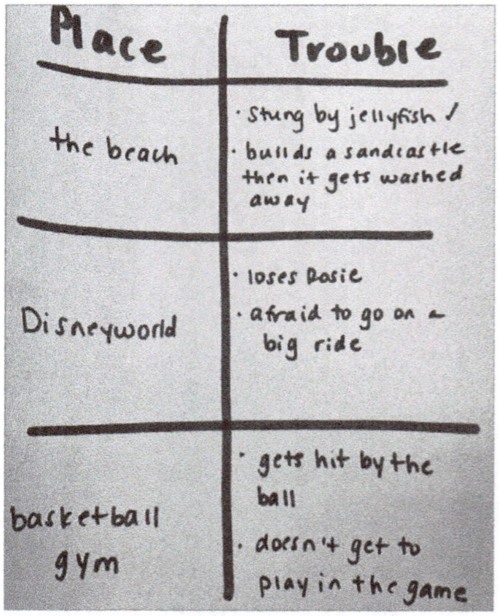

Photo 9.6 This chart shows the settings where Julie hangs out and the types of trouble she could get into.

Then, within the span of one to two days, students wrote their own versions of their character getting stung by a jellyfish. As you can see from the writing samples shared in Photo 9.7, the students wrote the same plot, but their stories are different.

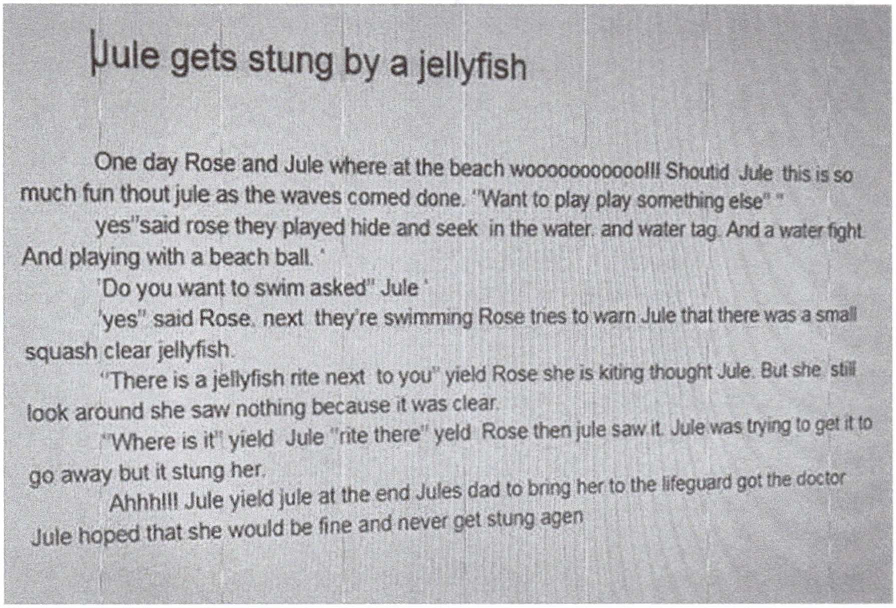

Jule gets stung by a jellyfish

One day Rose and Jule where at the beach wooooooooooo!!! Shoutid Jule this is so much fun thout jule as the waves comed done. "Want to play play something else" "

yes"said rose they played hide and seek in the water. and water tag. And a water fight And playing with a beach ball. '

'Do you want to swim asked" Jule '

'yes" said Rose. next they're swimming Rose tries to warn Jule that there was a small squash clear jellyfish.

"There is a jellyfish rite next to you" yield Rose she is kiting thought Jule. But she still look around she saw nothing because it was clear.

"Where is it" yield Jule "rite there" yeld Rose then jule saw it. Jule was trying to get it to go away but it stung her.

Ahhh!!! Jule yield jule at the end Jules dad to bring her to the lifeguard got the doctor Jule hoped that she would be fine and never get stung agen

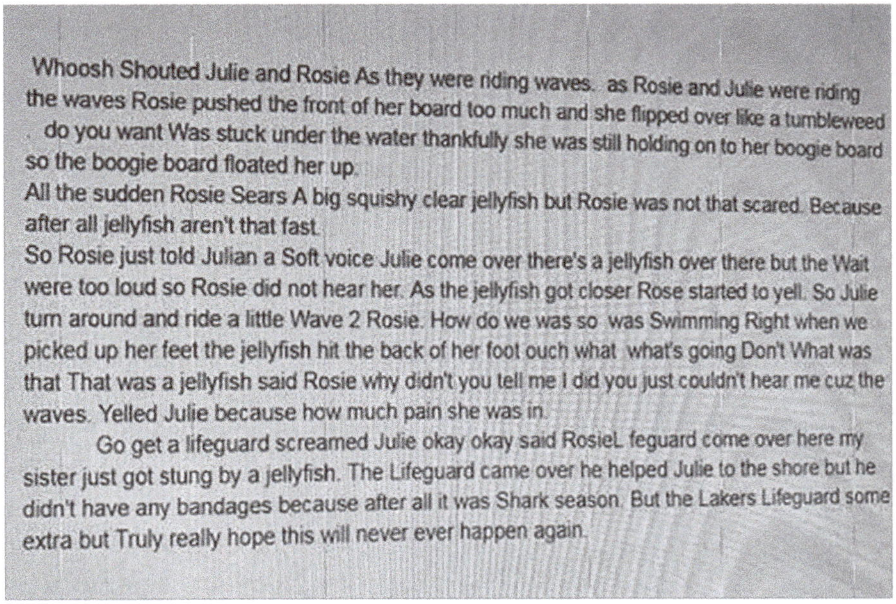

Whoosh Shouted Julie and Rosie As they were riding waves. as Rosie and Julie were riding the waves Rosie pushed the front of her board too much and she flipped over like a tumbleweed . do you want Was stuck under the water thankfully she was still holding on to her boogie board so the boogie board floated her up.
All the sudden Rosie Sears A big squishy clear jellyfish but Rosie was not that scared. Because after all jellyfish aren't that fast.
So Rosie just told Julian a Soft voice Julie come over there's a jellyfish over there but the Wait were too loud so Rosie did not hear her. As the jellyfish got closer Rose started to yell. So Julie turn around and ride a little Wave 2 Rosie. How do we was so was Swimming Right when we picked up her feet the jellyfish hit the back of her foot ouch what what's going Don't What was that That was a jellyfish said Rosie why didn't you tell me I did you just couldn't hear me cuz the waves. Yelled Julie because how much pain she was in.

Go get a lifeguard screamed Julie okay okay said RosieL feguard come over here my sister just got stung by a jellyfish. The Lifeguard came over he helped Julie to the shore but he didn't have any bandages because after all it was Shark season. But the Lakers Lifeguard some extra but Truly really hope this will never ever happen again.

Photo 9.7 While we have issues to work on with both of these writers, we celebrated the establishment of basic story structure that both were able to maintain.

From there, they each chose their own "trouble" they wanted to write about and spent another couple of days working on those stories. Since we'd essentially removed choice from their writing lives, as soon as we could give back elements of it, we did! During these days of writing, Lisa emphasized the importance of beginning, middle, and end, and students had the plan from their co-created chart as well as beginning-middle-end paper to keep them structured and organized. As that skill became more solid, she could work on the balance of dialogue, description, action, and inner thinking, but on *different* stories. Don't forget that not every story has to be perfect!

THINKING OUT LOUD

I recognize that not every classroom has the luxury of two certified adults in the room at the same time. A paraprofessional can frequently help you do this work. If you are by yourself, you can still do a shared writing experience, but the rest of the class will need to understand that for the first ten minutes after your minilesson, you will be working with a specified and predetermined small group. The job of the rest of the class is to work on their independent writing work with the tools and resources available to them within the classroom.

In addition to these pieces, students had their choice of continuing their work either by

- writing another independently written piece about Lisa's character; or
- writing a piece about a character that they made up themselves, creating their own plan and then initiating and completing the process on their own.

These processes were intentional. While we recognized that we were taking away the element of choice for this group of students, the shared writing experience enabled them to verbalize their ideas, lean on each other for developing details, and produce several stories both collaboratively and independently. Basically, using a gradual release model, we traded choice for a pattern of success and an increase in productivity, and the results paid off. After two weeks of heavier coaching and scaffolding, Lisa, as planned, was able to shift the responsibility of story development over to the students. This group of six students who were previously unable to sustain writing stamina for more than about five minutes and couldn't come up with any ideas, not only developed story ideas and plans, but also maintained writing stamina for over twenty minutes and created their own clearly structured stories.

TIP!

Look to Chapters 3 and 4 for more detail on these entry point strategies, as well as strategies for building bridges, specifically:

- Creating learning progressions (p. 59)
- Shared writing with older students (p. 80)

Building Independence for All

As Lisa worked with the six students, the structure of a workshop continued to strengthen. Her six students participated in minilessons, and the bulletin board developed and evolved. Additionally, as the tools and charts on the bulletin board became more and more important resources for students, we taught into partnerships. We taught students specific questions they could ask each other as well as phrases they could use to engage in conversations, as shown in Photo 9.8.

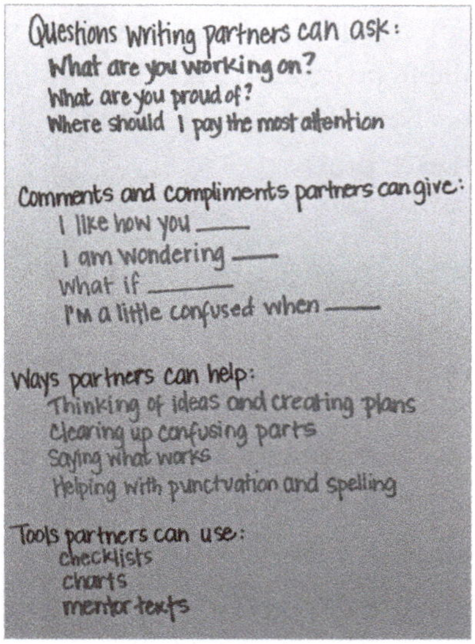

Photo 9.8 A chart like this one offers students possibilities for the types of questions, comments, and compliments partners can offer each other throughout the writing process.

Five students had met the goals of narrative writing, and we matched them up as a group of two and a group of three. We taught them ways to be strong writing partners. To reinforce the instruction, we created a partnership tool, pictured below. Lisa Corcoran, a staff developer at the Reading and Writing Project, had shared a more complex version, and I modified this progression for third graders. This partnership progression provides pictorial representation of some of the work and behaviors of strong partnerships, while it also emphasizes the importance of using tools to work with each other. This group of students improved in their ability to determine next steps for themselves with adult intervention.

Photo 9.9 Pictures and descriptions allow students to self-assess their partnerships.

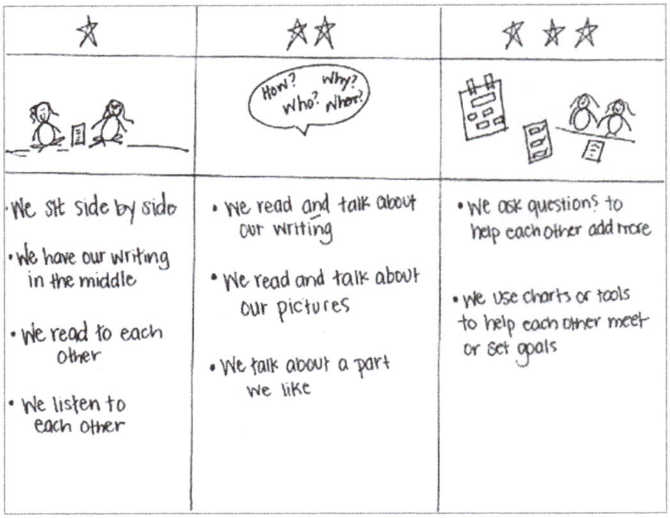

To support students' work with the partnership progression, we also gave them grade and genre-specific checklists, and they knew they had access to any and all of the charts on the bulletin boards. Through these strategies, we were confident that our stronger writers were also growing, both from our input and from the challenges they offered each other.

Expanding Paper Choice

Another important change for all of the students involved paper. Early on in our work together, we introduced students to some paper choices. We offered a choice of packets to begin with, with a page for the beginning, a page for the middle, and a page for the end. While the structure of the packets was consistent, we differentiated the number of lines, and students could choose the ones they felt most comfortable writing on. We created paper packets that had beginning, middle, and end written across the top, but the lines were spaced differently. Students had the choice of how large they wanted the picture box and how many lines they wanted to have. The backs of these pages also have lines so if students need extra space, they have access to it.

TIP!

Chapter 5 provides a number of ideas for paper choice, and sample paper choices are available for download from the companion website, resources.corwin.com/everychildcanwrite.

Lisa and I also emphasized the various ways to plan. Some students chose to plan by drawing pictures across the available boxes on the tops of the pages, while others made beginning, middle, and end charts that were modeled after mine. Photo 9.10 shows an example of a planning chart that students could use as a model.

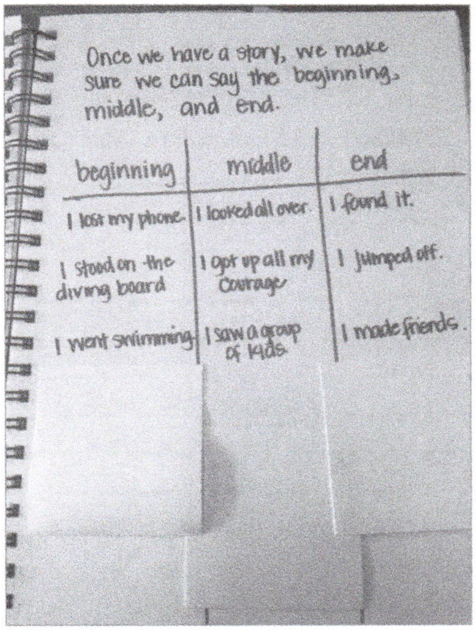

Photo 9.10 This chart that I have in my notebook serves as a model for students to create their own plan, or they can fill out sticky notes right on the spot and place them on their own pages, thereby creating a plan for their story.

Many students opted to fill out "Beginning-Middle-End" cards, which were available in one of the envelopes on the bulletin board; an example can be seen in Photo 9.11.

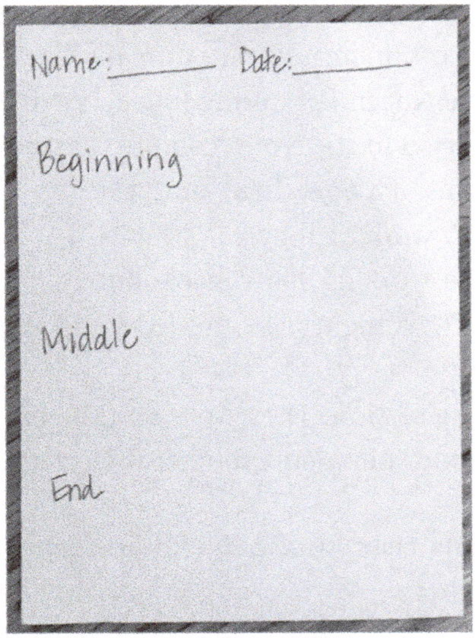

Photo 9.11 For some students, the Beginning-Middle-End cards were exactly what they needed in order to hold onto their idea and begin writing their story quickly and efficiently.

Assessing Engagement

During independent time, I spent a couple of days doing an engagement inventory, and I let students know I was doing that.

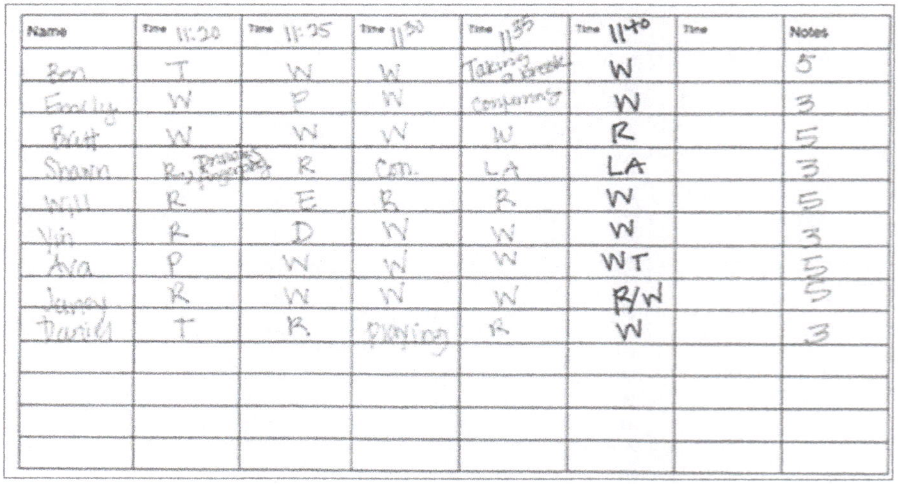

Name	Time 11:20	Time 11:25	Time 11:30	Time 11:35	Time 11:40	Time	Notes
Ben	T	W	W	Taking a break	W		5
Emily	W	P	W	Conferring	W		3
Britt	W	W	W	W	R		5
Shawn	R, [illegible]	R	Con.	LA	LA		3
Will	R	E	R	R	W		5
Yin	R	D	W	W	W		3
Ava	P	W	W	W	WT		5
Jenny	R	W	W	W	R/W		5
Daniel	T	R	Playing	R	W		3

Photo 9.12 I filled out this engagement inventory over a twenty-minute time period, having let students know that I'd be watching and recording their behaviors during their independent writing time.

"I'm watching you," I told them. "I just want a sense of how much time you actually spend on writing and how much time you spend doing anything but."

Because the students knew I was watching them, their engagement and commitment to their work increased. Additionally, we asked the students to self-assess their level of engagement during independent writing time, which is the number that is reflected in the Notes column. I asked students to rate their own productivity in terms of a one, three, or five:

- **One**—They weren't working much at all.
- **Three**—They were working fairly hard, but they definitely could have completed more. They might have needed some reminders to get to work or remain on task.
- **Five**—Great writing session. They were on task, excited about what they were working on, and they were proud of their output.

At the end of the writing class, students held up their fingers with their self-ratings, and I recorded them.

THINKING OUT LOUD

While I would not recommend students self-assessing their engagement every day, I do think it's important to teach and ask them to do it from time to time. As with the idea of asking students to "take inventory" from Chapter 2, I'd do it often as I'm first introducing it, then fade it to a tool that's effective and used intermittently.

Reflecting on Student Growth and Making Adjustments

Throughout our work, Lisa and I reflected on student growth and their responses to the changes. We agreed that their productivity and volume had already increased; I couldn't be there every day—only three times a week—and even without me there, that increase continued, probably because success leads to success. Like most of us, students develop habits, both independently and as a group. They had been in the habit of avoiding writing, and after even just a few days of sustained writing, that habit was changing.

Even still, a couple of students still concerned us because they were not producing enough writing. One child spent a lot of time erasing and rewriting her work. I taught her to make a line through parts she thought she should change and then move on. It became a joke between the two of us whenever she went to touch her pink eraser or turn her pencil upside down; if I even touched her shoulder or widened my eyes from across the room, she remembered her intention to use her eraser less. Just the awareness of how much she erased and the realization that a cross-out was acceptable—even something to celebrate since it represented a revision—helped her become a more productive writer during her independent work time.

One boy had a different productivity issues however. Both Lisa and I reminded him several times to get started, and even when he did initiate his writing task, he did not sustain productivity. We met and he filled out a Green Greatness Form (see Photo 9.13). Because he suggested a headset, we let him use one, but I employed another strategy as well to address his productivity levels: my set of Flair pens. Multi-colored Flair pens are powerful tools for several reasons. They don't require as much hand strength to use, which sometimes benefits striving writers. Students also feel special when they hold a pen they associate with adults or teachers, and that works as well. What students don't always realize is that if we hand out different colored pens on different days, then Flair pens offer quick and easy color-codes of day-to-day productivity. My being able to say to this student, "What's up with only five words in blue today?" was a great way to send him a message about his productivity (or lack thereof) and inspire him to get to work.

Photo 9.13 One of the boys recognized his challenge involved focusing and suggested a headset to help him concentrate.

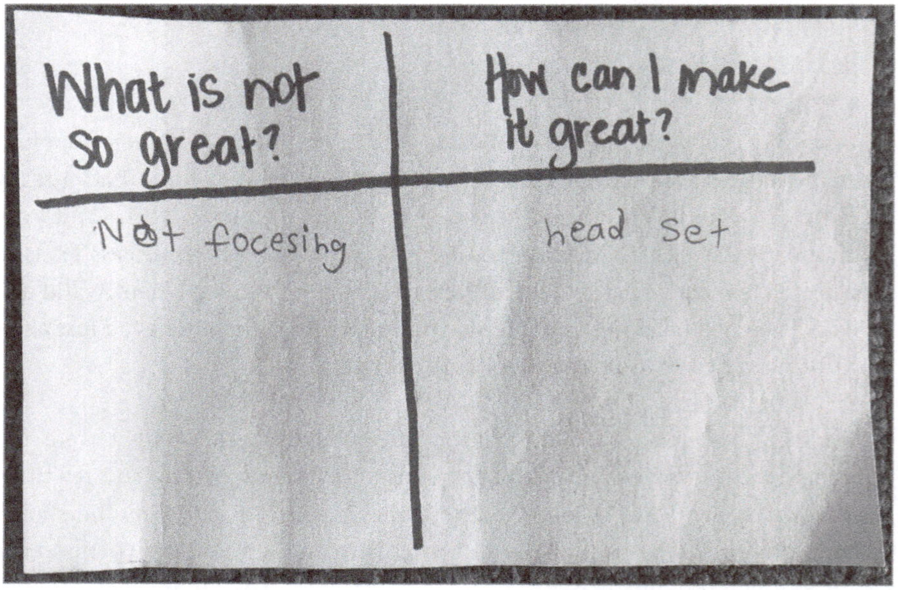

Every Child Can Write: Getting Closer to Our Goals

After four weeks of our work together, Lisa and I asked the whole class to write the best story they could within one class period. Our district scores writing across six traits: focus, organization, elaboration, fluency, voice, and conventions. The following chart shows the number of students who scored below expectations within the six traits of writing that we score. The first column indicates the number of students who scored below expectations on their narrative assessment before our coaching cycle, and the second column shows the number of students who did not meet standards on the same sort of assessment that we gave after the coaching cycle.

	Narrative 1	Narrative 2
Focus	7	1
Organization	7	3
Elaboration	15	5
Fluency	6	5
Voice	10	1
Conventions	13	6

As you can see from the chart, the number of students who met standards on specific traits improved in all areas, indicating strong growth in writing. We score students across all six traits, and they meet expectations if they score a 17 or higher. For the first narrative, 15 students did not meet expectations overall. After our work together, only four students did not meet expectations.

Unquestionably, the success of our work in this fairly short time period could be the result of several factors. Just the fact that we had two adults in the room instead of one 3 to 4 times a week for 4 weeks certainly could have an impact. But I believe that simply having students writing more helped tremendously. Volume and production usually lead to growth and achievement. We were able to see where kids were getting stuck, where they needed a new entry point, and where to build bridges of support. We also explicitly:

- Retaught the expectations for attending to instruction and working independently;
- Offered an increasing number of charts and tools that we could direct students to use or they could intentionally access;
- Utilized shared writing and a gradual release model for several of our most striving writers;
- Changed the paper choices to differentiate for various levels of output;
- Monitored volume and engagement by using engagement inventories as well as different colored pens, and;
- Taught students how to use each other as resources with productive, reflective, and insightful partnerships.

At the end of our four-week cycle, Lisa and I talked about what worked, what didn't, and why. We agreed that the paper choices as well as the availability of charts had been effective for many of her students. Because of these reflections, Lisa created similar resources and tools for the next unit on her curricular calendar. I did not continue to co-teach with her on a regular basis, but Lisa was able to implement many of the ideas and strategies on her own. Furthermore, her students believed in themselves as writers, and sometimes, that self-efficacy is the most powerful element of all.

In fact, the biggest evolution in Lisa's classroom over that four-week time period was the change in students' beliefs in themselves as writers. I saw firsthand what Smith meant when he wrote, "The only conclusion that can be drawn from masses of fragmented research is that there is no guaranteed method of turning students into writers, but that anything that encourages interest, effort, thinking, and pride is likely to do good, while anything that produces anxiety, resentment, despair, or a negative self-image can only do harm. . . . The cardinal rule is to watch for the effect on the learner, and on the learner's writing" (Smith, 1994, p. 221). I have followed the progress of Lisa's students over the course of the year, and most of them have continued to meet or exceed expectations on different genres of writing. The four students who were still striving in the fall have made gains, and they were just one point away from meeting expectations on their more recent assessment.

As I conclude this book, I hope that this look into Lisa's class illustrates the possibilities that exist within our writing instruction and demonstrates the truth that every child can write. Scripts and mandated lesson plans don't necessarily work, but instead a combination of best practices and commitment to build students' self-confidence, inspiring them to take risks, and showing them the value of their own words ensures that all children can write—even those who have struggled or have learning challenges. It's our job to provide the entry points, bridges, and pathways that lead them to success!

Appendix A: Favorite Mentor Texts for Writing Instruction

Narrative

Title	Author/Illustrator
Jabari Jumps	Gaia Cornwall
A Different Pond	Bao Phi Illustrated by Thi Bui
A Moon for Moe and Mo	Jane Breskin Zalben Illustrated by Mehrdokht Amini
Island Born	Junot Diaz Illustrated by Leo Espinosa
Sarabella's Thinking Cap	Judy Schachner
Yard Sale	Eve Bunting Illustrated by Lauren Castillo
Owl Moon	Jane Yolen Illustrated by John Schoenherr
Come On, Rain!	Karen Hesse Illustrated by Jon J. Muth

Information

Title	Author/Illustrator
Kids Get Coding	Heather Lyons and Elizabeth Tweedale
Be a Maker! Maker Projects for Kids Who Love Fashion	Sarah Levete
Move It!	Christa Schneider
Girls Play Softball!	Amy Rogers
Basketball in Action	John Crossingham and Sarah Dann
Deadliest Animals	Melissa Stewart
Big Blue Whale	Nicola Davies
Gentle Giant Octopus	Karen Wallace
What's a Robot	Melissa Stewart

Opinion

Title	Author/Illustrator
How to Be a T-Rex	Ryan North Illustrated by Mike Lowery
One Word From Sophia	Jim Averbeck and Yasmeen Ismail
The Big Bed	Bunmi Laditan and Tom Knight

Appendix B: Mentor Text Charts With Craft Moves

Narrative

Jabari Jumps by Gaia Cornwall

Page Number	Craft Move
1	Use of dialogue as a hook
2, 4	Power of three
4	Use of action
4	Figurative language—simile
4	Sound effect
4	Action that shows caring
8	Inner thinking
8	Blending of action, thought, and dialogue
14, 15, 16	Using small details when the moment matters
21, 23	Font size
26	Use of dialogue as an ending
26	Ending relates to the beginning

A Different Pond by Bao Phi

Illustrated by Thi Bui

Page Number	Craft Move
1–2	Establishment of characters and details
4	Use of similes
7–8	Blending of thoughts and talk
7–8	Establishment of setting
10	Establishment of setting through character action
12	Use of action to stretch important part
13	Blending of action and thought
16	Incorporation of backstory
18	Blending of action and description
20	Blending of action and inner thinking
21	Setting
25	Flash forward
26	Final thought to end

A Moon for Moe and Mo by Jane Breskin Zalben
Illustrated by Mehrdokht Amini

Page Number	Craft Move
1–2	Introduction of characters
3–4	Setting details: smells, colors, simile
6	Power of three
8	Purposeful repetition
11	Sensory details Intentional use of punctuation
13–14	Transitional words and phrases
17	Transitional words Power of three Blending of inner thinking, action, and talk
19	Transitional words Blending of feelings, action, and talk
21	Variety of sentence structures Transitional words
26	Purposeful repetition
27–28	Repetition
30	Circle ending

Island Born by Junot Diaz
Illustrated by Leo Espinosa

Page Number	Craft Move
1	Introduction of characters, specific names
2	Intentional use of punctuation
3–4	Scenes versus summaries
9, 22	Use of "what character always does" in order to build understanding of character
12	Character thinking
14	Different ways of talking
17	Intentional use of punctuation
20	Use of speech tags
23	Blending of feelings and actions

Page Number	Craft Move
25	Blending of action and dialogue
31	Use of action to show feelings
35	Use of summary
39	Transitional language
41	Setting Revealing character mood

Sarabella's Thinking Cap by Judy Schachner

Page Number	Craft Move
1	Introduction of characters, specific names Intentional use of punctuation
2–4	Repetition Poetic language
6–7	Scenes versus summaries Information about other characters Power of three
10–11	Scenes versus summaries
12–13	Scenes versus summaries
14	Scenes versus summaries Blending of action and dialogue
18	Establishing the setting
20	Blending of action, description, thinking, and talking
22–23	Transition words
24–25	Blending of action, thoughts, and dialogue
27	Establishing of time
30	Establishing of time Ending with dialogue

Yard Sale by Eve Bunting
Illustrated by Lauren Castillo

Page Number	Craft Move
1	Beginning with a clear problem
2	Inner thinking blending with talk
4	Showing of setting through action

Page Number	Craft Move
11,12	Blending of inner thinking with action
13, 14	Blending of talk and action
14	Detail of smell
16	Blending of talk, feeling, and action
18	Action to show feelings
21	Inner thinking that reveals a flash forward Action to show feelings
22	Transitional language
24	Careful and intentional choices of verbs
28	Ending with talk

Owl Moon by Jane Yolen

Illustrated by John Schoenherr

Page Number	Craft Move
1	Establishment of characters and setting Figurative language
2	Figurative language Sentence structure
4	Breakdown of actions
5	Repetition
6	Figurative language Description
8	Repetition Inner thinking
10	Simile Inner thinking
12	Description
14	Description Simile
17	Breakdown of actions to show important part
18	Repetition Power of three
20	Transitional language
25	Repetition Power of three
27	Blending of talk with action
28	Ending with a resolution

Come On, Rain! by Karen Hesse
Illustrated by Jon J. Muth

Page Number	Craft Move
1	Dialogue to begin story Blending of talk and action
2	Using action to show the setting
3	Figurative language Use of sounds
4	Description
5–6	Use of ellipse to add tension, suspense
6	Description
7	Figurative language
8–9	Breakdown of action
10	Breakdown of action
12	Conversation
13	Using action to show the setting
7, 12, 13, 15	Personification
18	Breakdown of action
20	Unusual sentence structures Strong verbs
21–22	Use of ellipse to add tension, suspense
23	Strong verbs
23–24	Alliteration Simile
25	Alliteration
28	Ending with talk and important action

Information

Kids Get Coding by Heather Lyons and Elizabeth Tweedale

Page Number	Craft Move
2	Table of contents
3	Content specific vocabulary
4	Headers
5	Questions and answers
6–7	How-to text feature
14	Craft moves using conventions

Page Number	Craft Move
Throughout entire story	Clever headers
16	Transitional language
24	Index

Be a Maker! Maker Projects for Kids Who Love Fashion by Sarah Levete

Page Number	Craft Move
4	Introduction that hooks readers Introduction with a quote in it Content-specific vocabulary
4	Alliteration in the text feature
5	Talking to readers
5	Close-up picture
6	Transitional language: however, instead, also, for example
6–7	Interesting headers
8	Interesting punctuation
9	Use of a quote from a historical figure
10	Example of a twin sentence (Sari) Explanation of unfamiliar vocabulary
11	Text box that talks to readers, challenges them to do some thinking on their own
12–13	How-to section with • Safety tips • Materials needed • Make it better section • Conclusion
30	Glossary
31	Learning more
32	Index

Move It! by Christa Schneider

Page Number	Craft Move
4	Introduction
6	Header as a question
6	Content vocabulary

Page Number	Craft Move
8	Pictures and labels
10	How-to examples
30	Conclusion
31	Glossary
32	Index

Girls Play Softball! by Amy Rogers

Page Number	Craft Move
4	Introduction
4–5	Ways to incorporate content vocabulary
7	Pictures and captions
9	Diagram with explanation
8	Sentence structures
10	Twin sentences to extend information and elaborate
12	Extending information Transitional language
22	Conclusion
23	Glossary
24	Index

Basketball in Action by John Crossingham and Sarah Dann

Page Number	Craft Move
3	Table of contents
4	Introduction "What is Basketball"
4	Picture with caption and explanation
4	Content vocabulary that is explained within the sentence
6	Twin sentences (first two sentences)
7	Diagram with labels
6, 8	Interesting headers
8–9	Headers
10–11	Captions of specific elements of the game
11	Talking directly to readers
12–13	Directives and descriptions of exercises

Page Number	Craft Move
14	Begins with an "Imagine" statement Talks to readers
22	How-to section
24	Sentence variety with various punctuation
25	Description of pictures
30–31	How-to sections
32	Glossary and index

Deadliest Animals by Melissa Stewart

Page Number	Craft Move
4–8	Introduction with checklists and surprising facts as hooks
8–9	Text features of "surprises"
10	Narrative features that include • Alliteration (clever carnivore) • A scene of the polar bear hunting
11	Riddles on the pages to add interest
12	Strong verbs to describe the behaviors
13	Interesting fact as a text feature
14	Strong verbs Weird but true fact
16	Compare/contrast between previous pages
20–21	Headers with alliteration
21	Repetition
23	Explanation of facts in the "Viper" section
25	Ask and answer a question Close-up picture
27	Power of three If . . . then statement
30–31	10 cool facts
33	Use of familiar object to show size (see basketballs)
40	Punctuation
44	Reason for organization—the deadliest of them all
45	Conclusion

Big Blue Whale by Nicola Davies

Page Number	Craft Move
6	Power of three Comparison to familiar animals Small facts to go with pictures
9	Talking to readers Similes (several of them)
10	Comparison/contrast
11	Simile Punctuation craft moves Change of font
13	Talking to readers Explanation of content vocabulary Change in font
14	Explanation of content vocabulary Comparison to familiar object
16	Simile
17	Simile
18–19	Beginning sentences with intentional conjunctions
20	Narrative technique: Making the whale into a character
Throughout entire story	Inclusion of facts with different text
27	Narrative techniques Punctuation craft moves
28	Ending that relates to the beginning

Gentle Giant Octopus by Karen Wallace

Page Number	Craft Move
6	Poetic language: alliteration and similes Hooking readers with an image
9	Fact and pictures to go with it
10	Comparison/contrast
13	Power of three Punctuation
15	Use of a scene to teach about a characteristic
16	Poetic language: similes and strong verbs Fact in separate font and structure
18	Use of a scene to teach readers about a fact

Page Number	Craft Move
22–33	Use of scene aligns to the facts that are being taught Variation of sentences
25	Similes Use of pronouns
29	Ending aligns to end of life cycle
Throughout entire story	Inclusion of facts with different text

What's a Robot by Melissa Stewart

Page Number	Craft Move
4	Introduction with questions Power of three
6	Ask a question and answer a question Caption on pictures Text box for definitions
8–9	Timeline
10	Twin sentence Comparison of unfamiliar to something familiar
12	Talking to readers Explanation of content vocabulary Using a list in a creative way
14	Power of three Pictures and captions
16	Transitional language Introduction of new word
17	Power of three
19	Using familiar to teach about unfamiliar Simile
21	Talking to reader Weird but true text box
24	Power of three
26–27	Appealing to readers Text feature that goes along with the text itself

Page Number	Craft Move
30	Ask and answer a question
32	Power of three Reaction to the facts that are listed
34–35	Punctuation as craft moves
36	Involving readers in a list—inviting reader interaction
45	Ending that thinks to the future

Opinion

How to Be a T-Rex by Ryan North

Illustrated by Mike Lowery

Page Number	Craft Move
1	Begin with a story State a claim
4	Restating a claim in a different way
5	Addressing counterarguments
10–11	Presenting reasons that support claim
12	Incorporation of a how-to within an opinion
14–17	Addressing counterarguments
19	Counterargument
22	Changing thinking, presenting compromise
29–20	Closure

Appendix C: Sample of Progressions

Creating a Beginning for a Narrative Story

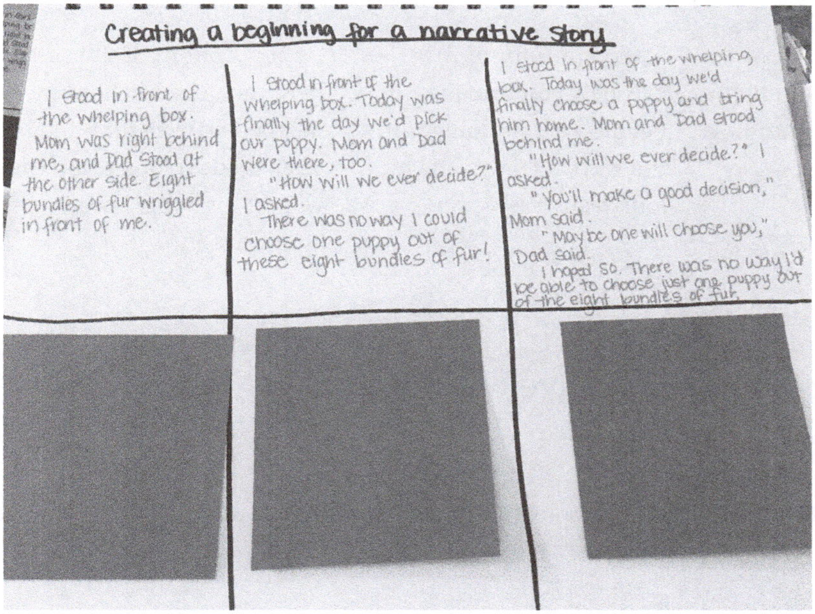

Creating an Ending for a Narrative Story

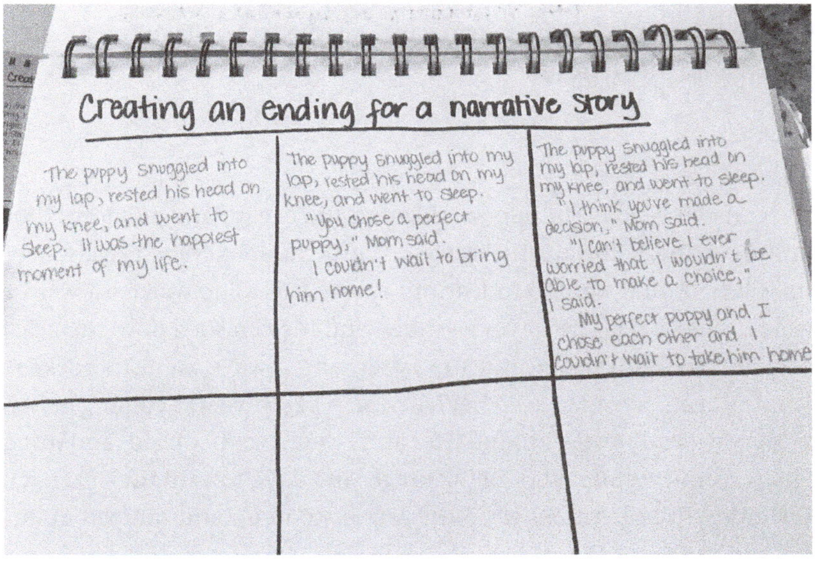

A Sample of a Progression of a Narrative Beginning Using Stars

☆	☆☆	☆☆☆
I stood in front of the ocean. All around me, people were jumping into the waves.	I stood in front of the ocean. All around me, people were jumping into the waves. They made it look really easy.	I stood in front of the ocean. Mom sat in her beach chair behind me. All around me, people were jumping into the waves. They made it look really easy. One boy was on his boogie board. He rode wave after wave in.

A Progression of Narrative Elaboration

LEVEL 1

Annie went to the beach. She wanted to learn how to ride a wave. She got up all her courage, and she rode a wave into the shore!

LEVEL 2

Annie arrived at the beach. The sun sparkled on the ocean, and all along the beach, families were beginning to head toward the waves. Annie wanted to learn to ride a wave. The waves were big, and they crashed onto the beach, banging and splashing. Annie got up all of her courage, and she rode a wave into the shore.

LEVEL 3

Annie arrived at the beach. The sun sparkled on the ocean, and all along the beach, families were beginning to head toward the waves. Many children were already beginning to head toward the waves. Annie wanted to learn to ride a wave. She walked toward the waves until her toes were in the water. The waves were big, and they crashed onto the beach, banging and splashing. Annie walked further into the water, and a wave almost knocked her down. She stumbled and swayed, trying to keep her balance. A big wave was coming at her. Annie studied the top of the wave and turned around. Her arms were over her head, and just as the wave was about to break, Annie got up all of her courage. She dove toward the beach, and she rode the wave into shore. When her ride was over, Annie stood up and jumped up and down before running back to catch another wave.

Introduction Progression for Information Writing

Have you ever heard of Geno Auriemma? He is the coach of UConn Women's Basketball. This text will teach you all about this amazing coach.

Imagine a man who dedicated himself to being the best basketball coach of all time. That's Geon Auriemma, the coach of the UConn Women's Basketball Program. Over the last decade, he has coached amazing players, developed inspiring drills, and won many memorable games.

There are many basketball coaches in this country. Some have even won multiple national championships. Geno Auriemma who coaches the UConn Women's Basketball Program stands out from the rest. Over the years in Storrs, Connecticut, he has recruited and developed many star players. He has successful practices and drills, and he has won many titles and championships. Get ready to be inspired by his successful players, his inspiring training techniques, and his most memorable games.

Conclusion Progression for Information Writing

In the world of women's basketball, Geno Auriemma is a star. Connecticut is lucky to have him.

If you want to be inspired, learn more about Geno Auriemma. His expertise about basketball stands way beyond the players he coaches, his drills, and the games he's won. If you go to a game, jump on that!

Geno Auriemma is a Connecticut hero for great reasons. He has brought many talented players into the state, and basketball coaches everywhere learn from his amazing drills and routines. And . . . if you want to see a winning record with wins upon wins, look no further. Take yourself to Storrs and learn about his amazing program.

Appendix D: Samples of Task Analyses

Sample Task Analyses for Narrative Story, Research-Based Essay, Information Writing

NARRATIVE STORY

1. Think of an idea.
2. Squeeze it down to a small moment in time.
3. State the beginning, middle, and end.
4. Say what the story is really, really about.
5. Make a plan, deciding what sort of plan works best.
6. Draft, adding action, description, talk, and inner thinking to the important parts.
7. Use all you know about conventions as you draft.

RESEARCH-BASED ESSAY

1. Read articles and understand some of the issues on either side.
2. Watch videos if available.
3. Take notes.
4. Develop a claim.
5. Sort notes.
6. Establish reasons that support claim.
7. Create an organizational structure/a plan.
8. Find additional research if necessary.
9. Draft.
10. Revise as you go.

INFORMATION PIECE

1. Think of an idea or a topic.
2. Make a plan for how sections could go.
3. Think about questions that relate to the topic.
4. Find resources that could answer the questions.
5. Read or watch the resources.

6. Take notes that help to answer the questions.
7. Revise questions and sections based on the information that you find.
8. Draft, paying attention to blending facts and information with thoughts and reflections.
9. Use all you know about conventions as you draft.
10. Add text features that could add to enhance your piece.

Classroom Example: Narrative Story

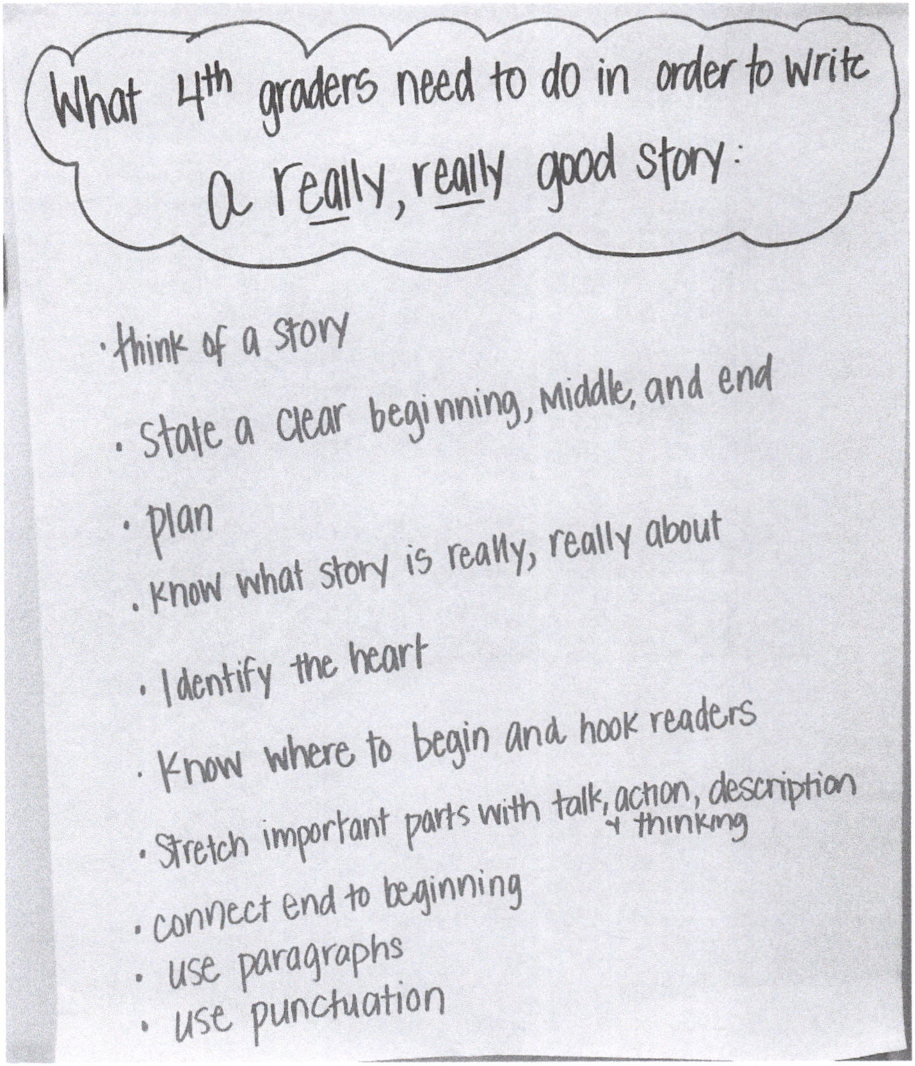

Classroom Example: Information Book

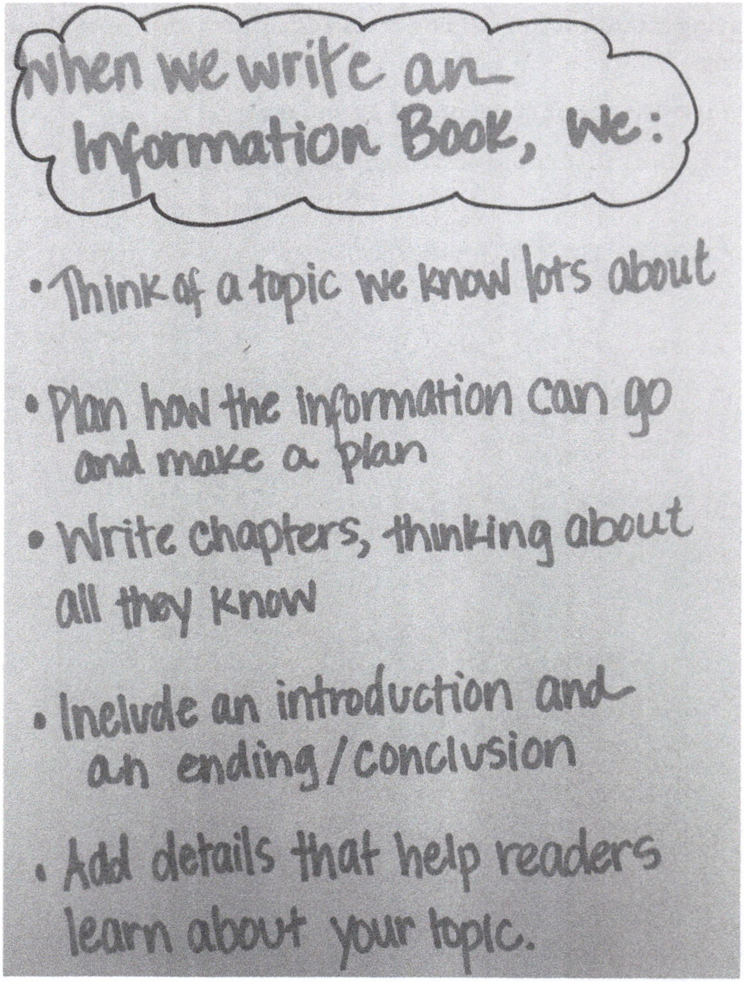

Appendix E: Anchor Charts

Narrative Writing Anchor Chart Sequence

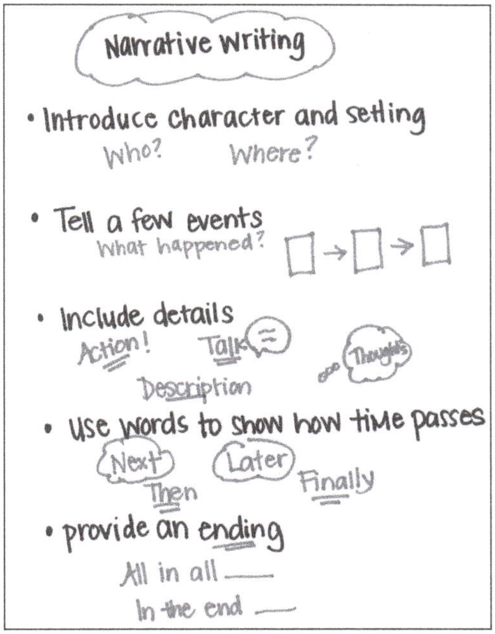

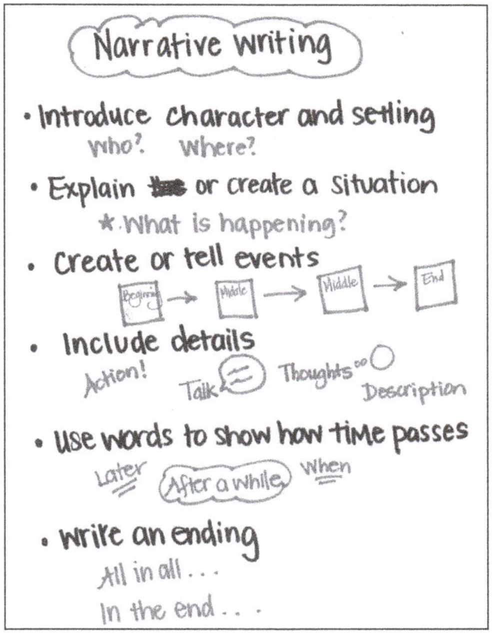

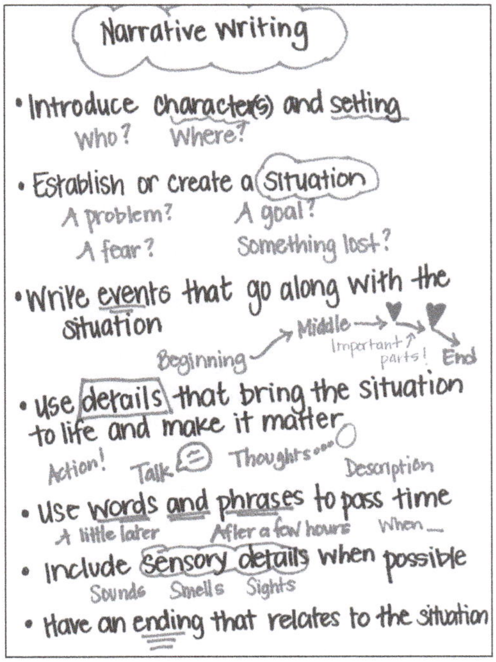

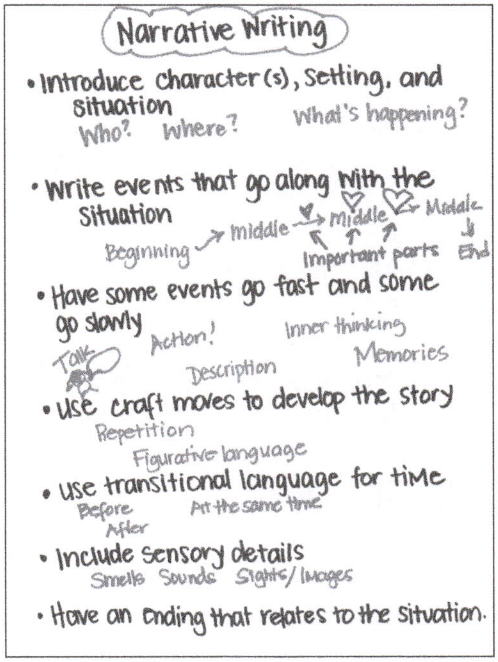

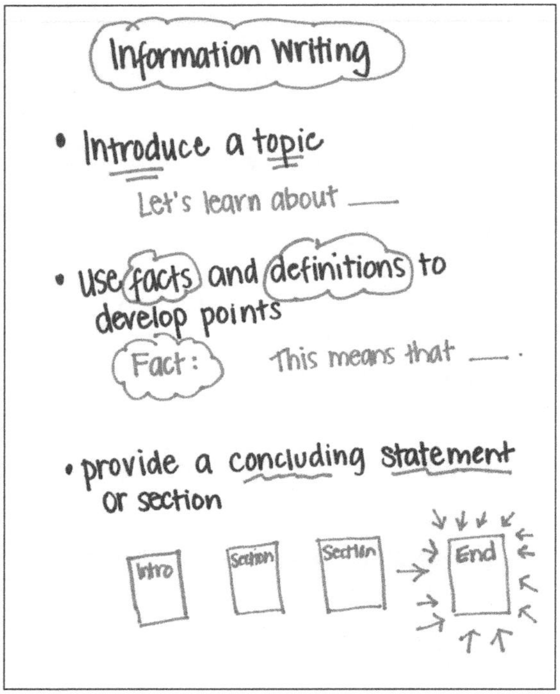
Information Writing
• Introduce a topic
Let's learn about ___
• Use facts and definitions to develop points
Fact:
This means that ___.
• provide a concluding statement or section
Intro
Section
Section
End

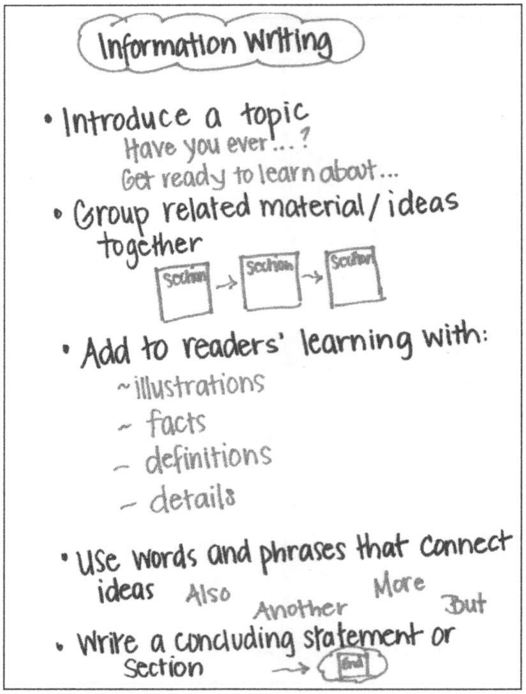
Information Writing
• Introduce a topic
Have you ever...?
Get ready to learn about...
• Group related material/ideas together
Section
Section
Section
• Add to readers' learning with:
~illustrations
~ facts
– definitions
– details
• Use words and phrases that connect ideas
Also
Another
More
But
• Write a concluding statement or section
End

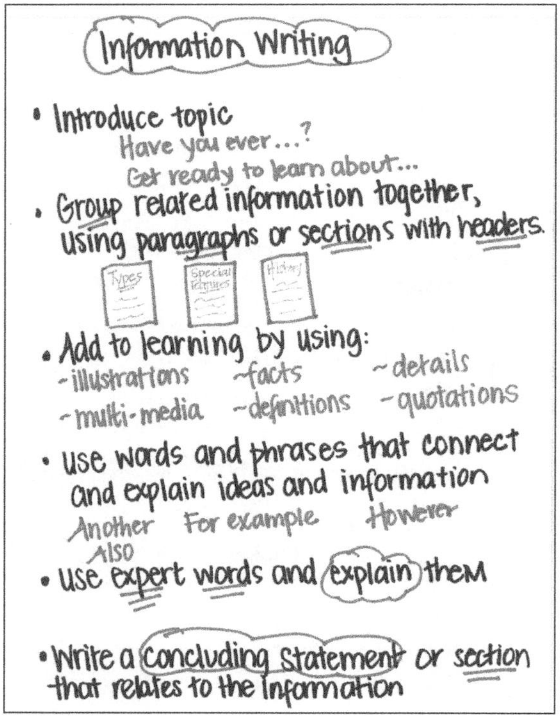
Information Writing
• Introduce topic
Have you ever...?
Get ready to learn about...
• Group related information together, using paragraphs or sections with headers.
Types
Special features
History
• Add to learning by using:
-illustrations
~facts
~details
-multi-media
~definitions
-quotations
• Use words and phrases that connect and explain ideas and information
Another
For example
However
Also
• Use expert words and explain them
• Write a concluding statement or section that relates to the information

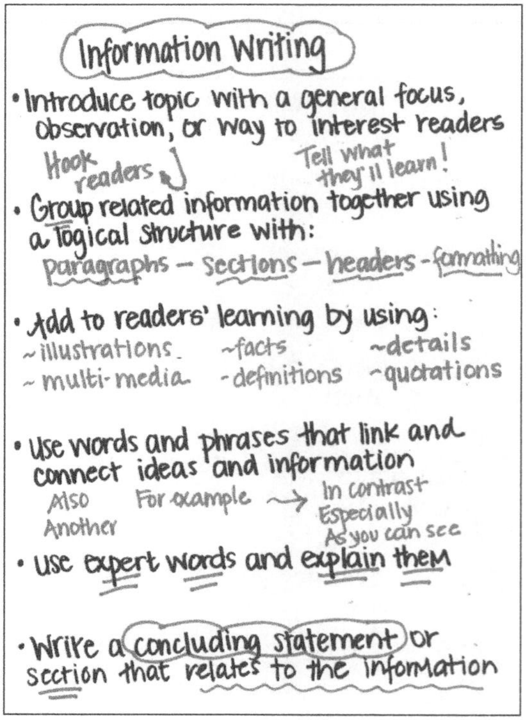
Information Writing
• Introduce topic with a general focus, observation, or way to interest readers
Hook readers
Tell what they'll learn!
• Group related information together using a logical structure with:
paragraphs – sections – headers – formatting
• Add to readers' learning by using:
~illustrations
~facts
~details
~multi-media
-definitions
-quotations
• Use words and phrases that link and connect ideas and information
Also
Another
For example
In contrast
Especially
As you can see
• Use expert words and explain them
• Write a concluding statement or section that relates to the information

Appendix F: Writing Standards

Narrative Writing Standards

KINDERGARTEN

Use a combination of drawing, dictating, and writing to narrate a single event or several loosely linked events, tell about the events in the order in which they occurred, and provide a reaction to what happened.

GRADE 1

Write narratives in which they recount two or more appropriately sequenced events, include some details regarding what happened, use temporal words to signal event order, and provide some sense of closure.

GRADE 2

Write narratives in which they recount a well-elaborated event or short sequence of events, include details to describe actions, thoughts, and feelings, use temporal words to signal event order, and provide a sense of closure.

GRADE 3

Write narratives to develop real or imagined experiences or events using effective technique, descriptive details, and clear event sequences.

- Establish a situation and introduce a narrator and/or characters; organize an event sequence that unfolds naturally.
- Use dialogue and descriptions of actions, thoughts, and feelings to develop experiences and events or show the response of characters to situations.
- Use temporal words and phrases to signal event order.
- Provide a sense of closure.

GRADE 4

Write narratives to develop real or imagined experiences or events using effective technique, descriptive details, and clear event sequences.

- Orient the reader by establishing a situation and introducing a narrator and/or characters; organize an event sequence that unfolds naturally.
- Use dialogue and description to develop experiences and events or show the responses of characters to situations.
- Use a variety of transitional words and phrases to manage the sequence of events.

- Use concrete words and phrases and sensory details to convey experiences and events precisely.
- Provide a conclusion that follows from the narrated experiences or events.

GRADE 5

Write narratives to develop real or imagined experiences or events using effective technique, descriptive details, and clear event sequences.

- Orient the reader by establishing a situation and introducing a narrator and/or characters; organize an event sequence that unfolds naturally.
- Use narrative techniques, such as dialogue, description, and pacing, to develop experiences and events or show the responses of characters to situations.
- Use a variety of transitional words, phrases, and clauses to manage the sequence of events.
- Use concrete words and phrases and sensory details to convey experiences and events precisely.
- Provide a conclusion that follows from the narrated experiences or events.

GRADE 6

Write narratives to develop real or imagined experiences or events using effective technique, relevant descriptive details, and well-structured event sequences.

- Engage and orient the reader by establishing a context and introducing a narrator and/or characters; organize an event sequence that unfolds naturally and logically.
- Use narrative techniques, such as dialogue, pacing, and description, to develop experiences, events, and/or characters.
- Use a variety of transition words, phrases, and clauses to convey sequence and signal shifts from one time frame or setting to another.
- Use precise words and phrases, relevant descriptive details, and sensory language to convey experiences and events.
- Provide a conclusion that follows from the narrated experiences or events.

Information Writing Standards

KINDERGARTEN

Use a combination of drawing, dictating, and writing to compose informative/explanatory texts in which they name what they are writing about and supply some information about the topic.

GRADE 1

Write informative/explanatory texts in which they name a topic, supply some facts about the topic, and provide some sense of closure.

GRADE 2

Write informative/explanatory texts in which they introduce a topic, use facts and definitions to develop points, and provide a concluding statement or section.

GRADE 3

Write informative/explanatory texts to examine a topic and convey ideas and information clearly.

- Introduce a topic and group related information together; include illustrations when useful to aiding comprehension.
- Develop the topic with facts, definitions, and details.
- Use linking words and phrases (e.g., also, another, and, more, but) to connect ideas within categories of information.
- Provide a concluding statement or section.

GRADE 4

Write informative/explanatory texts to examine a topic and convey ideas and information clearly.

- Introduce a topic clearly and group related information in paragraphs and sections; include formatting (e.g., headings), illustrations, and multimedia when useful to aiding comprehension.
- Develop the topic with facts, definitions, concrete details, quotations, or other information and examples related to the topic.
- Link ideas within categories of information using words and phrases (e.g., another, for example, also, because).
- Use precise language and domain-specific vocabulary to inform about or explain the topic.
- Provide a concluding statement or section related to the information or explanation presented.

GRADE 5

Write informative/explanatory texts to examine a topic and convey ideas and information clearly.

- Introduce a topic clearly, provide a general observation and focus, and group related information logically; include formatting (e.g., headings), illustrations, and multimedia when useful to aiding comprehension.
- Develop the topic with facts, definitions, concrete details, quotations, or other information and examples related to the topic.

- Link ideas within and across categories of information using words, phrases, and clauses (e.g., in contrast, especially).
- Use precise language and domain-specific vocabulary to inform about or explain the topic.
- Provide a concluding statement or section related to the information or explanation presented.

GRADE 6

Introduce a topic; organize ideas, concepts, and information, using strategies such as definition, classification, comparison/contrast, and cause/effect; include formatting (e.g., headings), graphics (e.g., charts, tables), and multimedia when useful to aiding comprehension.

- Develop the topic with relevant facts, definitions, concrete details, quotations, or other information and examples.
- Use appropriate transitions to clarify the relationships among ideas and concepts.
- Use precise language and domain-specific vocabulary to inform about or explain the topic.
- Establish and maintain a formal style.
- Provide a concluding statement or section that follows from the information or explanation presented.

Opinion Writing Standards

KINDERGARTEN

Use a combination of drawing, dictating, and writing to compose opinion pieces in which they tell a reader the topic or the name of the book they are writing about and state an opinion or preference about the topic or book (e.g., *My favorite book is . . .*).

GRADE 1

Write opinion pieces in which they introduce the topic or name the book they are writing about, state an opinion, supply a reason for the opinion, and provide some sense of closure.

GRADE 2

Write opinion pieces in which they introduce the topic or book they are writing about, state an opinion, supply reasons that support the opinion, use linking words (e.g., *because*, and, *also*) to connect opinion and reasons, and provide a concluding statement or section.

GRADE 3

Write opinion pieces on topics or texts, supporting a point of view with reasons.

- Introduce the topic or text they are writing about, state an opinion, and create an organizational structure that lists reasons.
- Provide reasons that support the opinion.
- Use linking words and phrases (e.g., because, therefore, since, for example) to connect opinion and reasons.
- Provide a concluding statement or section.

GRADE 4

Write opinion pieces on topics or texts, supporting a point of view with reasons and information.

- Introduce a topic or text clearly, state an opinion, and create an organizational structure in which related ideas are grouped to support the writer's purpose.
- Provide reasons that are supported by facts and details.
- Link opinion and reasons using words and phrases (e.g., for instance, in order to, in addition).
- Provide a concluding statement or section related to the opinion presented.

GRADE 5

Write opinion pieces on topics or texts, supporting a point of view with reasons and information.

- Introduce a topic or text clearly, state an opinion, and create an organizational structure in which ideas are logically grouped to support the writer's purpose.
- Provide logically ordered reasons that are supported by facts and details.
- Link opinion and reasons using words, phrases, and clauses (e.g., consequently, specifically).
- Provide a concluding statement or section related to the opinion presented.

GRADE 6

Write arguments to support claims with clear reasons and relevant evidence.

- Introduce claim(s) and organize the reasons and evidence clearly.
- Support claim(s) with clear reasons and relevant evidence, using credible sources and demonstrating an understanding of the topic or text.
- Use words, phrases, and clauses to clarify the relationships among claim(s) and reasons.
- Establish and maintain a formal style.
- Provide a concluding statement or section that follows from the argument presented.

Appendix G: Convention Station Samples

Periods and Capitals

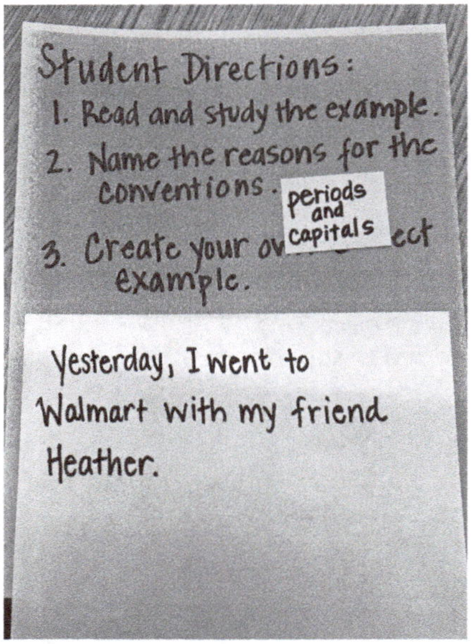

Capitals

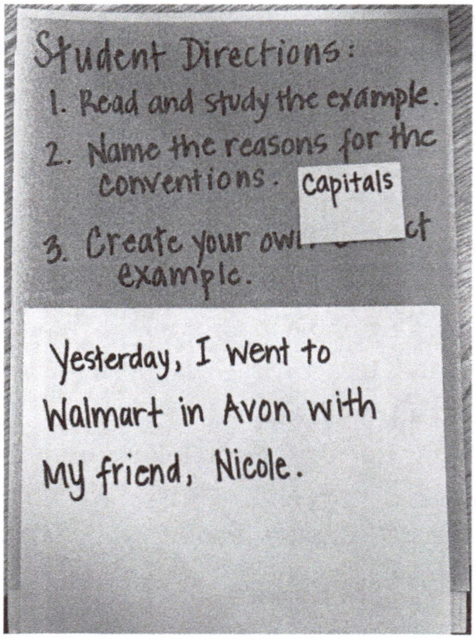

Commas

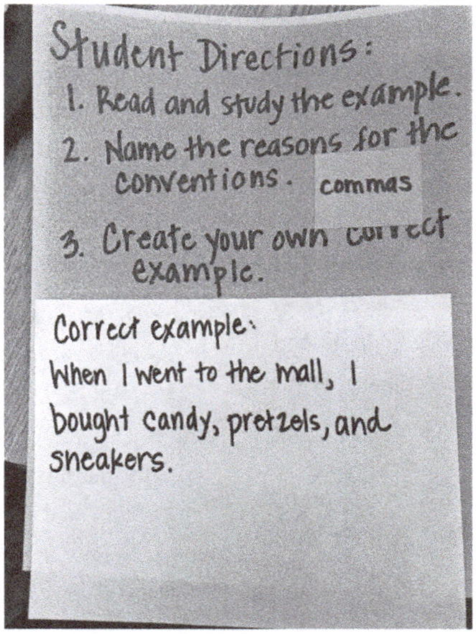

Tricky Words

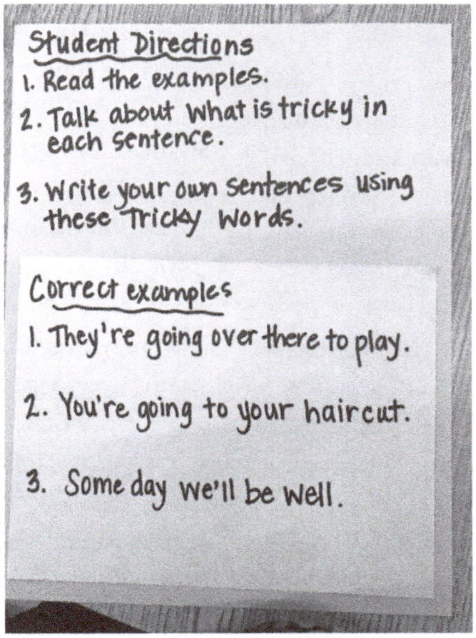

References

Bandura, A. (1997). *Self-efficacy: The exercise of control.* New York, NY: W H Freeman/Times Books/Henry Holt & Co.

Barrett, P. Barrett, L., & Zhang, L. (2015), Teachers' views of their primary school classrooms. *Intelligent Buildings International, 8*(3), 176–191. doi:10.1080/17508975.2015.1087835

Berger, R., Rugen, L., & Woodfin, L. (2014). *Leaders of their own learning: Transforming schools through student-engaged assessment.* San Francisco, CA: Jossey-Bass.

Calkins, L. (1994). *The art of teaching writing.* Portsmouth, NH: Heinemann.

Calkins, L. (2014). *Writing pathways: Performance assessments and learning progressions, Grades K–8.* Portsmouth, NH: Heinemann.

Calkins, L. (2016). *Units of study in opinion, information, and narrative writing, grade 5, with trade book pack.* Retrieved from https://www.heinemann.com/products/e08958.aspx

CAST. (n.d.). *Universal design for learning guidelines.* Retrieved from http://udlguidelines.cast.org/

Clark, R. P. (2006). *Writing tools.* New York, NY: Little Brown and Co.

Clark, R. E., Feldon, D., van Merriënboer, J. J. G., Yates, K., & Early, S. (2008). Cognitive task analysis. In J. M. Spector, M. D. Merrill, J. J. G. van Merriënboer, & M. P. Driscoll (Eds.). *Handbook of research on educational communications and technology* (3rd ed., pp. 577–593). New York, NY: Macmillan/Gale.

Cooper, J. O., Heron, T. E., & Heward, W. L. (2019). *Applied behavior analysis* (3rd ed.). New York, NY: Pearson.

Common Core State Standards Initiative. (2019). *English language arts standards.* Retrieved from http://www.corestandards.org/ELA-Literacy/

Davis, H. A., Summers, J. J., & Miller, L. A. (2012). *An interpersonal approach to classroom management: Strategies for improving student engagement.* Thousand Oaks, CA: Corwin.

Dorfman, L., & Cappelli, R. (2007). *Mentor texts: Teaching writing through children's literature, K–6.* Portsmouth, NH: Stenhouse.

Dweck, C. S. (2012). *Mindset: How you can fulfill your potential.* New York, NY: Little Brown Book Group.

Ericsson, K. A., & Kintsch, W. (1995). Long-term working memory. *Psychological Review, 102*(2), 211–245.

Fisher, D., & Frey, N. (2010). *Guided instruction: How to develop confident and successful learners.* Alexandria, VA: ASCD.

Fisher, D., & Frey, N. (2013). Gradual release of responsibility instructional framework. *IRA e-ssentials, 1–8.* doi:10.1598/e-ssentials.8037

Fisher, D., Frey, N., & Hattie, J. (2016). Visible *learning for literacy, grades K–12.* Thousand Oaks, CA: Corwin.

Fisher, D. Frey, N., Amador, O., & Assof, J. (2018). *The teacher clarity playbook: A hands-on guide to creating learning intentions and success criteria for organized, effective instruction: Grades K–12* (1st ed.). Thousand Oaks, CA: Corwin.

Fisher, A. V., Godwin, K. E., & Seltman, H. (2014). Visual environment, attention allocation, and learning in young children. *Psychological Science, 25*(7), 1362–1370. doi:10.1177/0956797614533801

Gawande, A. (2007, December 30). A lifesaving checklist. *The New York Times.* Retrieved from www.nytimes.com/2007/12/30/opinion/30gawande.html?_r=1&oref=slogin

Gentry, J. R. (2016). 5 brain-based reasons to teach handwriting in school. *Psychology Today.* Retrieved from www.psychologytoday.com/us/blog/raising-readers-writers-and-spellers/201609/5-brain-based-reasons-teach-handwriting-in-school

Graham, S., Bollinger, A., Olson, C. B., D'Aoust, C., MacArthur, C., McCutchen, D., & Olinghouse, N. (2012). *Teaching elementary school students to be effective writers: A practice guide* (US DE Report NCEE 2012-4058).

Graham, S., Harris, K. R., & Santangelo, T. (2015, June). Research-based writing practices and the common core. *The Elementary School Journal, 115*(4), 498–522. doi:10.1086/681964

Graves, D. (1994). *A fresh look at writing.* Portsmouth, NH: Heinemann.

Hattie, J. (2009). *Visible learning: A synthesis of over 800 meta-analyses relating to achievement.* New York, NY: Routledge.

Hattie, J. (2018). *Visible learning: Feedback.* doi:10.4324/9780429485480

Hattie, J., & Zierer, K. (2018). *10 mindframes for visible learning.* New York, NY: Routledge.

Hogan, K., & Pressley, M. (Eds.). (1997). *Scaffolding student learning: Instructional approaches and issues.* Cambridge, MA: Brookline Books.

Horn, M., & Giacobbe, M. E. (2007). *Talking, drawing, writing: Lessons for our youngest writers.* Portsmouth, NH: Stenhouse.

Jang, H., Reeve, J., & Deci, E. L. (2010). Engaging students in learning activities: It is not autonomy support or structure but autonomy support and structure. *Journal of Educational Psychology, 102,* 588–600.

Laberge, D., & Samuels, S. J. (1974).Toward a theory of automatic information processing in reading. *Cognitive Psychology, 6*(2), 293–323.

Marks, H. M. (2000). Student engagement in instructional activity: Patterns in the elementary, middle, and high school years. *American Educational Research Journal, 37,* 153–184.

Marzano, R, J., Pickering, D. J., & Heflebower, T. (2010). *The Classroom Strategy Series: The highly engaged classroom.* Centennial, CO: Marzano Research Laboratory.

Marzano, R. J., Pickering, D. J., & Pollock, J. E., (2001). *Classroom instruction that works: Research-based strategies for increasing student achievement.* Alexandria, VA: Association for Supervision and Curriculum Development.

Miller, G. A. (1956). The magical number seven, plus or minus two: Some limits on our capacity for processing information. *Psychological Review, 63*(2), 81–97.

Newkirk, T., & Kittle, P. (2013). *Children want to write: Donald Graves and the revolution in children's writing.* Portsmouth, NH: Heinemann.

Newman, J. (1991). *Interwoven conversations: Learning and teaching through critical reflection.* Toronto, Ontario: Canadian Scholar's Press.

Puentedura, R. R. (2009). *Technology, change, and process.* Retrieved from http://hippasus.com/resources/actem2009/TechnologyChangeProcess.pdf

Popham, J. W. (2007). All about accountability/The lowdown on learning progressions. *The Prepared Graduate, 64*(7), 83–84.

Puntambekar, S., & Hubscher, R. (2005). Tools for scaffolding students in a complex learning environment: What have we gained and what have we missed? *Educational Psychologist, 40*(1), 1–12.

Rodrigues, P. F. S., & Pandeirada, J. N. S. (2018). When visual stimulation of the surrounding environment affects children's cognitive performance. *Journal of Experimental Child Psychology, 176,* 140–149. doi:10.1016/j.jecp.2018.07.014

Serravallo, J., & Calkins, L.(2010). *Teaching reading in small groups.* Portsmouth, NH: Heinemann.

Slocum, S. K., & Tiger, J. H. (2011). An assessment of the efficiency of and child preference for forward and backward chaining. *Journal of Applied Behavior Analysis, 44*(4), 793–805. doi: 10.1901/jaba.2011.44-793

Smith, F. (1994). *Writing and the writer* (2nd ed.). Routledge.

Sousa, D. A., & Tomlinson, C. A. (2011). *Differentiation and the brain: How neuroscience supports the learner-friendly classroom.* Bloomington, IN: Solution Tree Press.

Vygotsky, L. S., & Cole, M. (1978). *Mind in society: The development of higher psychological processes.* Cambridge, MA: Harvard University Press.

Index

CORWIN Literacy

Because...

ALL TEACHERS ARE LEADERS

This Is Balanced Literacy, Grades K–6

Tap your intuition, collaborate with your peers, and put the research-based strategies embedded in this road map to work in your classroom to implement or deepen a strong, successful balanced literacy program.

Writers Read Better: Nonfiction & Narrative

By flipping the traditional "reading first, writing second" sequence, this innovative series lets you make the most of the writing-to-reading connection via 50 carefully matched lesson pairs.

Word Study That Sticks & The Word Study That Sticks Companion

Word Study That Sticks and its resourceful companion deliver challenging, discovery-based word learning routines and planning frameworks you can implement across subject areas.

The Ramped-Up Read Aloud

With 101 picture book experiences, a thousand ways to savor strategically, this is the book that shows how to use ANY book to teach readers and writers!

Text Structures From Fairy Tales, Text Structures From Nursery Rhymes, & Text Structures From the Masters

Centered on classic fairy tales, nursery rhymes, and literary masters, these lessons include writing prompts and planning frameworks that lead students to organize writing through a text structure.

To learn more, visit corwin.com/literacy

9 781544 355078

Printed at Repro India Ltd.